The Freedom to Choose Hell

◆ ◆ ◆

John C. Rankin

TEI Publishing House
www.teii.org; www.teipublishinghouse.com

All biblical translations are the author's own unless otherwise noted.

Cover design by David R. Clarkin.

Other books by John C. Rankin:

- *The Six Pillars of Biblical Power*
- *The Six Pillars of Honest Politics*
- *Jesus, in the Face of His Enemies*
- *Genesis and the Power of True Assumptions (Second Edition)*
- *The Real Muḥammad: In the Eyes of Ibn Isḥāq*
- *The Judas Economy*
- *Changing the Language of the Abortion Debate*
- *Moses and Jesus in the face of Muhammad*

◆ ◆ ◆

Content

♦ ♦ ♦

Introduction

There is a verse in the RSSV: "For God so loved the world, that he gave us each the freedom to choose to go to hell if we damn well want to."

Now, I would give caution on how we use this verse, since it is from the Rankin Sub-Standard Version (i.e., my biblically informed imagination). But if we grasp the interface of theology between Genesis 2:7-17 and John 3:16-21 – and across the whole biblical text – it will stand the test of time.

Or to put it another way: Heaven is for the many who love mercy; hell is for the few who guard bitterness.

I am an evangelical Christian, in the trajectory of a biblical and classical ecumenism. The Greek for the "good news" in Mark 1:1 is *euangelion*, from whence we derive the word "evangelical." In the face of the debate over the nature of "hell," what is the Good News of Jesus Christ?

The Good News is rooted in human freedom as God's gift. Too, freedom and the love of hard questions go hand in hand. We lose freedom to the extent that any powers restrict the questions we ask. I thrive in posing questions of God and one another, of being posed questions reciprocally.

In five noteworthy instances in the past dozen years, I have been asked to address the question of "universalism," the doctrine that everyone will be "saved," or "ultimately be saved." It is not a question I ever intended to be the subject of a book, but here we are. I had already written on heaven and hell in the context of freedom, but without addressing the question of universalism per se. Thus, in these modest pages, we will enter the debate through the lens of these five invitations that came my way. It is otherwise a very large subject, but in this specified approach, I believe a good contribution can still be made.

The first invitation came in the summer of 2005, when the Rev. Kalen Fristad contacted me. He is a Methodist minister in Iowa who rejects an "orthodox" position on hell, and instead embraces one of an "ultimate reconciliation" universalism, or as others put it, an "ultimate restoration." This is where hell is real but limited. After a person dies in unbelief or in some rejection of the Gospel, God will ultimately persuade him or her of his love, no matter how long it takes. In the end, all people will accept God's love (even the devil and the demons will be persuaded in some versions of this doctrine). Hell will thus be emptied. Kalen published his book in 2003, *Destined for Salvation: God's Promise to Save Everyone*.

Kalen was traveling across the country, coming also to New England, contacted me de novo, so we set up five forums to address the question together.

The second invitation came from a friend in Wyoming, Pieter Crow, who knows Julie Ferwerda, author of *Raising Hell*, published in 2011. She was raised in a strict "evangelical" background, and came to challenge it, especially saying that the church's doctrine of hell is a nasty fiction. Pieter wanted me to write a critique that he could forward to her, and so I did.

The third invitation came from Pieter at the same time, as he also asked me to read Rob Bell's 2011 best-selling book, *Love Wins*. Rob had founded and pastored the well-known Mars Hill Bible Church in Michigan, until that time, but his book caused controversy and he moved on. In it he focuses on an implicit but relentless trajectory toward an "ultimate restoration" universalism.

The fourth invitation came from a friend here in Connecticut, Jeff Reynolds, M.D. (we both graduated from Denison and Harvard). This followed the 2017 publication of *Lies We Believe About God* by W. Paul Young, author of the huge bestseller, *The Shack*. Jeff and I have heard Paul speak on several occasions, and his testimony in the face of the real hell of his childhood is dynamic. In *Lies*, Young raises many questions where he challenges variously accepted church beliefs, opens the door to an "ultimate reconciliation" universalism, and does not close it. Jeff was deeply concerned, and had read critiques that said Young espouses universalism. We had lunch, and I agreed to write a personal review of *Lies* for him.

And fifth, I have a long-time friend, George Sarris (we both graduated from Gordon-Conwell), who also published a book in 2017, *Heaven's Doors: Wider Than You Ever Believed!* Several years ago, George had me review, first a paper, then an early draft manuscript, and give input. He argues for an "ultimate reconciliation" universalism.

The books by Paul and George have caused much discussion and debate among a circle of friends here in the Northeast, I have joined in, but was unsatisfied with my review of *Lies*. I needed to give the matter more time, and expand it. The questions raised by these five authors are important and needful for the church to address. Jeff made a passing reference about how I should write a book, and given that I had so much in the pipeline already, here it is.

In my first five chapters, I review each of these writers as they organize their thoughts, their self-defined "methodologies." They each, from one angle or another, do so topically. My purpose is to 1) sum up the salient arguments they make, 2) affirm all good questions they raise, and 3) pose further questions I believe are necessary, in the contexts they arise, with appropriate observations. And I will be candid about where I agree and disagree.

Now, none of our five writers start with a biblical organization of thought. This I will seek do in Chapter Six, one which is able to define and address any and all questions in the Bible. As issues of freedom, hell and cognates arise, I will note them in context. In so doing, I am eschewing the common methodology of merely arranging topics through a post-biblical prism. I seek to observe the issues as they arise within the Bible, on the terms of the storyline itself, making no retrofit for the sake of a topical checklist. This takes more work on the reader's part. But the difference is enormous and satisfying – a Biblical Literacy 101 is my deepest purpose and goal. And too, I honor the storylines each of our five writers, and hopefully such a pursuit of the biblical storyline will edify them as well.

My longest review is on Kalen, mainly because he is the first one reviewed, the first one who approached me to delve into this debate, and the first to publish a book on this subject among the five, and thus the first one here to address a given subject. No need thereafter to rehash the same, only to review new angles. And though it is in writing my paper on *Lies* where I now enter this debate, my review of it is the shortest, narrowing my focus to that which relates to the question of universalism. But too, Paul's impact is so large that I needed to include him here.

There are six major themes these five hold in common, or with interface:

1. They each start from some reactive and/or experiential posture, with visceral repulsion against a doctrine that believes God sends people to hell arbitrarily. I am repulsed by the same.

2. They each are highly or strategically selective in how they treat Scripture in the process. I do not thus select.

3. They are each willing, at points, to jettison or sublimate the Scriptures in framing their arguments. I am not thus willing.

4. They each minimize the question of God's judgment. I do not.

5. They each articulate no biblical structure for interpreting the text on its own terms. I do – this is my life's work.

6. They each fail at the most important question of all – the biblical nature of freedom. This is crucial to address.

I trust these pages will be rigorously challenged wherever any of these five writers, or others, believe needful. The power to love hard questions – in all directions and equally – is intrinsic to a biblical faith.

A personal note. I write about this debate as it is presently taking place within the evangelical church. These five writers either grew up in such a church milieu, or same such.

For myself, I enter this debate as one who grew up outside the evangelical church – in the Unitarian Universalist Church, and was taught by agnostic Sunday School teachers – and too, in a town with the largest Jewish population in New England. Yet, I also come from a long line of Presbyterian ministers, including many abolitionists.

But my father left a local Presbyterian Church around the time of my birth, because he found it "insufferably judgmental." He moved on to a Congregational Church a mile north, with a famous preacher later found to be having an affair with a woman in the church, and it reverberated nationally. My father left that church too.

He cared neither for judgmentalism nor hypocrisy. Thus, Dad sojourned another mile north to the First Universalist Church, just prior to the national merger of the Unitarian and Universalist churches. He enjoyed the minister because a) "he was intelligent and worth listening to," and b) "he was faithful to his wife."

I met the Lord supernaturally as a fourteen-year-old in 1967, for which the Anglican liturgy in prep school served as a backdrop. I moved naturally into an evangelical faith, but too, in that world I ran into an ugly doctrine of hell I had to process. Happily, I also soon delved into C.S. Lewis, found solid and biblical respite, but later got involved in a church for several years that partially reversed course for me. Then I spit out its doctrines and ugly ethics, left, and have prospered well in the Word ever since.

When Dad was 90, I was reading one of my books to him (due to his failing eyesight). In our interactions, I saw the biblical faith of his youth, and especially in his deeply honed ethics. He was a medical doctor who simply loved caring for and helping people. He had found refuge in the Unitarian Universalist church, not in fleeing the Bible on its own terms, but in rejecting judgmentalism and hypocrisy. These five writers have similar reasons for fleeing toward or into some form of universalism. They love people who are made in the image of God.

But what is the most honest way to define and implement such love?

Thus. my experience thus places me in both camps, but more importantly: What do the biblical texts say, and how do they address the universal thirst for genuine freedom?

♦ ♦ ♦

Chapter One

Questions for Kalen Fristad

In James 3:1, we read: "Not many of you should become teachers, my brothers. I know there is great judgment for we who take it up."

- These five authors step forth as teachers, from their various backgrounds. They are accountable to what James says, and I no less. Accordingly, even as I honor the very good reasons for various questions they pose, I will also not shy away from posing questions, including some very tough ones, as they arise.

The Preface of *Destined for Salvation* begins accordingly: "I have written this book to let the world in on a secret that the Church has kept away from most people for the last 1,400 years" (p. ix). Kalen starts with this critique of church history, and makes his specific case in Chapter Ten.

1. If universalism is so deeply biblical, how is it possible for it to have been kept secret for so long?

2. What is the theological understanding of such a possibility?

3. What places Kalen – among all the believers across history – in position to declare that he can now reveal such a "secret?"

4. And if he does hold such a position, what exacting standards of biblical exegesis and knowledge of church history must he meet?

Kalen continues with the *raison d'etre* for his concern:

"The hope for universal salvation stands in bold contrast to what many people claim to be good news. That is, God succeeds in saving those who have the good sense to become converted before death, but for others, God throws them into hell and tosses away the key.

"Thoughtful people are justified in rebelling against a God who would do such a thing. They seem to instinctively know that God is not condemning,

9

but loving and saving. They consider the perception of the God of eternal damnation, as commonly taught by most Christian churches, to be incredibly bad news. The belief that God will not or cannot save everyone, and even imposes and enforces everlasting punishment, turns many people against God ...

"I too rebel against the teaching of a God of eternal damnation. Two of the basic tenets of my faith are that God is unconditionally loving and is all-powerful. It is because of these two foundational beliefs and the specific support of universalism in the Bible that I am compelled to believe in it. A God who, out of love, desperately wants to save everyone but is unable to accomplish it, isn't much of a God. By the same token, a God who is quite capable of saving everyone but callously chooses not to do so is not much of a God" (pp. ix-x).

5. How are "basic tenets" and "foundational beliefs" defined and determined?

6. By the Bible on its own terms, or in the advance of supporting universalism?

7. How helpful are sarcasm and clichés (e.g., "good sense to become converted" and "throwing away the key") in making a serious argument?

8. Is "conversion" merely a conscious single act in time, or are their deeper dynamics involved?

9. Does God condemn sin?

10. What is the difference between the idea that God condemns people, and that people condemn themselves?

11. If it turns out biblically that God allows people the freedom to eternally damn themselves, does Kalen rebel likewise?

12. To rebel in reaction to a negative is therefore a double negative, but what is the prior articulation of the original positive?

13. What is the definition of "unconditional" love, and does it necessarily mean universal salvation?

14. Is God subject to "desperate wants?"

15. In this construct, is there a dichotomy between God being desperate and being all-powerful?

In the Introduction, Kalen starts from a reactive posture: "Speaking from my own personal experience as a minister, I have found that by making the slight mention of it [universalism], I run the risk of experiencing judgment and wrath ... I am so misguided I am in serious jeopardy of spending eternity in hell ... As a result, most people who believe in universal salvation have been intimidated into silence" (p. 2).

This is deeply visceral in face of a genuine lack of Christian charity (to understate it). And too, this is an indictment on certain church subcultures.

16. If we start with the reactive, how can we avoid the slippery slope of reactions to reactions with no end in sight?

17. To what extent do portions of the church place codified doctrine over the biblical ethics of love of God and neighbor?

18. Biblically, does the storyline emerge out of codified doctrine, or does life-giving doctrine emerge out of the story?

19. If we start with a personal reaction in our hermeneutic (method of interpretation), how does this color or distort our grasp of the Bible on its own terms?

20. How does such a visceral and reactive starting point measure up, versus that of biblical exegesis (to dig out of the origins) as the foundation?

And our personal experiences do matter. In the Second Westminster Catechism, we learn that our first purpose is to glorify God, and then "to enjoy him forever."

And, in the Wesleyan Quadrilateral, we see the four ordered sources for authority in the Christian faith – Scripture, tradition, reason and experience. We start with 1) the biblical text on its own terms, then 2) learn through the prism of church history and tradition how given questions have been understood or misunderstood, 3) accordingly we employ our reason as it flows out of the prior two realities, which includes the freedom of unlimited questions, and finally 4) we thus have the foundation to experience love of God and neighbor.

21. To what extent does Kalen mix-up, even reverse this order, where he starts with experience, and then employs reason, tradition and Scripture to ratify such subjective experience?

As we read through *Destined For Salvation*, Kalen repeatedly appeals to his personal experience or opinion as the prism for judging the question of God's nature and of hell.

22. If idolatry is the worshiping of something good instead of the God who creates the good, can experience become an idol?

At this juncture, Kalen quotes the parable of the two sons in Luke 15:11-32, and sums it up:

"This parable captures perfectly the letter as well as the spirit of Jesus's teachings. What Jesus taught regarding unconditional love and acceptance of sinners is illustrated by the father accepting with open arms his wayward son. In the parable, the father represents God. This Scripture gives us confidence that God will eventually welcome into heaven not only those who remain faithful throughout their lives, as did the older son, but those who go astray as well" (p. 4).

Now, across his book, Kalen makes many such generalizations and extrapolations.

23. How can one passage from the whole Bible, and its interpretation, give "confidence" for a formally developed doctrine that is not mentioned within the passage?

24. Is this a "confidence" before the whole biblical testimony is reviewed, before a bevy of questions are posed?

"To exegete" means to "dig out of the guide" or "origins," to find out what is there on its own terms. The opposite verb is "to eisegete," that is, to "place something into the guide" or "origins," later discover it, and pretend it was there all along. Continually, as we read Kalen's argument, we must ask ourselves:

25. Is biblical exegesis or human eisegesis the basis for claims made?

With respect to the parable of the two sons, Tim Keller, in his widely read and definitive book, *The Prodigal God*, exegetes it so very well, and with pastoral focus. He points out that the word "prodigal" means lavish expenditure, not lostness. The first son lavishly wastes his father's inheritance, then his father lavishly spends resources on welcoming him back once he repents.

26. Is Kalen aware that Jesus speaks this parable (like so many others), not in immediate reference to heaven, but to the Pharisees (the "older son") on the one hand, and the sinners (the "younger son") such as tax collectors and prostitutes, on the other?

27. And that the older son is not the faithful one, as it were, but rather he legalistically violates his father's love the way his younger brother violates it through sinful waste?

28. And that the younger son accepts his father's love, but that the older son in the end refuses his father's love?

It is a parable about pride versus humility. Indeed, if Kalen were applying the parable consistently – even absent knowledge of Keller's exegesis – it means that the older son refuses to enter heaven. Generalizations in service to specific agendas run into many shoals.

Kalen titles Chapter One: *Dare to Possess the Truth: What Does the Bible Say About Salvation?* His instincts begin well: "It is a good thing to ask questions and struggle with what God would have us believe" (p. 6).

29. When Kalen speaks of God having us "believe," to what extent does this clause reflect a church subculture of believing "the right thing" even apart from how we live our lives?

He then says: "We put ourselves in jeopardy of not having well-founded beliefs if we accept a philosophy that runs contrary to the Bible. It is also important that we not blindly take someone else's word for what the Bible says, instead of reading the Word for ourselves … We also risk failing to possess ultimate truth if we come to believe a conclusion prematurely or stubbornly cling to what we believe even when we receive information to the contrary" (pp. 6-7).

Kalen and I agree in this: Consistency with the Bible, and an active faith as opposed to a passive one, are good and to be pursued.

30. Thus, what is the biblical theology, what is the biblical basis for the goodness of questions in the face of God, especially as in much of history, church authorities have prohibited the same?

31. And to what extent is he writing in reaction to a specific church culture of his own experience, one that is rooted in such passive acquiescence?

32. What is the church milieu that "possess(es) ultimate truth?"

Kalen says, "Salvation is what this book is all about" (p. 8), then defines "salvation" as meaning "eternal life" in the context of quoting John 3:16: "For God so loved the world that he gave his only Son, so that everyone who believes in him may not perish but have eternal life" (Kalen uses the 1989 Revised Standard Version [RSV] in all his biblical quotations). Now salvation is in view here, but the word for salvation is not in the text.

33. But how can a word like "salvation" be properly defined without first looking into its etymology, its word history?

It would be helpful to look at *yesa* in the Hebrew (the verbal predicate for the name *Yeshua*, transliterated into the Greek *Iesou*, Jesus), and then explain how in the New Testament, its parallel, *soza*, is directed toward

14

eternal life. The context is far richer than the church subculture to which he reacts.

He then looks at five passages that raise "questions about universal salvation." Here we run into a defining problem for the whole book, already touched on, but here it is front and center:

34. To what extent is Kalen looking at everything through an eisegetical lens of "universal salvation," to find it where he can?

Kalen's first selected passage is Matthew 13:24-30, 36-43, the parable of the weeds. The good seed is gathered into the barn, and the weeds are burned. Jesus then makes analogy to the "sons of the kingdom" versus the "sons of the evil one," where the sons of the evil one will be thrown into a furnace of fire. But Kalen then says: "This passage makes it very clear that hell is terrible and that it will be experienced by the unsaved following death. It does not indicate that hell is without end" (p. 9).

35. Why then is the word "hell" not even mentioned in this parable?

36. What is the history of the language of judgment in Scripture?

37. Very clear in what terms?

38. Also, if the "sons of the evil one" are eventually saved from hell, what about the evil one himself?

39. An argument from silence?

Thus, an important question:

40. If hell is limited in duration for sinners, why would this not also apply to the ancient serpent, Satan, the one who sets sin into motion?

41. And what about the demons?

42. What in this language says anything about there being no end to hell?

43. As Jesus uses the art of analogy, and to be consistent with it in Kalen's mind, does it mean the weeds are later saved, after they have been burned?"

Analogies, being tertiary or quaternary in nature, do not aim at precision, for they jump contexts for illustration. Nonetheless, Kalen has pulled out something very precise here – no "hell without end."

44. Why has Kalen not defined the word "hell," upon which he bases so many assumptions about its nature?

"Hell" as a word originates in the proto-Germanic *halja* dating to the fifth century A.D. – for "one who covers up or hides something." By the eighth century, in Old English, the word was *hel* or *helle*, signifying a dark nether world of the dead. Note how the darkness of covering something over migrates to a destination of darkness – yet without the literal fires of hell's popular imagination. Yet, here, it is only the question of an English word that Kalen has thus far raised. There is the need for the Hebrew and Greek antecedents.

His second text is Matthew 25:1-13 concerning the bridesmaids, with a final presupposed conclusion: "Again, however, this passage gives no indication that finding oneself excluded from the wedding banquet is a permanent situation" (p. 10).

45. How can this analogically work?

46. Is not a wedding banquet a time-bound event, and once it is over, it is over?

47. Or is the wedding banquet in this parable endless?

48. In first century occupied Israel, do wedding banquets have an encore for those who failed in the instructions to attend the first one?

49. How does this parable of a wedding banquet relate to the wedding banquet of the Lamb in Revelation 19:9?

50. In terms of the trajectory, is there a second wedding banquet after the Book of Revelation scheduled for those who miss the first one?

51. Would not Kalen need to argue this possibility to make his case?

52. Again, an argument from silence?

The third text is Matthew 25:31-46, on the separation between the sheep and the goats at the Judgment, parallel in purpose to the separation between the wheat and the weeds. It contrasts the inheritance of the sheep (the righteous) as prepared since the creation, to the goats (the evildoers) joining the "eternal fire" prepared for the devil and his angels, and concludes with the contrast of "eternal punishment" with "eternal life."

Kalen says the key to understanding this text is in knowing the Greek term for "eternal."

53. If it is key to know the Greek for "eternal," why not likewise for "hell."

His sequence of thought is thus: 1) "The Greek word *aionios*, translated 'eternal' does not necessarily apply only to the length of life," but to the quality of life as well. 2) "... the English words 'eternal' and 'everlasting' both mean 'without end,' but the Greek words from which they are a translation don't have exactly the same meaning." 3) If the New Testament writers had meant "the concept of punishment without end," they would have used the word *aidios* for "perpetual." 4) He then jumps to Origen of Alexandria (in the third century) who translates it as an "indefinite but limited duration." 5) Kalen then says: "A Greek English lexicon defines *aionios* as "lasting for an age." 6) And finally, "*Young's Analytical Concordance to the Bible* gives the definition "age lasting."

He concludes: "By virtue of the definition of *aionios*, therefore, we can conclude that eternal punishment in hell will eventually come to an end" (p. 11), making reference to v. 46.

54. Is this meant to pass muster as scholarship?

55. Is this an accurate rendering of *aionios*?

Without an accurate definition, his language of "does not necessarily apply" reflects his genre of vagueness and generalization, as is "they don't have exactly the same meaning."

56. Is not Kalen's introduction of *aidios* is an example of "word shopping," one that does not address the text in question, thus, second guessing the biblical use of *aionios*?

57. How much of Kalen's work is rooted in taking the human chronological reckoning of time as the key prism?

58. Thus, when issues of time and quality interface, what is the prism of the Creator?

Origen is not a primary source, writing some two centuries after the fact, and Young's Concordance is not a lexigraphical source for the Greek, but a 1970 analytical concordance that hardly qualifies.

59. "A Greek Lexicon?" Which one?

Scholarship starts with the most primary sources available, and the ones with the greatest attribution in the checks and balances of all other resources on the subject.

In the *Liddell and Scott Unabridged Greek-English Lexicon*, and in the *Bauer, Arndt and Gingrich Greek Lexicon*, *aionios* means "without beginning and end." Never in classical or New Testament Greek does it refer to a limited time frame. Its root word (*aion*) does so occasionally, but that word is not used here. In fact, in the thirty major English translations of this word in Matthew 25:46, it is only translated as "eternal," "forever" or "everlasting."

Thus, for Kalen to not reference *Liddell and Scott*, or in *Bauer*, and to cite an anonymous Greek Lexicon, is "source shopping." It is an eisegetical means that runs contrary to his own earlier exhortation not "to believe a conclusion prematurely or stubbornly cling to what we believe even when we receive information to the contrary" (p. 7).

- Now, critically for Kalen, if *aionios* does not mean "eternal," but only to a penultimate time-bound reality, this means there is no eternal life for believers on the other side of the coin. The same word applies both to the sheep and the goats, applicable likewise to the sons of the kingdom and the sons of the evil one. Either life and death are both set to come to a complete end at some point, or they both have eternal, endless destinies. Kalen cannot have it both ways, but his visceral reactions to bad doctrine and bad church culture has boomeranged him into an untenable position. Reactions to reactions only beget further reactions and spin us out of control. We need a truly proactive theology, and honest scholarship.

When Kalen cites John 3:16 as his definition of "salvation," upon which his whole book focuses, he says it is the same as "eternal life" used by Jesus here in Matthew 25. But the word is *aionios,* which now Kalen has just tried to mean something less than everlasting.

60. Therefore, by Kalen's own interpretive logic, must not both hell and heaven be limited in duration?

In my final 2005 forum with Kalen, he could not give one example of *aionios* ever being translated as limited in duration of time. He only cited Origen.

61. How can Kalen's citation of Origen be trusted?

For, according to his footnotes, Kalen's reference on Origen is from the 1883 *Columbian Congress of the Universalist Church.*

62. When using such an obscure secondary source to ratify a primary and central point in his argument, is this not a quintessential example of eisegesis?

63. And what confidence in the argument is thus possible?

In the same footnote, he also references an 1876 Universalist work: "John Wesley Hanson: Aion-Aionios: the Greek Word Translated Everlasting – Eternal, in the Holy Bible, Shown to Denote Limited Duration."

In terms of primary sources, Origen, in his argument for universal salvation in Book 1, Chapter 6, and Book 2, Chapters 5 and 10 of *De Principiis*, does not examine the Greek term *aionios* at all. Maybe he does elsewhere in his large corpus of writings, but Kalen gives us no source material here to know how, if at all, Origen translates *aionios*. In his argument for universalism, he cites certain biblical verses atomistically, and does not address the deep range of biblical texts which might state otherwise.

> 64. If Kalen's cited ancient source, even if through secondary means, does not examine the defining word Kalen attributes him, does not a major stilt in his argument collapse?

Origen's work moves toward a form of universal salvation, and he starts in the Preface, section 4, by citing "points clearly delivered in the teaching of the apostles." This includes a statement in section 5, that after death human souls are "destined to obtain either an inheritance of eternal life and blessedness" or "to be delivered up to eternal fire and punishments." Now Origen says that the teaching of the apostles is subject to review – which is what he is doing – but the question remains for him is one of biblical fidelity.

The fourth text is the parable of the rich man and Lazarus in Luke 16:19-31. The text speaks of a great chasm fixed between Abraham and Hades, one that cannot be crossed. Kalen again gives generalizations that have no basis in the actual text. First, he says that Hades is the same as hell, and this is not linguistically true. They are different words with different meanings, as we will later note in specificity. "Hell" is used concomitant with final judgment, and Hades as a prior penultimate way-station to either eternal life or death. He also assumes that "the side of Abraham" is the same thing as heaven, and the text does not say this.

> 65. How does Kalen assume a parable can be so blithely attributed to doctrinal conclusions on a larger subject?

66. Are we reading an exercise in mere wishfulness?

His fifth citation is in 2 Thessalonians 1:5-9, with reference to the "eternal destruction" of those who do not obey the Gospel. He says: "This passage of Scripture, along with the others I have quoted above, apparently supports the idea of hell in the next life, but there are legitimate reasons to conclude that, for individuals, hell is not necessarily without end" (p. 12).

Same train of thought, and generalized opinion. In reactively being appalled at truly bad doctrine, subjective criteria govern. Kalen has defined an assumption that needs to be negativized, as opposed to simply starting where the Scriptures start, across the board.

67. Are these five cited texts supposed to represent the entire biblical argument that oppose his doctrine of universal salvation?

68. And we can ask here: Is Kalen merely selecting passages via his chosen issue, or does he have comprehension of an overall biblical structure?

69. And if he does, what is it, and why is not employed up front?

Kalen now turns his focus: "Many Bible passages suggest everyone will eventually be saved. Some present the concept that God will even save people from hell" (p. 12). He lists eleven passages.

70. Do interpreted "suggestions" and some "concepts" equal biblical exegesis, especially as the foundation for a given argument?

First, in Matthew 18:21-22, he cites how Jesus answers Peter on the matter of forgiving others, even seventy-seven times. Second, in Luke 15:3-6 (as he cites it; v. 7 completes the parable), Jesus speaks of leaving ninety-nine sheep on the hillside to search for the one lost sheep. In other words, the pursuing love of Jesus is interpreted as one that will not stop – across eternity – until all people choose to receive salvation. From the general to an unspoken specific doctrine.

Third, Kalen lifts out the verse of John 12:32, where Jesus speaks of how he will draw all people to himself. This introduces the question of how "all" is used in Scripture.

71. In drawing "all" people to himself, what in the text says that therefore "all" people will be saved?

For example, a huge range of people come to Jesus, many love him, many prove fickle, and a few (especially self-serving elitists) hate him.

72. Why does Kalen not especially review this crucial and often debated word?

The concept of "all" is ubiquitous in Scripture. In New Testament Greek, *pas*, *pasa* and *pan* are the words, and capable each of being used, in three distinct categories for "all." They can refer to 1) completeness; e.g., "From him and through him and to him are all things" (Romans 11:36). Or 2) to comprehensiveness; e.g., Moses was instructed in "all" the wisdom of Egypt (Acts 7:22).

73. Can any person know "all" wisdom in the sense of completeness, even if limited to that of one culture?

And they can be used 3) for the sake of emphasis or representation; e.g., "all" Judea and Jerusalem and the surrounding region coming to see John the Baptist at the Jordan River (Matthew 3:5).

74. Does this mean, per Kalen, that hundreds of thousands of people, if not more, trekked out to the wilderness – men, women, children, the aged and infirm, Jews, Gentiles and Roman occupiers – to see John?

75. Or is "all" representative of the people across the whole region?

In other words, "all" is far greater than a numerical construct.

76. How therefore can it be used to imply universal salvation unless the numerical construct is evident in the text?

In the Hebrew Bible, the clause "all Israel" (*kol yisrael*) is used often (e.g., Joshua 3:17 vis-à-vis completeness; Joshua 3:7 in the comprehensive sense, and 1 Samuel 2:22 in the emphatic/representative sense). It can refer to the leaders of the tribes representing all their members, and it represents genealogies where only leading, representative and specifically noteworthy names are listed. And it often refers to the whole nation.

In the Book of Chronicles (originally one unit), and in comparison with a different purpose in the construct of the prior Book of Kings, the emphasis is on the unity of the "whole nation," of *kol yisrael* in the face of its many divisions across the centuries. And in Romans 11:26, when the apostle Paul declares "all" Israel will be saved, he is especially treating Israel as a unit, the chosen people through whom salvation comes to all people.

> 77. But in coming to "all" people, are "all" automatically saved, now, or past the grave?

Kalen's fourth selected passage to support universal salvation, is also lifted from John 12 (vv. 46-47), where Jesus comes as the light of the world, not to judge it but to save it. Kalen then says: "Jesus came to save everyone in the world!" (p. 14). Note how in his enthusiasm, he here inserts "everyone" into the biblical text.

Thus far, we see how Kalen selects sundry passages and verses for his argument, but little or no attention is given to the context of his selections, and original purposes for their intent. This is classic "proof-texting" – stringing passages or verses together from disparate contexts, and atomizing them in service to a presupposed idea or doctrine. For example, here, contrary to Kalen's issue of being "non-judgmental," in John 5:26-27, Jesus speaks of how the Father has given him the authority to judge.

But far more discomfiting for Kalen is the very next verse after his chosen text, John 12:48, which continues the discussion of Jesus on the subject of judgment: "The one who rejects me and does not receive my word is himself judged; the word I speak will judge him on the last day."

- This is a dangerous point for Kalen. He has selectively lifted out two verses, splitting them from the succeeding verses, indeed, splitting v. 47 from v. 48, purposing to use the Scriptures falsely, to remove from Jesus his authority to judge. The simplicity of this context, and others like in in John's Gospel, is that Jesus is showing how he is coming as the Savior, and with the authority to judge (e.g., John 5:19-47, as already referenced in part, and John 8:15ff.).

78. Is Kalen able to read this very passage in the whole, and grasp such a straightforward tension?

79. If he were self-assured, why not quote the whole text, and then give interpretation?

Fifth, he lifts out another verse, Romans 5:18, where Paul speaks of how one man's sin leads to condemnation for all, and one man righteousness leads to justification and life for all, e.g. Adam and Christ. He also cites 1 Corinthians 15:22 as a corollary: "For as all die in Adam, so all will be made alive to Christ."

80. Why does Kalen not quote the whole argument Paul is making in Romans 5:12-20, one of the most thoroughly debated biblical texts in church history concerning universalism?

81. Is "all" being used in a sense of completeness, comprehensiveness or emphasis/representation?

Sixth, he quotes Romans 8:38-39, in that nothing in all creation can separate us from the love of Christ. Here we hit another crucial juncture.

82. Why does Kalen not at least reference the larger context of vv. 18ff.?

This text builds from defining God's wrath against sin, apparent to all peoples in Romans 1. Paul builds his theology through to the beginning of Romans 8 where he then segues from the condemnation in the law to its abolition provided in Christ. And this is necessary to understand the crescendo of vv. 38-39. As well, in vv. 28ff., we have one of the two most debated texts in Scripture concerning predestination.

83. How can Kalen's argument be taken seriously with such a huge lacuna?

84. Thus, for Kalen, by definition, does the love of God prohibit people from the freedom to eternally reject it?

85. If people cannot thus reject God's love, can they remain free, is God therefore coercive, is he a slavemaster like pagan deities who are finite?

86. If those who end up in hell, according to Kalen's doctrine, are eventually persuaded of God's love after the grave, has something changed either in God's character or human nature?

87. Accordingly, if God cannot persuade certain people in this life, despite remarkable patience (e.g. the 120 years in Noah's day, the years prior to Sodom and Gomorrah, the 400 years between Abraham and Moses, in Romans 1, and across the whole trajectory in the Book of Revelation), what changes after the grave?

88. In other words, has the patience of Kalen's God in this life proven insufficient, so that a Plan B must be adopted?

89. If ultimate universalism is so fundamentally biblical, why is it not stated explicitly in one or more of the various passages Kalen cites?

90. Why not, therefore, did Jesus not speak of the eternal fire with an exception clause?

- E.g.: "You will suffer the fire of hell, but no sweat, I will get you out after a period of time." Or: "You missed the wedding banquet, but relax, I will get married again so you can be a guest."

Seventh is Philippians 2:10-11 (part of an early church hymn) where Paul quotes Isaiah 45:23, applying it to Jesus, that every knee will bow to him and confess his Lordship. Kalen takes this to mean the possibility of eventual universal salvation.

91. Does bowing the knee always reflects chosen worship?

25

92. And again, why lift central verses from the richness of their context?

The theology vv. 5-11 is perhaps the most dynamic incarnational text in the New Testament. And for the two verses in question, the tapestry is complex. In pagan antiquity, bowing the knee is virtually universal, in acknowledgement of the superior position of the given ruler, chosen or forced. Friends and enemies alike must kneel. In Esther 3, the pagan royal officials kneel down to Haman (a hater of the Jews), Mordecai the Jew refuses, and sets in motion a series of events that saves the Jews from annihilation. Matthew quotes Psalm 110:1, in 22:44 of his gospel. Jesus, as Messiah, fulfills it, and all his enemies are placed under his feet – an ultimate kneeling in the face of reality for those who still reject belief in the goodness of the Creator and/or his Messiah. In Matthew 27:29, some soldiers kneel down before Jesus, and mock him as King of the Jews. In James 2:19, the apostle says that even the demons believe in God – and shudder. They believe God is God, but they reject his goodness. In other words, kneeling is an inescapable reality in the presence of tangible authority, for those who either love or hate the one in authority.

In the eighth case, 1 Peter 3:18-20; 4:6, Kalen again lifts verses out of the larger context, i.e., vv. 8ff. on the question of suffering. Yet, this is a most interesting text, as it is unique and has occasioned much debate in church history. Kalen quotes how Peter writes about Jesus preaching to the spirits in prison, to the dead who have been judged in the flesh … so they might now live in the Spirit. Kalen then says: "This passage makes a clear and specific reference to Jesus saving people from hell" (p. 15). It is neither clear nor specific.

First, it is not a singular passage, but is the linkage of two passages in sequence from Peter's letter. Second, as Kalen links quotes between 3:18-20 and 4:6, he eclipses the very context of those to whom Jesus is preaching – they who perished in Noah's flood. Third, hell is not mentioned. Fourth, Kalen continually conflates *sheol* (in the Hebrew Bible) and *hades* (in the New Testament) with the English word hell (none of which he has attempted to define). Fifth, with the understanding that *sheol* is a place for the dead, righteous and unrighteous alike, and likewise for *hades*, this is the natural context for "the spirits in prison." Sixth, in Luke

4:18-19, where Jesus fulfills Isaiah 61:1-2, he proclaims freedom to the prisoners, and this has foundational theological interface with 1 Peter 3:19. Seventh, in the Apostles Creed, the early church proclaims that Jesus "descended into hell," and this is a dynamic part of this debate (he only alludes to it later, whereas this is the more natural place to make such reference). And eighth, Kalen here has an opportunity to dig into all this material and make a case for "ultimate restoration," as have others in church history. But he does not.

93. How can Kalen be taken seriously when he so easily glides over such a central text that relates to his concerns?

The ninth passage Kalen cites is Colossians 1:19-20, lifting two verses that focus on Paul's declaration that "all" the fullness of God dwells in Jesus, and Jesus reconciles "all" things in earth and heaven to himself. As we have already noted in the treatment of "all" in the biblical texts, there is so much rich tapestry in need of review, in order to understand whether a given reference is to completeness (the numerical quality Kalen always assumes for his purposes), comprehensives, or emphasis/representation.

94. Too, does reconciliation mean the same thing as automatic willing belief?

95. Where is the review of how the Bible uses the language of "reconciliation?"

96. E.g., In Psalm 110:1 and Matthew 22:44, with the enemies under the feet of Yahweh, of Jesus, what is left unreconciled, as it were?

Reconciliation includes both to Jesus as Lord and Savior, and not just the latter as we see Kalen earlier indicate. There is no Hebrew word for reconciliation, and as such, the nature of the atonement (*kaphar*) is the theological backdrop. The Greek term in Colossians 1:20 is *apokatallassa*, and it indicates man's need for reconciliation, not God's need to change his character to accommodate us as sinners. It means to "change" or "to exchange," and that is what the cross of Jesus is all about. But it still requires repentance (the Greek verb *metanoeo* means a change of mind, and hence a change of direction). Thus, Kalen cannot argue for universal salvation based on "all" or on "reconciliation." He has to show, that after the grave, the Scriptures show that all people will ultimately repent of their sins, and this idea has yet to be evidenced in his argument.

97. Just as knees can bow in the face of reality, without choosing to embrace to the goodness of God, is not the same reality also present here?

• We are reconciled to the Lordship of Jesus, he is not reconciled to human sinfulness. The "all" is thus subsumed.

The tenth passage cited is lifted out of 1 Timothy 2:4-6, where Paul says that God our Savior "wants all men to be saved and come to a knowledge of the truth."

98. Curiously here, why does Kalen not also quote from 2 Peter 3:9 where the apostle says that God is patient, "not wanting anyone to be destroyed, but for all to make room for repentance?"

The passage in Peter is perhaps a bit stronger for Kalen's purposes, but still there is the deepest question yet.

• Here Kalen hits on one of the most salient questions of all, as he then says: "If God desires everyone to be saved, will God not succeed?" (p. 16).

99. But is desire the same thing as will?

100. What exactly is God's will?

101. What is the definition of God's sovereignty and human freedom in this regard?

102. If everyone is not saved in the end, has God thus "lost"?

103. Why not ask instead: Why does man choose to become and stay lost?

104. What are the biblical definitions of winning and losing, how to they apply to God, and to what extent can the idea of winning and losing become a modern construct myopically applied to God and Scripture?

And here follow two of the most dynamic questions for Kalen:

105. Is universal salvation – and if necessary through the means of an
✳︎ ultimate "reconciliation" – so completely intrinsic to the Scriptures that it is an assumption that interprets all else?

There is nothing in his book I have read that indicates otherwise. Thus:

106. Why did Paul and Peter not make it clearer, instead of mixing in
✳︎ the language of "want" and "desire?"

- They could have simply said: "For God knows that all people will be saved in the end." Period. But they did not.

Kalen's eleventh and final verses are from 1 John 2:1-2, where the atoning sacrifice of Jesus is for the sins "concerning the whole world." This returns us to the discussion on "all" and is not a new issue, just another passage Kalen cites accordingly.

Kalen concludes his chapter by saying there are conflicting passages of Scripture on both sides of the issue, but in our review, his presuppositional interpretive views are all slanted in one direction. Thus, he calls for a review of "many general biblical themes and profound implications we need to think through" (p.16).

107. What biblically self-defining hermeneutic defines the "general."

108. How does the "general" interpret the "specific?"

109. Or does the "general" serve as a last refuge for the many "specific" questions that have been neither considered nor addressed?

Thus, Kalen introduces these general themes in Chapter Two, "Seeing the Bigger Picture." The first theme is "God's quest to save us." He argues that the "evidence" first shows up in Genesis 3 in the promise for the serpent's head to be crushed.

110. Why does Kalen not first tell us why we need to be saved?

111. Saved from what?

112. What is the nature of Genesis 1-2 that precedes Genesis 3?

113. And who is the serpent?

His next theme is judgment, and he begins with Hebrew 9:27 ("It is appointed for mortals to die once, and after that the judgment" [1989 RSV]), and then cites John 3:19-21.

114. What is the original cause for the need of judgment, and what is the biblical trajectory that brings us to the New Testament?

In other words, Kalen's "general" themes are based on specific verses he places into a general theme. And here again, we see how Kalen elucidates his presuppositions from specific passages without specific linkage other than his wishes.

In John 3, the nighttime conversation with Jesus and Nicodemus (the whole chapter) ends with Jesus, as he notes the difference between a) "men who love darkness more than light because their works are evil" and b) those who live in the light because they are confident that their works have been done though God.

115. Is Kalen familiar with how radical the language here is concerning love?

Namely, classical and *koine* (New Testament) Greek have many words for love that are specific in focus. For example, we can note four differentiated loves (specific relational focuses each): *storge* is an instinctive familial love; *philadephia* is a brotherly love; *philos* is the love of close friends; and *eros* is unbounded sexual love. Then we have the undifferentiated love, applicable to any and all, namely, *agape*. It is a self-giving or self-emptying love for the sake of the other. Everything is given to the object of the gift. Now, *eros* is not used in the New Testament, and *agape* is a rare word from early classical Greek. *Agape* was employed by the Jewish writers of the Septuagint (LXX) in the third century B.C. translation of the Hebrew Scriptures into Greek. They needed a word to express a self-giving love applicable to God, and this was the closest they found. And the New Testament picks it up.

It may be the closest the Septuagint scholars could locate, but it is not synonymous with the character of God. Rather, God's character modifies the application of *agape*, quintessentially in the incarnation and on the cross. So too can sinful people modify its usage. This we see in John 3. First, the apostle John uses *agape* when he says, "For God so loved the world" (v. 16). This is the very text Kalen started with earlier in defining salvation. Then second, the apostle John uses *agape* for the "love" of darkness (v. 19) – not *philos*, not even *eros* – but a total self-giving love to darkness as an idol. Here again, Kalen skims the surface of biblical verses to substantiate his doctrines, and this leads to two critical questions:

116. How well has Kalen studied the actual Greek text?

117. And if not in reality, how does this accord with the warning by James, of judgment upon we who take up teaching the Word?

Anyone who knows the lexigraphical and grammatical force of *agape*, used for opposite loves in this context, is floored by Kalen's cavalier oversight as he then says without evidence: "But I want to make it very clear that if someone chooses to go to hell, it is not a final choice. I believe God will not let it be so. It is not as if people have complete free will, that whatever they choose is acceptable to God and will stand forever" (p. 19).

He is rooted in feelings, not biblical exegesis.

- Here again, Kalen steps into dangerous theological currents. First, the *agape* of God versus the *agape* of darkness versus carries with it the force of a most fully and time invested decision to accept or reject God. Second, Kalen has now rejected what he calls "complete free will" (a term begging definition) for human beings, which is to say, that in the very end, he says God will employ some force or coercion to get people into heaven.

118. How can Kalen insinuate a presupposed doctrine into a biblical text, and furthermore, without knowing the dramatic nature of the Greek term *agape* and syntax that argue so forcefully the opposite?

119. If Kalen's "God" employs any coercion of the human will, and thus dehumanizes, how is this god different than pagan deities?

120. Thus, how can this god truly "save," unless it is a "salvation" to some form of slavery?

For example, in Hebrews 6:4-8, the author (I am convinced it is Barnabas) speaks of the impossibility of restoring to repentance those who have once been enlightened, shared in the power of the Holy Spirit, and tasted of "the powers of the coming age" – if they fall away by crucifying the Son of God all over again in a way that publicly disgraces his once-and-for-all atonement for sin.

This language has much texture that flies against Kalen's cavalier treatment of Scripture. If we understand Barnabas as one of the early Jewish priests who converted to Jesus as Messiah, and if we grasp the biblical sophistication of the letter to the Hebrews, we can see him writing to some of his fellow priests who converted but later apostasized. For a Jewish priest to accept Jesus as the Lamb of God who paid the atonement price for sin once and for all, and then to return to the annual sacrifice for atonement, it is a deliberate and deeply thought out mockery of the sacrifice of Jesus. And as well, 2 Peter 2:20 describes the same intentionality in turning away from Jesus, in the context of the whole chapter dealing with the deliberate evil of false teachers. In both cases, repentance is declared beyond reach.

121. If Barnabas and Peter speak of those who are beyond the reach of repentance through such patterned and willful evil, why does Kalen not address this as he explains how they reconsider their reconsideration after the grave?

122. If the same *agape* can apply to the Light of the World as it does to the Prince of darkness, what does this say about the nature and possibility of "settled choices" in the human soul?

123. If in view of such a dramatic "impossibility" for the living human soul to again choose repentance, how does Kalen linguistically segue this into a possibility, after the grave, to repent of having forsaken repentance?

Kalen continues nonetheless: "I'm convinced Jesus understood judgment as a beginning, not as an end. Therefore, rather than focusing on the past, our attention should be on the future ... Our task is to move beyond judging people and assessing whether they deserve our compassion" (p. 20). In other words, sans cause and effect. And: "Could heaven truly be heavenly for anyone if even one soul is forever forbidden from entering in?" (p. 21). Feelings apart from wrestling with biblical theology and anthropology.

124. If Kalen were to examine the whole theme of judgment across the Bible, where and how can he say it is a beginning, not an end?

125. Is there no final judgment, or just his insistence of massaging the finality out of all such texts?

Kalen continues with the "general themes" of God's grace, the purpose of punishment or suffering, and the love of God. No new material, just the appeal to sundry verses to serve his organization of thought. Then he touches on expiation of sin with a reactive feeling: "Christ's death was not for the purpose of appeasing an angry God" (p. 26). Yes, a doctrine of "appeasing an angry God" is ugly. But too:

126. How does Kalen address Paul's definition of God's wrath in Romans 1, as it reflects all biblical history?

127. Can God be angry with sin (e.g., Mark 3:1-6) without forcing on us a need to "appease" him?

Then he concludes Chapter Two with the general themes of a diagnosed lack of urgency of the part of Jesus in this regard, and questions of life after

33

death. In terms of the latter, he says it is "totally logical" that Jesus would "not spend all of his time exclusively with people enjoying heaven while ignoring those who suffer in hell" (p. 29). And: "I believe Jesus will never rest as long as anyone remains in hell. I am confident that countless Christians will join with Jesus their leader, in a great mission to rescue those who suffer. And they will not quit, either, until the last person is liberated from hell" (p. 30).

128. In terms of literary structure, as we see Kalen insinuating the "totally logical" projections of his presuppositional theology, and here on the person of Jesus, does this express confidence, or the making of a case that is not self-persuasive?

129. Why not simply make the proactive case, then answer the reactionaries, and let the argument stand?

Chapter Three is titled, "Amazing Grace," and Kalen again resorts to his projections of the human upon the divine. "As for me, as imperfect as I am, I would never consider abandoning even one person to endless hell … I absolutely cannot believe God is morally or ethically inferior to me or other humans, so I cannot believe God would abandon anyone in hell" (p. 33). Here, as through the entire book, Kalen assumes "endless hell" would be an imposition of God upon the human will, and he spits this idea out. But too, he has said that human freedom is not complete, and thus God has to use some coercion to ultimately empty hell. He cannot have it both ways.

130. Crucially here, do we start with a human perspective in grasping God's character?

131. Are we made in the image of God, or is Kalen's "God" made in Kalen's image?

Now Kalen does concede that there is a real hell with all the descriptions of unmatched suffering.

132. Does he have in mind how long the most stubborn people will persist in suffering it before becoming "persuaded of God's love?"

133. A year, 10,000 years …?

134. Would current U.S. law consider even ten minutes of hell as a form of "cruel and unusual punishment?"

135. Thus, has not Kalen conceded to an opinion that God is an unjust ✳ God, and why argue the difference between ten minutes and forever?

136. And would not any hell sufferer be so traumatized after ten minutes (!) that all rationality is forfeit, and the possibility of reconsideration becomes moot?

137. And with Kalen's emphasis on the persuasive love of God, is hell an act of love or is it intrinsically destructive?

138. Thus, is not the only possibility one where unending judgment is only chosen by a minority, those who have patterned their lives in a perverse love of darkness rather than light, evil rather than the good, bitterness rather than forgiveness – and thus they deaden their own consciences, and would rather stew in their juices (too literally) than anything else?

From here, Kalen continues judging God through a human perspective by talking about human parental love, then projecting the same on God, not vice versa. Then he muses on ideas about those who have not heard the Gospel, but without any review of salient biblical texts or theological study. This is a rich field, with many excellent questions to raise and address, such as his concern of "fairness," but Kalen skims over it most briefly. Then he diagnoses Dante's *Inferno* as "an attempt to get God off the hook" (p. 37).

139. What does Kalen know about the biblical, literary, cultural, political and ecclesiastical depths of Durante degli Alighieri?

140. Is it Dante who wants to get God off the hook, or is his life and work far more deeply textured?

141. Or is it Kalen who wants to "get God off the hook?"

Kalen then adds several paragraphs about the completeness of Christ's victory, concluding with a "joyous affirmation" of an "ultimate heaven." Chapter One is his framing of the issue, and Chapters Two and Three come across as a bucket list of assorted ideas into which he can place his generalizations about the whole topic.

In Chapter Four, Kalen focuses on free will. "Some people put much emphasis on free will. Obviously, we do have freedom. We make choices every day. But are we totally free? That is the question we must address as we deal with the issues of how we are saved and whether anyone might spend eternity in hell" (p. 40).

142. "Obviously?" Not "totally?" What is required to "address" this huge subject?

"I get the impression that some people are not particularly bothered by the prospect that certain other people might be consigned to hell forever" (pp. 40-41). These are meandering thoughts, with such imprecise language as "much emphasis," "obviously" and "totally."

143. For people who embrace a biblical belief of final judgment, does Kalen accuse them of not being "bothered" about the well-being of "certain other people?"

He also says: "Do we have total free will? Are we completely free to make choices that result in either happiness or misery? ... And if we continue to have freedom of choice in the next life, wouldn't it be utterly absurd to choose to continue to suffer in hell forever? ... Choosing eternal life is an easy choice, it seems to me" (p. 41).

In contrast to Kalen's sentiments, we can consider Revelation 6:16, where in response to the opening of the sixth seal, the peoples of the earth call on the mountains and rocks to fall on them and "conceal us from the face of him who sits on the throne and from the wrath of the Lamb!" In other words, at the Second Coming of Jesus, they prefer to be crushed to death rather than look at Jesus.

144. On what basis can the continuation of the freedom of choice, after death, change the choices made before death?

145. If people want to hide from Jesus in the face of the Judgment of his Second Coming, why would they later choose the light?

146. Does a new post final finality now appear?

147. If people love bitterness more than forgiveness, because they become their own gods in passing judgment on others, why would they ever give up the perverse satisfaction of being their own gods?

Indeed, Jonah states in 2:8 of his book: "Those who cling to worthless idols depart from steadfast love." Even more so, Jeremiah states: "They walked after worthless idols and became worthless themselves" (2:5).

148. Kalen may think eternal life is an easy choice for himself, but does he then impose this sentiment on those who might believe otherwise?

149. Does Kalen believe human freedom can only make one ultimate choice, namely salvation, and if so, is not his freedom a form of pre-destined fatalism?

He continues: "Does God allow some people to condemn themselves forever of their own free will?" (p. 42). Then he quotes one writer: "He is either the weak God of unlimited love but limited power, or else he is the cruel God of limited power but limited love" (p. 43).

150. What is Kalen's biblical theology of "free will" if any?

151. Are these the only two options for God's nature and character – and as posited through one individual human perspective?

In both these options, Kalen says they make God into a monster: "The teaching of eternal damnation makes it impossible to believe God is both loving and all-powerful" (ibid).

152. Is, perhaps, Yahweh Elohim simultaneously unlimited in both love and power?

153. And can Kalen comprehend what this might look like?

In Mark 10:17-23, a rich man asks Jesus what he must do to inherit eternal life: "And Jesus looked at him and loved him, and said to him, 'You lack one thing. Go and sell all your holdings and give to the poor, and you will have a storehouse in heaven. Now come follow me' " (v. 21). The man walks away in sorrow for he will not give up his idolatry of wealth, and Jesus thus remarks how hard it is to enter the kingdom of God.

This text is in the wheelhouse of Kalen's concern – the inheritance of eternal life. Jesus, as he calls the man to flee idolatry, "loved him." The man clings to his idol, and thus volitionally excludes himself from eternal life.

154. Here, according to Kalen, is Jesus lacking in power or love?

155. And is the love of Jesus ill-affected by the man's rejection?

156. Does love need to be loved in order to qualify as love?

Kalen then sets up Martin Luther as someone who is grateful for not having free will in the matter of salvation, that it depends entirely on God. Here, Kalen takes an isolated quote from Luther, suitable for his purposes, but through the prism of a secondary source (a writer in 1961).

157. Why does Kalen not use primary sources, especially when easily available, with all their richness of context, e.g., Luther's definitive work, *The Bondage of the Will*?

Luther is deeply passionate in his discovery of grace as he rejects Roman Catholic legalism, as he opposes the manipulation of the masses through the sales of indulgences as a hellfire or purgatory escape. But much of his life remained viscerally reactive to many things, and this context informs *The Bondage of the Will*. Kalen lifts Luther out of his deep texture as well, all for the purpose of a presuppositional doctrine.

Kalen then continues with his next brief section on "the idolatry of free will," saying: "It is of great significance that when Jesus was on the cross, he did not pray, saying, 'Father, throw them all into hell because they have free will and they know very well what they are doing.' Instead, he said, 'Father, forgive them; for they do not know what they are doing' " (Luke 23:34).

At this juncture, Kalen's personal sentiments continue to drive the discussion, not Scripture. He uses biblical passages and verses so often as props for his presuppositions.

158. What about the nature of unilateral forgiveness, where it is given before someone asks for it (e.g., Mark 11:25)?

159. For forgiveness to be real, is it a requirement for someone to accept and act on it?

160. Or are forgiveness and heaven passively experienced realities?

Kalen then says Scripture is denied if we say we are saved by free will. But this idea is only critical of a Pelagian position, a minority position in this debate. It is a set up to answer a largely unasked question.

161. When a person comes as drawn by the Father, as Kalen quotes John 6:44 (p. 44), is he saying this is therefore a compulsion of the will?

162. When Kalen quotes John 15:5 (ibid.), "You did not choose me but I chose you," does he have any sense of what Jesus is saying to his disciples?

Namely, in the first century, a young Jewish man at about age 13 would have to approach and ask a given rabbi to accept him as his student. For Jesus, he was saying that his twelve disciples – those who did not seek to become rabbis or had been rejected – were now being chosen. The opposite, a divine gift. But not compulsion – they each chose to accept the calling to follow Jesus.

Kalen concludes this chapter by defining the "irresistible God."

163. How does this line up with Calvinism's "irresistible grace" that teaches an unending hell?

Kalen says: "Just as loving parents would restrict the freedom of their children, so too we can be sure that if it were necessary, God would restrict the freedom of the children of God loves in order to save them" (p. 46).

164. How can this be understood other than an opposition to human freedom in the sight of God?

Thus, ultimately, there is no freedom for Kalen, here in utilizing another analogy of judging God by human actions. As well:

165. In Kalen's theology, do children never grow up, never to learn responsibility?

In Chapter Five, Kalen throws in various subjects, but without direct import to the subject at hand. He says: "Now I would like to share some other important thoughts about what God is like. First of all, we must move beyond 1,000 B.C. in our understanding of God. Before that time, God was perceived to be a family, tribal or national deity" (p. 60).

Pagan gods yes, not so Yahweh Elohim. Kalen continues to say that God is not just the God of "Abraham, or the Israelites, or even Christians ..." (ibid.). Again, he is reacting to an unbiblical notion of God. The one true Creator makes us all equally in his image, a reality found nowhere outside the Bible.

166. Is Kalen saying the biblical portrayal of Yahweh Elohim in the days of King David is in error or not fully evolved?

He also adds to this confusion: "And saying that God loves Billy Graham more than Adolf Hitler must be challenged" (p. 61). Hitler was a man of long simmering and deliberate evil that metastasized into the sufferings, tortures and deaths of many millions.

167. Is God great enough to love those who hate him by giving them what and whom they loved – even hell itself?

168. What is the thoughtful biblical theology and anthropology that says such a human conscience wants to change such adopted, indeed, loved hatreds?

169. What are the chosen depths of Hitler's love (*agape*) of darkness, and thus, the Prince of Darkness?

This question of Hitler finds place as he quotes another obscure writer: "We have created a chasm between the sacred and profane, heaven and earth, divine and human, spirit and matter, good and evil" (ibid.).

170. Is there no chasm between good and evil?

This is a mishmash along with the other dualities cited, all of which can fit into distinct if not opposite categories compared with the others. And out of it his theme is that we should treat all people well since we are all "divine."

171. Why not then start with the biblical theology of Yahweh Elohim in Genesis 1-2, and the nature of being made in God's image?

172. Thus, in this chapter, what have we learned from Kalen of anything that approaches a theology of freedom?

173. Why such a diatribe against freedom?

In Chapter Six, Kalen continues with ideas sans biblical foundation. "The environment of hell is not necessarily different from that of heaven, but what one does within is what makes it heaven or hell" (p. 63).

174. Based on what?

175. Why does Kalen never exegete the biblical language of hell and its relationship to the larger reality of judgment?

He continues with the force of an earth-bound analogy. Namely, people can be unhappy in the "paradise" of Hawaii. Here again, Kalen uses the temporal to judge the eternal.

176. What is the biblical language of paradise?

Continuing: "The real issue is not that people will exist in hell, but that hell will exist within them … We can appropriately conclude that God did not create hell as if it were in a geographical location such as Siberia where a person might be sent off for punishment. It is more appropriate to consider hell the creation of sinners" (p. 64).

177. To what extent does Kalen not await the establishment of cross-checked facts before reaching "appropriate" conclusions?

178. Biblically, how is hell the creation of sinners, since the eternal fire is prepared by God for the devil and his angels (e.g., Matthew 25:41)?

And thus, hell is a perverse choice of humans, not their ex nihilo creation.

179. How can Kalen draw such a conclusion without looking at the biblical definitions?

180. And to what extent is Kalen battling a straw figure in a reactive posture, or namely: Who argues hell is a "geographical" destination or location, again as he makes an earth-bound analogy?

Only after his "conclusion" does Kalen attempt a biblical reference, returning again to the parable of Lazarus and the rich man in Luke 16:19-31: "Again, it is important to realize that heaven and hell are not so much places as they are spiritual states of being" (ibid.).

181. What is the nature of a parable?

182. Since Kalen has never defined the biblical language of heaven and hell, does he also not realize that the word used here is *hades* and not *gehenna*?

183. Does Kalen not realize, as we have noted before, how so much of the parables of Jesus are aimed at the self-righteous religious elitists versus the poor and needy?

184. Does Kalen not see how the rich man is trying to bring Abraham's domain down into *hades*, and thus making the good submit to the domain of those awaiting the Judgment?

185. Namely, for evil to define the good?

And Jesus makes this clear in concluding that it is unbelievers who will not listen to Moses and the prophets. They will not listen to one who is raised from the dead, whether the rich man in his plea in this parable, or to Jesus after the third day.

186. If they will not listen to Jesus as raised from the dead, what changes after they die, and opens their reconsideration of the Lordship of Jesus?

187. Does Kalen know of the nature of the kingdoms of the heavens and earth from Genesis 1 through Revelation 22, and what the new heaven and new earth in Revelation 21 are predicated upon?

188. What is Kalen's biblical basis to declare something as "spiritual" as opposed to otherwise?

Thus, as Kalen makes reference to this parable and does not examine such pertinent questions, he then uses an analogy to a concert of classical music, as told by one of his seminary professors.

The rest of the chapter is again a bucket for miscellaneous ideas, but the most creative one is his argument that "original sin" is laziness. Now, sloth is not good. And Kalen is reacting to Augustine's definition of the term.

In the rabbinic practice of *mishrashim* – telling stories in the Jewish community is a means to reflect on a biblical text – all ideas are welcome, even of those poorly educated or socially and mentally unbalanced. All people are image-bearers of God, and all have their own unique observations borne out of living life. So, whereas I must necessarily be candid in my critiques of Kalen's theology, he has started from a point of real reaction to bad doctrines in certain parts of the church.

- Thus, Kalen raises here an excellent question concerning the nature of "original sin," for it has polluted so much in church history to the extent that people believe they are merely passive victims to it. Consider Yahweh Elohim's rebuke to Cain (Genesis 4:6-7).

As Kalen moves into Chapter Seven, he starts out: "What great news we have! We will all eventually be converted, transformed, and enabled to live in a new way so we and those we influence will be able to experience heaven to the fullest" (p. 73). Kalen's purpose here is to then explain the power of "unconditional love" as the mechanism that makes this possible. He then says this is what the term *agape* means.

Specifically: "*Agape* is the spiritual love of one person for another, corresponding to the love of God for all people. It is unselfish love for others without sexual implications" (ibid.). Here Kalen attempts to define a word he finds crucial, and appeals to New Testament Greek – but displays ignorance of the Greek itself. This is an interpretation placed ahead of the actual etymology.

189. What is a "spiritual "love?

190. Does this reflect a Gnostic dualism of flesh versus spirit?

191. In his contrast, is *agape* not possible in sexual context between a husband and wife?

This is a sloppy attempt to distinguish *agape* from *eros*. For, indeed, the sexual love between a man and woman in marriage, rooted in Genesis 1-2, is the opposite of the lustful and manipulative "love" which is found within the classical Greek use of *eros*.

In terms of the root classical Greek definition of *agape*, as we have already noted, it means a "self-emptying" love. Thus, the idea of an unselfish love is taken to apply to the context God's love, as chosen by the Jewish translators of the Septuagint.

192. As Kalen uses so many secondary sources in his research, has he done so in term of his use of *agape*?

For if he had translated John 3:16-21, he would know *agape* applies to men's "love" for the darkness as well as God's "love" for the world. These are self-emptying but opposite loves. But such texture does not serve Kalen's all out drive to impose universal salvation on the biblical text.

Kalen states: "If we believe in eternal damnation, wouldn't that also mean we believe there is no such thing as unconditional love? … If, on the other hand, we embrace the teaching of universal salvation, haven't we recognized that unconditional love is not only possible, but that it is the force that is essential to bring about the salvation of everyone?" (p. 74).

193. To what extent is this a false dichotomy?

Only by ignorance of the biblical language at play. Kalen's motivating hermeneutic is again visceral: "What power is there in 'be-good-and-you'll-be-rewarded-religion' or 'don't-be-bad-or-you'll-be-punished' religion?" (ibid.). Yes, such a religious and childish construct is facile, but:

194. Is a facile religious construct best answered by a different and reactionary facile religion?

One of the most often repeated ideas in Scripture, and a reality in all human literature, is that what we reap we sow, we all experience cause and effect. In Galatians 6:9, Paul speaks about the contrast between sowing to the sinful nature, and reaping "destruction" and sowing in the Spirit and reaping "eternal (*aionion*) life."

195. How does Kalen's construct here reflect a childish faith (contra 1 Corinthians 13:11)?

The balance of this chapter is mostly occupied by various meanderings that add nothing new. But one section is salient: "The Non-judgmental

45

Nature of God" (p. 79). Its argument is brief and resides in a comparison between how God and Jesus are perceived, according to Kalen.

196. With the Hebrew Bible and the New Testament full of stories on and teachings about God's judgment, how is it possible for any serious writer to make such a comprehensive statement, not only on the thinnest of gruel, but without even attempting to address such a pervasive biblical reality?

197. Has Kalen considered Noah's Flood, Sodom and Gomorrah, the Canaanites, the Babylonian exile, or the texts of Matthew 23, Romans 1 and Revelation 20?

198. Has he grasped this trajectory that begins after the fall, its forfeiture of eternal life, then through the grueling travails of this earthly broken life, and finally to the resurrection and the new creation?

199. Or does he simply ignore this as unsuitable for his purposes, and dichotomize the earthy and resurrection lives?

In Chapter Eight, Kalen talks about going "beyond forgiveness" and how to grow in God's image.

200. What is the biblical exegesis on the nature of God's image?

In another chapter of miscellaneously organized topics, he then turns to the "four stages of spiritual growth" as identified by psychologist M. Scott Peck in his sequel book, *Further Along the Road Less Traveled.* These are 1) "chaotic/antisocial," 2) "formal/institutional," 3) skeptic/individual" and 4) "mystical/communal" (pp. 93-94). Now this is interesting material, and Kalen weaves so much into his definitions of heaven and hell as primarily states of the mind, but:

201. What has this to do with putatively biblical review of heaven and hell?

202. Is it an antidote to hell?

In Chapter Nine, "Misery Loves Company," Kalen seeks to identify why some people "cling to the idea of eternal damnation" (p. 101). Apart from supposed biblical texts they may cite, Kalen says: "I believe there often exists an unhealthy co-dependent relationship between the Church and its members. Unfortunately, co-dependency gives people a psychological reason to cling to the idea of eternal damnation" (p. 104). In other words, mutual manipulation, and to this Kalen reacts.

He then argues that universal salvation was hidden from believers as the church manipulated them from Augustine to the Reformation, by holding onto the power of excommunication. Then on to the enforced use of Latin, and the Roman Church's opposition to the Bible in the vernacular. But his treatment is superficial, even as he identifies real issues that need address.

In Chapter Ten, Kalen attempts his only systematic treatment in his book, on church history and universalism. "The doctrine of endless punishment in hell for the unsaved was widely believed by pagans and heathens ... before the time of Christ and into the early years of the Church" (pp. 114-115). And in saying this, Kalen cannot be referring to the actual world "hell" (*gehenna* in the Greek), but to other definitions, however murky, of final judgment.

As early advocates of universalism, Kalen cites Anaxagoras, Pantaenus, Clement of Alexandria, and Origen. Anaxagoras is given no historical reference, but is Kalen somehow referring to the fifth-century B.C. pre-Socratic philosopher?

For these first three references, he resorts again to the obscure secondary source, the 1883 *Columbian Congress*. Apart from Kalen's appeal to this *Congress*, we know that Pantaenus was Clement's teacher, and traveled widely in missionary endeavors, including India and possibly well into East Asia. However, there are no extant remains of his writings.

203. On what historically attributed basis, therefore, can Pantaenus be claimed as advocating universalism?

204. Assumedly because he was Clement's teacher?

Without citing him, this *Congress* states: "Clement would not tolerate the thought that any soul would continue forever to resist the force of redeeming love. Somehow and somewhere in the long run of the ages that love must prove weightier than sin and death, and vindicate its power in one universal triumph" (p. 115).

205. "Somehow and somewhere?" as an argument?

In the *Ante-Nicene Fathers*, we have over 400,000 words of Clement's writings.

206. Where are the actual words of Clement in this regard?

207. How can a secondary source that cites a secondary opinion about a primary source, without citing the primary source, be taken seriously?

208. Maybe this is an accurate reference to Clement, but how can we know without a citation in immediate and greater context?

Here, Origen is the only one of these four writers for whom a real citation is made: "… in his book, *On First Principles*, 'There is a resurrection of the dead and there is a punishment but not everlasting. For when the body is punished the soul is gradually purified' " (p. 116, cited from a 1966 English translation of the original). Yet, as we already noted, Origen did not use the key Greek term *aionios* at all in his argument.

For Tertullian, a contemporary of Origen, he "believed in the everlasting punishment of the wicked" (p. 116). Kalen then says universalism was not only taught in the theological school of Alexandria, but also in Antioch and Edessa, as cited in the *Columbia Congress*. Gregory of Nyssa, in the fourth century "believed evil was merely the corruption or disfigurement of the good. Evil, therefore, had no substance in its own right, and had to eventually come to an end, in contrast to good, which would endure forever since it was genuine substance. Gregory of Nyssa rejected the idea of everlasting punishment because such punishment could only be vindictive" (pp. 116-117).

Now, the idea of evil as having no substance, and being the absence of the good, is biblically compelling. But:

209. How does this idea contribute to universalism, as opposed to annihilation?

210. Does the end of evil mean all are converted to the good?

211. Or does the end of evil means the end of evil's power to pollute the good in a broken world?

212. Why must a chosen and everlasting punishment be vindictive?

213. If only an arbitrary deity would impose salvation, cannot the good God honor people's settled choices?

Augustine opposes universalism, as noted variously already, and Kalen then says that Ambrose and Jerome supported it, but only in citing a secondary source.

214. Might Kalen's readers be better edified with the most original sources always referenced?

Many of the conclusions he draws here might be reasonably accurate, but we have already seen various of his other conclusions where they cannot be substantiated, or contrary factors are overlooked.

From here, Kalen addresses the theological imposition in "stopping the spread of the belief that God would eventually save everyone" (p. 119). This he attributes to Emperor Justinian in the sixth century, and the convening of the Fifth Ecumenical Council in Constantinople. Some of Origen's teachings were thus condemned.

Then Kalen says: "The meaning of the Greek word *aionios* was central to the issue of Origen's theology, because it relates to punishment in hell. Origen believed *aionios* meant, "indefinite but limited duration ... basic to his belief in universal salvation" (p. 120). This, as already noted, is simply untrue. *Aionios* is never once used this way in *Liddell and Scott*, or *Bauer*, nor in thirty major English translations, and Origen does not cite the word in this context (unless it is found miscellaneously in an unrelated context in Origen's writings, but if so, why not give the citation?).

Still, Kalen cites an 1876 work by a Universalist minister and historian, John Wesley Hanson, demonstrating "that even as late as A.D. 540 *aionios* meant limited duration, and required an added word to impart the force of endless duration" (ibid.).

- In academic research, we begin first with the most current and well tested scholarly writings, and judge their knowledge and fidelity to represent original sources on forward. Kalen, in contrast, skips through selected materials best suited to serve his visceral presupposition.

Still, back to the biblical Greek text in the New Testament, not secondary, tertiary or quaternary sources. As noted earlier, in public forum, when I asked Kalen for one example in the New Testament where *aionios* is translated other than "eternal," "forever" or "everlasting," he could not do so. Here is a crucial question:

215. If the meaning of *aionios* is supposedly "central" to Origen, according to Kalen, and Origen does not use it in his argument, has a "central" stilt been removed from Kalen's argument?

Kalen then argues that John Wesley, in the eighteenth century, started by not embracing universalism, but eventually converted to it in a well-known 1782 sermon, *On the Fall of Man*.

216. But is this really the case?

Kalen points out in partial paraphrase and partial quote from near the end of the sermon, how God does not despise the works of his own hands, and that Wesley says: "God in his mercy has provided a universal remedy for a universal evil!" (p. 123) through Jesus as the Second Adam (i.e., Romans 5:12-20).

The problem here is that Wesley says nothing about universal salvation in these words, nor his whole sermon. Now, some in church history have tried to use Romans 5 accordingly, but this comes back to the use of "all," a term unexamined by Kalen, which we have reviewed. Thus Kalen, again, makes an unexamined assumption about biblical language. He takes some words of one of the greatest leaders in the Reformation, and adds his gloss to make Wesley say what he did not say.

217. What is the nature of willful eisegesis?

From this juncture, Kalen makes passing reference to the origins of Universalism in the American colonies, and refers to some subsequent theologians of disparate theologies and contexts.

In commenting on Paul Tillich, Kalen says: "Predestination means that God ordained or determined from eternity what must take place, including fixing each person's destiny for happiness or misery. So, to believe in double predestination is to believe that God arbitrarily decided before the beginning of time which people will go to heaven and which people will go to hell" (p. 126).

Kalen says this is contrary to the "very good" creation of man and woman in Genesis 1:31, and Tillich says such a doctrine is demonic. Deeply agreed – God is not arbitrary. And the debate over predestination in church history, beginning with John Calvin, is central to the question of heaven and hell. But:

218. Why has Kalen not defined the doctrine of "predestination" in its historical origins, and has not referenced it until now?

In Chapter Eleven, the final one, Kalen returns to his reactionary motivations. He says that the preaching of hell – as it is wont to be preached – drives people away from the church and into atheism, Communism, pessimism, Satanism and lukewarm Christianity. It creates unnecessary agonizing among people, meaninglessness and meanness, creates fear and is bad news. We should instead be hopeful and loving toward our enemies.

Now, I see readily – and through decades of ministry to skeptics of the Gospel – that bad church doctrine and hypocrisy drive countless people into painful belief systems and lifestyles. But too:

219. How many people also rebel against the true Gospel?

220. And how might a weak universalism drive people away from living lives accountable to Jesus as both Lord and Savior?

In his appendix, Kalen gives tips for advancing universalism in the face of its opposition.

In sum, Kalen 1) starts with a reactive experiential posture, a visceral repulsion against a doctrine that believes God sends people to hell arbitrarily; 2) is highly selective in how he cites Scripture; 3) resorts at places to challenge the integrity of the whole inspiration of Scripture; 4) minimizes the question of God's judgment; 5) does not give a biblical interpretive structure; and 6) poorly addresses the underlying question of biblical freedom, indeed, while choosing to mute if not eviscerate it.

♦ ♦ ♦

Chapter Two

Questions for Julie Ferwerda

In *Raising Hell*, Julie Ferwerda makes her case that hell is an unbiblical concept. There are four dominating realities in the book.

First, Ferwerda writes experientially throughout. She, like each of the other four writers, has visceral reactions to any church doctrine that views hell as arbitrary in nature, and for whom most people are destined. I agree.

1. Does Julie understand the Wesleyan quadrilateral of Scripture, tradition, reason and experience?

2. If we start with an experientially reactive posture, do we not reverse this classical interpretive leverage?

3. Accordingly, can she articulate a different, proactive and better starting point for understanding the Bible and any church doctrine?

4. Otherwise, how can a cycle of reactions to reactions not take over and pollute the whole discussion?

Second, Julie embraces the freedom to pose any and all questions, and this is good. She asks many very valid questions that need a biblically literate response.

Third, Julie uses the English word "hell" as the lynchpin idea, but never defines its etymology.

5. If the word "hell" is the foundational idea for critique, why is it not defined properly?

And fourth, Julie does not know the biblical Hebrew, Aramaic and Greek, yet is willing to tell translators, who know the original languages, where they have made mistakes. The resources she uses to critique the translators are in fact dependent on the same translators who are trained to do what she is not trained to do.

6. In reactionary mode, is this not still an act of remarkable hubris?

This matter deserves some up-front attention.

In her Introduction, Julie states, "You might also be asking, who am I to question or doubt the majority of today's mainstream Bible translators, theologians, and pastors?" (p. 5). In also including "scholars" in a subsequent list, she then asks, "which ones should I listen to?" (ibid.).

7. To what extent do scholars serve as scapegoats for Julie's angst?

She then posits that "*Arminianism* declares that God desires but is not able to save all people because he cannot infringe upon the 'free will' of man ... *Calvinism* declares that God is unwilling – does not desire – to save all of his children because He has only 'elected' a few for salvation" (ibid).

This may be a caricature of a far larger historical reality, but it does honestly represent how many people view this theological debate. And all of us should recoil at the idea that God is either 1) weak or 2) arbitrary toward those made in his image.

8. What is the responsibility of biblical scholars and pastors to listen to, understand and address such a heartfelt concern?

In an appendix that pits "scholars" versus "common people," in reference to "Bible study tools online," Julie states: "Through these resources, practically *anyone* can learn basic study of Hebrew and Greek Scripture in order to begin identifying problematic translation issues and correcting them on their own. In fact, learning how to identify and improve many translation errors is so simple, a little kid could do it" (p. 239).

9. Is this not dangerous and facile language?

10. Is Julie able to debate face-to-face Hebrew, Aramaic and Greek scholars, sustain her online abilities to "correct them," fix their "translation errors," and also make her claim that such scholars are often dishonest?

11. How can Julie be so categorical, herself being without the training to know the nature of translating from one culture to another, from antiquity to the present age?

Whereas Julie shows real aptitude to grasp certain ideas, she is nonetheless ill equipped to make such translation judgments. For example, she makes assumption that words or phrases are stand-alone units, in the English, with no knowledge of the proto-Ugaritic etymology of the Hebrew, and no recognition of grammar, syntax, mood, tense and voice in both the Hebrew and Greek.

Julie states: "We've already discovered that often times when words are being mistranslated, nouns are swapped out for adverbs or adjectives, or other variations. This is a fundamental no-no when translating any language. There must be consistency, and if you find an adverb or adjective replacing a noun (or any other substitution), be suspicious" (p. 251).

12. How can Julie define what a "no-no" is when "translating any language"?

13. What are her translation skills that give her such expertise to make such a judgment?

14. Julie only uses English, her entire grammatical prism, but how can that suffice as the reference point for translation choices?

15. With English, or even Latin-based assumptions, how can parts of speech be defined and understood as used in Hebrew or Greek?

16. What is an adjectival noun in any language, and thus what happens when, grammatically speaking, one form of a noun replaces another form of a noun due to different linguistic use of nouns and/or various modifiers?

17. What is the nature of one-for-one word comparisons across languages and cultures?

Translation is an art form that requires great inter-cultural and trans-historical knowledge and skills. It is not a mathematical science where equivalencies are easily swapped. Here are three specific examples:

First, in Exodus 34:6 the Hebrew text states literally that "Yahweh has a long nose" (cf. the same construction and content in Numbers 14:18; Nehemiah 9:17; Psalms 86:15, 103:8 and 145:8; Joel 2:13; Jonah 4:3 and Nahum 1:3). Julie can certainly go to these verses in an English translation and see how it is translated as "slow to anger."

  18. What is the Hebrew word for "nose," and why is it not translated here "literally?"

  19. And thus, does Julie define this as a mistranslation, a dishonest substitution of "slow to anger" for "long nose?"

A verbal clause indeed renders an adjectival noun to convey an honest translation. In Hebrew, the word for "nose" is *anap*. Hebrew men in the first two millennia B.C. had high cheeked thick dark beards, and when they got angry, it did now show up as flushed cheeks, but only when the heat of it reached the nose did it become visible. And thus *anap*, in context, is the word for anger. To have a "long nose" means it takes a long time for the anger to reach the end of patience, thus "slow to anger."

In English, we do not have this metaphor, so a word for word translation makes no sense. And if we say God has "a long nose," one of our literary metaphors would be Pinocchio, and this does not work, as though God were being called a liar. A workable metaphor is "a long fuse," but too, the ancient Hebrews did not have dynamite.

Second is the well-known text in Isaiah 53 where the prophet states, according to an English translation: "But he was pierced for our transgressions, he was crushed for our iniquities; the punishment that brought us peace was upon him, and by his wounds we are healed" (v. 5 in the 1984 New International Version [NIV]). Without getting too technical here, the simple reality is that the past tense is used three times, and the present tense is used once, all in reference to a future event.

20. The dishonest switching of tenses?

21. Why does the Hebrew text use the past and present tenses to indicate the future?

22. Does Julie know that <u>biblical Hebrew has no future tense</u>, and accomplishes the purpose with grammatical dexterity? ٦

23. Or does Julie also call this a mistranslation?

And third is a text we have already noted, Jonah 2:8. The NIV renders it: "Those who cling to worthless idols forfeit the grace that could be theirs." A wooden translation straight from the Hebrew is: "They who honor themselves with empty vapors leave steadfast love."

The NIV, in its use of "cling," does well enough. The first verb in play, *shamar*, is strategically important across the biblical text. In Genesis 2:15, Adam is charged to "guard" (*shamar*) the Garden from what proves to be the entrance of the serpent. "To guard" is the principle understanding, with a cognate "to keep." In the piel (intensive) form in Jonah 2:8, it is "to honor" that which is being guarded, and hence "to cling" is a reasonable choice for readers in the English.

To the one literate in the Hebrew text, we see opposite guardianships, the former guards the good, and the latter guards evil. Complete opposites. Also, the word for "idol" here is one of various terms used in the Hebrew, *hebel*, for a "vapor" or "emptiness."

When Paul says that idols are both nothing and demons at the same time (1 Corinthians 10:19-21), he is tracing a line of biblical theology back to the Garden and through Moses, Jeremiah, Jonah and others. We may think of physical idols in antiquity, but Jonah is writing about the underlying reality that idols are demons that are vapors in the presence of the steadfast love of God. Evil has no intrinsic power.

The verb "to leave" can be synonymous with "to forfeit" as context has its input, and the word the NIV translates as "grace" is another strategically important word in the Hebrew Bible, *hesed* – the "steadfast love," "lovingkindness" and "gracious love" that is only found in Yahweh Elohim. And we could parse this text further into the weeds. No translation can be fully satisfactory, by definition, so when we translate we make the best interpretive (hermeneutical) choices rooted in good exegesis, and then start mining the riches.

24. Is this a rich field in which Julie can find mistranslations, mistakes and dishonesties?

25. Or might she – like all of us – be humbled and edified by such a rich text?

26. And thus, might she see how an English language perspective cannot interpret the Hebrew text?

And thousands of examples here can easily multiply. Let's walk through *Raising Hell* and identify the salient questions.

As already noted, Julie places experience first in her undefined and visceral reaction to the English word "hell." It is in her book title, and it is the word and concept to which she objects consistently. Yet she never defines it.

27. What is the biblical source and definition for the word translated in the English as "hell?"

This we have already touched on. Rather, the book starts with her daughter's uneasiness with the concept of hell as taught in their church upbringing, and an overseas missions trip where she could not reconcile a message that damned people to hell if they did not hear the Gospel before they died. Later Julie embraces the same, and finally she arrives at a point of declaring *"there is no hell!"* (p. 17). Julie starts with an English word, and then looks backward into the subject via interlinear Bibles.

On page 15, in Chapter One, she states: "The Bible mentions hell repeatedly, doesn't it?"

28. How tricky is it to use a loaded rhetorical question to serve a serious concern?

29. In other words, exactly how many times is "hell" mentioned in English translation?

In her introduction, *Setting the Stage*, Julie says "I was born to ask questions" (p. 3). Good. But then she makes analogies to the stereotypes of Jim Jones and Hare Krishna: "… but please keep reading and give me a fair chance to build my case. I'm not asking you to go to South America to drink Kool-Aid, or to wear a toga and sell flowers at the airport …" (p. 4).

30. Why such reactive, hyperbolic and petty reactions?

31. Is the pain that deep?

32. And if so, how is it best addressed?

The reactive is not consonant with asking good questions, and does not serve a proactive argument as to the nature of the Bible on the question at hand.

In Chapter One, Julie begins by raising questions about the inclusive love of God, as she does often, and quotes lists of atomized Scripture verses.

33. How can selected verses suffice for a biblical argument apart from their contextual linkages?

And likewise, with various quotes from church history.

34. Likewise?

In Chapter Two, Julie hits the ethical core with her daughter's concerns as raised in missions-work: "She couldn't accept the seeming contradiction of God's 'character' and 'injustice' that billions of people would be eternally punished because they had no knowledge of Jesus (p. 17). This is the strength and appeal as she speaks for so very many who are in the evangelical church.

On page 22, Julie demonstrates a monstrous interpretive mistake and in the process, challenges biblical integrity:

"Ironically, what initially encouraged me that we were not getting off base in discovering so many translation errors and at all times even suspecting foul play or agenda was a verse I happened upon in Jeremiah 8:7-9: 'But my people do not know the ordinance of the LORD. *How can you say, "We are wise, and the law of the LORD is with us"? But behold, the lying lips of the scribes have made it into a lie.* The wise men are put to shame, they are dismayed and caught; Behold, they have rejected the word of the LORD, and what kind of wisdom do they have?' " (italics added by Julie).

She then gives her diagnosis: "Right there, Jeremiah confirmed that the scribes had inserted lies into the Old Testament writings, many centuries before a Bible was ever published or canonized." This is not true, even apart from the question of what "publication" means. The scribes here are not writing the Hebrew Bible, but they are misrepresenting the Law of Moses for their own purposes, for their own lies. They are false prophets, and Jeremiah is exposing them.

35. If "lies" have been inserted into the Bible, and if a biblical prophet confirms such an insertion, what else in the Bible is thus liable to being charged as false?

36. Therefore, how can any argument for or against "hell" by appeal to the Bible be trusted, and therefore why does the subject matter at all, since biblical trustworthiness is eschewed in the priority of a presuppositionally visceral and reactive agenda?

37. Does Julie know the nature of and differences between exegesis and eisegesis, and thus the concern for idolatry?

38. Does Julie know the context of Jeremiah as the final prophet in Jerusalem before its Babylonian exile in 586 B.C.?

39. Does she know the decades-long tussle Jeremiah has with false prophets who embrace or turn a blind eye to the pagan practices of

sorcery, sacred prostitution and child sacrifice that are ripping Judah apart at that time?

40. Has she considered Jeremiah 7-8 in the whole context, as opposed to proof-texting a verse or two out of context?

On p. 23, Julie compounds this error, asserting that "somewhere along the line" it is "not a stretch to imagine that 'stuff happened' " – leading to serious translation mistakes.

41. Where is the evidence in point concerning the Jeremiah text?

42. How can broad sweep and amorphous generalizations be taken seriously, without factual basis, as they apply to two select verses or any biblical context?

On p. 25, Julie lists a series of questions, and they are all sound, but also rooted in certain presuppositions of a slice of the American church. Then, on pp. 27-28, Julie says: "If you look into it, Jesus never even spoke to the crowds about 'hell' (that we read about), only privately and in smaller contexts to His disciples and the Pharisees – religious people – and only, at the most, on three or four unique occasions."

Not true. First, e.g., Jesus speaks about it most often to the crowds; and second, he does not teach it privately to the Pharisees, but confronts them in public. Here are the seven contexts, six unique, plus one partial parallel, for the thirteen uses of the word of *gehenna* (actual Greek term properly translated as "hell"): In Matthew 5, the Sermon on the Mount, Jesus teaches his disciples in the presence of multiple thousands who had gathered to hear him; in Matthew 10, Jesus sends out the twelve to heal and drive out demons, and teaching/preaching the Good News is assumed as always for their given "authority"; in Matthew 18, Jesus is teaching the disciples in public, and as he calls a little child to stand in their midst; in Matthew 23, Jesus rebukes the religious elitists before large crowds in the Court of the Gentiles; in Mark 9, he is teaching the disciples in public, partly parallel to Matthew 18, but with additional text; in Luke 12, he addresses the disciples in the presence of a crowd of thousands; and in James 3, the apostle – half-brother to Jesus – is writing a letter to the wide Jewish Christian diaspora.

43. Why does Julie not quote and review these texts?

44. Why has Julie tried to make the teaching about hell, by Jesus, into a "private" and "smaller" setting, when the biblical texts show the opposite?

45. What point is being made that ignores or misses the context?

46. To minimize the importance Jesus places on hell when he brings it up?

Julie then reaches beyond sound reason when she states on p. 30: "Did you know that if Evangelical America just put their church building funds toward feeding the poor that they could drastically reduce, if not eradicate, world hunger?"

This is facile – to thus imagine eradicating world hunger – and used as a supporting argument for *Raising Hell*, even though many churches can readily make an idol of a church building project. But too, without church property, and its good stewardship, the church would be seriously handicapped in organizational efforts needed to minister to the world at many fronts. As well, this is neither a biblical nor an economically sound strategy, where it is not a mathematical quid pro quo of wealth transference that serves justice, but healthy relationships rooted in the family unit defining honest government. The Greek word for economics is *oikonomos*, referring to the management of the household, the family unit. The chosen absence of the biological father, in concert with corrupt government, are the overwhelming reality of poverty worldwide.

47. Has Julie been burned by the idolatry of church-building programs?

To add one component to a statement John Wesley once said: The power of sound economics is when we "earn all we can, save all we can, employ all we can [or invest all we can], and give away all we can." Charity or investment needs prior production rooted in biblical ethics. Poverty and hunger need the prophetic presence of the church in undergirding the faithful marriage of man and woman, and parenthood, then in challenging the idolatry of "big daddy" government.

48. Is Julie aware of how her reactions to reactions beget further reactions that spin her so far afield?

On pp. 33-34, Julie speaks of the Good News of the Gospel – amen. She raises good questions about motivation v. manipulation – amen. But then on p. 35, Julie steps into it again.

In citing Acts 17:31, Julie renders it this way: "He has fixed a day in which He is about to be judging the inhabited world in justice through a Man whom He has appointed, *furnishing belief to all* by raising him from the dead" (MLT).

She cites the MLT, her own definition of a "More Literal Translation" from her use of interlinear Bibles. Yet she has no knowledge of biblical Hebrew or the *koine* Greek or the art of translation.

- This is a foolishly wanton act of eisegesis, where Julie critiques the honest art of translation as though it involves changing words, as it were, in the English. Yet here she changes a word deliberately.

Straight from the Greek text, here is a literal, if wooden, translation of Acts 17:31: "Accordingly, he has caused to stand a day in which he judges the household world in righteousness in the man he has set aside. He offers trust to all, causing to raise him from the dead." In order to make this substance easy to read and honestly understood, translators need to know the art of going from one culture to the next. There are different as well as overlapping grammatical rules at play, for example, between Hebrew, Aramaic, Greek, Latin, German, French and English. And thus, necessary flexibility where the "literal" is honored, but not the "literalistic."

Julie's MLT is neither. It is a hopscotch skip through an interlinear, and English translations, where she places into the text what she wants to be there.

49. *Furnishing belief?*

There is no such verb for "to furnish" present. As well, the verb commonly translated as "believe," *pisteo*, is rooted in a deeper and prior reality of "trust." We can only believe in whom or what we trust. Then, when Julie inserts the idea of *furnishing*, she does so by changing the Greek term for "offering." And the difference is both subtle and dramatic. To "offer" gives active freedom to say no. "To furnish" implies, at the level of the metaethics of language, a simple supply in a passive capacity.

Trust cannot be just supplied, in the implicitly passive sense that Julie's language intends. Trust is first earned, then chosen. The ministry of Jesus offers us the opportunity to trust him, but he does not do the trusting for us. Julie here – as is her wont across the whole book – challenges human freedom. She says God is *furnishing* belief to all in a passive capacity, in the context of saying there is no hell.

50. By depending on interlinear translations of given words, is Julie aware of the assumed trust she places in the expertise of these scholars as true, to thus buttress her presuppositions through which she challenges other scholars whose expertise she claims are suspect?

51. Can she delineate the difference between what is "literal" (and thus the larger reality of biblical literature and its multiple genres) and what is "literalistic," and how can she say she is doing a "translation?"

52. And too, how can she reconcile this with the warning in Revelation 22:18-19 not to add to or subtract from the words of this Book, which itself wraps up all Scripture, tying together the themes traced from Genesis 1-3ff.?

53. And how would her MLT render Revelation 20:11-15 and its final judgment?

In terms of sovereignty and choice, Julie has missed an opportunity to look at the larger context in Acts 17, of Paul's entire address to the Greek Philosophers in Athens. God "commanded the appointed times for them and their fixed dwelling places ... so that men would seek and grope about for him ..." (vv. 26-27). Sovereignty and choice, the latter made fully possible by the former. But no passive "belief" furnished.

54. Does Julie, in her "translation," provide a new twist on hyper-Calvinism, a "single-predestination" as opposed to a "double-predestination," where in both cases the human will is ruled over by a supreme deity for whom fate is reality?

55. Though she has made early and passing reference, what is Julie's depth of knowledge about the Calvinistic and Arminian debate in church history?

Of critical importance on p. 40 (the beginning of Chapter Five) is where Julie says that Genesis should be the obvious first place to find the doctrine of hell if such a doctrine exists, but it is not there. On the back of the book cover, she states it this way: "Why does He fail to mention hell in Genesis as the price for sin?"

 This proves to be the most strategic and important question raised among these five writers.

Julie says that the language, "you will surely die," in Genesis 2:17 (from an English translation) means: "It just says they will die, as in stop breathing, or kick the bucket."

- The use of this English language, and her definitive statement of what it means, is completely wrong. The actual Hebrew usage in Genesis 2:16-17 is so dynamically different, that once the actual, yes, the literal translation is grasped, we will see how it interprets all biblical language of blessings versus judgment, of heaven versus hell.

56. Given that Julie has identified this as a key leverage point in Genesis 2:17, and if my translation of vv. 16-17 proves satisfactory in showing a radically different understanding, and is indeed beautiful in its context, what impact would this have on the rest of her theological construction?

In the balance of Chapter Five of *Raising Hell*, Julie raises many interesting questions, all of which deserve proactive attention. In Chapter Six, Julie talks about "assumptions I grew up with" (p. 51). Okay, but such experiences need to be interpreted by the Bible first. She then delves into some church history (okay), but history or tradition is always subject to the Scripture.

57. As Julie uses many biblical verses atomistically, does she do so likewise with church history?

58. How much church history does Julie know apart from scouring it to furnish her objections to hell?

On p. 56, Julie then lists "the astonishing incongruency" of how many times "hell" appears in 14 chosen English translations, from 56 down to zero. Again, this is backward, as she has no reference point in the Hebrew and Greek. If she had, she would know the lexigraphic answer is that *ge'hinnom* (Hebrew antecedent for the Greek *gehenna* for hell) has seven explicit references and one dynamic allusion. And, as we have already noted, there are thirteen explicit uses of *gehenna* in the Greek New Testament. Now I agree that "hell" is a wrong translation too often. But still:

59. What difference does it make on the putative number of times a word is mentioned?

60. Is the Bible interpreted by stand-alone words or verses, or through the whole storyline, its wide variety of literary genres, constructions and strategic leverage points?

In Chapter Seven, Julie raises the question of God or Satan "winning" in the question of heaven and hell.

61. What is the biblical definition of "winning" and "losing?"

62. If there is no hell for human beings, what is the final identity and abode of Satan and his demons?

63. Heaven?

In this chapter, Julie again steps into dangerous territory, approvingly quoting scholar Bart Ehrmann, who has discarded trust in the Bible – due principally to personal ethical reasons:

" 'There came a time when I left the faith. This was not because of what I learned through historical criticism, but because I could no longer reconcile my faith in God with the state of the world that I saw around me. There is so much senseless pain and misery in the world that I came to find it impossible to believe there is a good and loving God who is in control, despite my knowing all the standard rejoiners [*sic* in Julie's quote] that people give.' "

Ehrmann places subjective experience first, not exegesis of the text. He says he has heard all the rejoinders.

64. What does it mean to be "in control?"

65. What is the biblical definition of power?

66. For Ehrmann, if there is no "good and loving God who is in control," what then controls the universe?

67. Is it a godless cosmos that is dehumanizing at the beginning and the end, like evil and the abyss that is nearly co-extensive with the place of hell?

68. Has Julie gone "scholar shopping" for a fellow traveler in all her questions?

In this chapter, Julie also speaks of whether God is angry forever, with death being swallowed up and the language of fire. These are secondary and real issues, needing proactive address.

In Chapters Eight through Ten, pp. 73ff., Julie raises many good questions in the experiential mode. Yet, on p. 100, she states: "I now know that the ultimate atonement for sin is not throwing someone away, or damning them to everlasting punishment, but providing a way for that person to repair damages they've caused and to restore their relationships between God and their fellow man."

She says this is not a "works-based salvation," making a distinction that people are only *"saved from death,"* and thereafter, they somehow can make things right.

69. Is a classic Roman Catholic doctrine of purgatory in view?

70. Does Julie believe salvation is only *from*, and not also *for*?

71. How deep is her theology mired in growing internal incongruencies because she starts in a reactive posture?

Also here, Julie addresses *lex talionis*, the "law of equal justice," a vital topic worthy of proactive address, but she is in way over her head. Then, beginning in Chapter Eleven, she rehashes the issues of "only one chance?"

72. Does this also allow for some definition of hell, as with those who advocate an "ultimate reconciliation" universalism?

Julie also raises the good question of whether God could have prevented sin, which needs proactive address, and the meaning of "all" as we have already touched on.

In the middle of these catch-all categories, Julie states: "I love looking for common themes or threads because, at closer inspection, the Bible is really one big interwoven Masterpiece" (p. 120). Good.

73. But, has Julie biblically defined such a theme?

74. Does "one big interwoven Masterpiece" include her charge that there are errors in the Bible, and that Jeremiah supports a lie as part of such a Masterpiece?

In Chapter Twelve, Julie again traces some church history, but still, Scripture defines all. In Chapter Thirteen, she steps into it again, in seeking

68

to teach about "Hebrew ABCs." She gleans some interesting data, but only in piecemeal ability in the English.

So, when she says there is no reference to eternity in Hebrew, she is mistaken. This is a classic example of not knowing Hebrew.

For example, *olam*, the main word in the Hebrew for "forever" is not a word of strictly linear quality – a human grasp of time without end, as it were. It aims to define the human perspective for that which is greater than space, time and number. In its 300 or so uses in the Hebrew Bible, it touches on the remote past as well as the distant future, and with certain prepositional uses in the Hebrew Bible, it means unlimited, incalculable, continuance, eternity.

It is likely rooted in the word *alam*, which means something "hidden" from human comprehension. In the prior Ugaritic, of which Hebrew is a cognate, the word *lm* means "eternity." In Ecclesiastes 3:11, Solomon states: "He has also set eternity (*olam*) in the hearts of men; yet they cannot fathom what God has done from beginning to end." The last three words here would be literally "upon the days."

In the Hebrew, Yahweh Elohim is greater than space, time and number, as his name indicates. Adam and Eve are not created to die (but to live forever). And the language of *olam*, along with other constructions in the Hebrew, aim beyond the limits of human understanding to relate to Yahweh Elohim.

75. If Julie were convinced there is no Hebrew reference to eternity, where does the concept enter in, what is the nature of life and death in Genesis 2, and how then can she believe in eternal life but not eternal death?

In Chapters Fourteen and Fifteen, Julie continues her errors, depending on interlinears and her perspective within the English language. In Chapter Sixteen, she addresses the Abrahamic and Mosaic covenants, and issues of the millennial kingdom. This covenantal treatment is a secondary matter to her defining question about hell.

In Chapter Seventeen, she addresses the harvests of the Hebrew festival seasons, but this again is secondary material to the question at hand. It is as though she is glad to impart her understandings on many interesting issues, but without the textual ability to relate them to a cohesive whole, and keep a simple focus on her main question.

In Chapter Eighteen, Julie looks at the question of evil, and comes up with a dualistic understanding that it is necessary in order for us to know the difference between good and evil.

- Here, Julie has identified a foundational question, one in need of biblical review.

In Chapter Nineteen, she states in its title, "What God Wants, God Gets," a topic we have already reviewed.

76. What, again, is power, and how does God define and use it, and does he force his way?

In Chapter Twenty, Julie addresses "Lazarus and the Rich Man," as we have already reviewed. In Chapter Twenty-One, Julie purports to redefine the soul. This is at best a reactionary position relative to its misuse, and she does come up with the right understanding that *nephesh* and *psuche*, the Hebrew and Greek terms for soul, or personhood, is what we are, not what we have.

So, she doesn't redefine it, but she rediscovers it. But she also here touches on Plato and the Jews – this is an enormously huge and defining topic, but way beyond the scope of her passing reference.

- *Nephesh* proves to be the most crucial leverage point in Scripture for defining "salvation."

Chapter Twenty-Two is Julie's formal conclusion before many afterthoughts, experientially rooted in a story. In Section Four, she then addresses a series of addenda, first with "The Scriptures: For Scholars or Common People?"

She then gives "Simple Steps for Identifying Mistranslations," again rooted in the same folly of comparing English translations side-by-side as though this gives any understanding to the Hebrew, Greek, and nature of translation. Julie then continues with "Common Misunderstandings of Scripture" in the same vein, and then with a section on "You've Got Questions for Me?"

Here the book concludes its long descent into potpourri feelings about various subjects, closely or distantly related to the central question at hand. It continues to its conclusion with a section on "Talking Points," largely with a list of proof texts, a section on "Verses Proclaiming God Will Save All," and finally, "Further Reading and Study."

In sum, Julie 1) starts with a reactive experiential posture, a visceral repulsion against a doctrine that believes God sends people to hell arbitrarily; 2) is highly selective in how she cites Scripture; 3) is willing at points to challenge the integrity of the whole inspiration of Scripture; 4) minimizes the question of God's judgment; 5) does not give a biblical interpretive structure; and 6) confusedly addresses the underlying question of biblical freedom, even muting it.

◆ ◆ ◆

Chapter Three

Questions for Rob Bell

The full title for Rob's book is: *Love Wins: A Book About Heaven, Hell, and the Fate of Every Person Who Ever Lived.* He certainly follows this progression of thought, but in the end, "the fate of every person" is left open-ended on the hand, while he presses to open the door to an "ultimate restoration" universalism, on the other.

Rob's book is written conversationally, in pastoral concern for what he considers poisonous doctrines, graciously blunt oftentimes, swimming in many questions, and with an agenda that becomes relentlessly clear even if not explicitly defined.

In the Preface, he begins with a proactive declaration of the love of God: "It is a stunning, beautiful, expansive love, and it is for everybody, everywhere" (p. vii). This "expansive love" is the thesis of his book, touched on repeatedly, and indeed provides the interpretive leverage for all he does.

1. What is the biblical definition of an "expansive love?"

2. To what extent does Rob preset this term, so that of its own inertia it moves toward a form of universalism, even though at places he gives circumscribed caveats otherwise?

3. Thus, what are the metaethics of his language and how do they establish the expectations of his readers?

"Metaethics" is a philosophical word from the Greek terms *meta* (that which is above, about or surrounding), and *ethikos*, from *ethos* (for how, in our social customs, we treat other people). Thus, metaethics touches on the assumptions our hearers and readers bring to the table when we say or write something. It is the air or fog we breathe in a given setting, into which we seek to communicate. We may say something that we understand clearly – as to nature, purpose and intent – but our hearers think something else entirely. We need to know our audiences.

For example, what would be the response if we were to happily slap someone on the back in Times Square, New York, and ask: "Brother, have you been washed in the blood of the Lamb?" How many people would know the biblical reference? Or if we chance upon a member of People for Ethical Treatment of Animals in such a greeting, the police might be called in. This is a failure at the metaethics of language. Otherwise, in a range of contexts, the question of forgiveness is universal. If we know to whom we are speaking, there are many ways to speak about the biblical reality of Jesus as the atoning Lamb of God, and only using the biblical metaphor when it can become understandable and helpful.

Rob knows his audience, yet:

4. How can his readers not follow the inertia toward some form of universalism?

Rob's starting point of the love of God is wonderfully and biblically proactive. But then, the angle changes sharply. "I have written this book for all those, everywhere" who have reacted to a non-biblical version of Jesus … "A staggering number of people have been taught that a select few Christians will spend forever in a peaceful, joyous place called heaven, while the rest of humanity spends forever in torment and punishment in hell with no chance for anything better" (p. viii).

Rob calls this doctrine "misguided and toxic" and I agree, for it is indeed facile and unbiblical. Yet he so quickly defines a point of honest reaction as his motivational starting point. Thus, the question of the metaethics of language again rises:

5. When we start at a place of reaction, indeed, a visceral one, how can we avoid catalyzing a cycle of reactions to reactions?

6. Thus, before we address reactions, what proactive foundation must first be defined, so as to prevent the cycle of reactions from taking control?

Rob is wired for the proactive, but in the end, he faces a self-conscious tension with the reactive. Heaven is the redemptive proactive, hell is the epitome of the reactive. Thus:

7. The very title *Love Wins* is a proactive statement and hope; thus, so long as any domain of hell remains, has "love" failed to "win?"

8. And what is the biblical definition of "winning" and "losing" in the cosmic sense?

He wraps up his preface with something dynamically true: "There is no question that Jesus cannot handle, no discussion too volatile, no issue too dangerous. At the same time, some issues aren't as big as people have made them. Much blood has been spilled in church splits, heresy trials, and raging debates over issues that are, in the end, not that essential" (p. x). Of course, we need to discern what is essential or nonessential.

9. Are heaven and hell essential questions?

10. How do we distinguish whether cognate questions are such or nonesuch?

I embrace this challenge; let the questions fly in all directions.

In Chapter One, Rob raises the perennial and compelling question of unbelievers who die, even those who have never heard or truly understood the Gospel, as well as cognate circumstances. "Does God punish people for thousands of years with infinite, eternal torment for things they did in their few finite years of life?" (p. 2). And in contrast, Rob posits, why is it that only a select few happen to gain heaven? Thus, a comparison is made based on a definition of a human timetable and mathematical comparisons between opposite destinies. It seems so unfair, as it were, that a brief few years can pollute the unending years that follow …

11. What then is the biblical definition of space, time and number, and how does the Creator relate to it?

12. Is a human reckoning of time and number the real question, or is it a matter of human character, and choices made, which are judged from the perspective of the Eternal One?

This doctrine of a select few is such a wild and arbitrary one, incongruent with a message of hope in Rob's view, and this grinds against his soul. I agree.

He next poses the question of what it is that qualifies one for the select few – a rite, a class, baptism, church membership, an experience, or some other outward criteria, etc.? "Which leads us to a far more disturbing question. So is it true that the kind of person you are doesn't ultimately matter, as long as you've said or believed the right things?" (p. 6). Rob is probing well the question of the inner and the outer person, and ultimately, if unwritten here, the question of predestination.

13. What does Rob, and what do we understand by the biblical teaching on predestination?

Rob continues: "One way to respond to these questions is with a clear helpful answer: all that matters is how you respond to Jesus. And that answer totally resonates with me; it is about how you respond to Jesus. But it raises another important question: Which Jesus?

"Renee Altson begins her book, *Stumbling Toward Faith* with these words:

'I grew up in an abusive household. Much of my abuse was spiritual – and when I say spiritual, I don't mean new age, esoteric, random mumblings from half-Wiccan, hippie parents … I mean that my father raped me while reciting the Lord's Prayer. I mean that my father molested me while singing Christian hymns.'

"That Jesus?"

In other words, Rob's "disturbing question" leads to the illustration of the visceral hell of a girl being soul-beaten by self-acknowledged hypocritical evil. And the struggle to understand its place in God's cosmos.

- Such extraordinary evil lies at the heartbeat of this whole debate. It is a protest against an arbitrary and unjust present hell, and its future prospects.

Here and prior, to the end of Chapter One and to the end of the book, Rob addresses various biblical vignettes and verses in service to these good concerns. But it can also seem like a game of hopscotch, a meandering path through much and varied biblical topography from the hiker's view.

14. What would an aerial view of biblical theology first teach us?

Thus, we have the need for grasping how the Bible structurally interprets itself.

15. Does the biblical storyline inform sound doctrine (teaching), or vice versa?

16. To what extent has bad doctrine poisoned the biblical storyline for so many people?

In Chapter Two, Rob focuses on defining the proactive of heaven and its nature. I affirm his biblical grounding, in that the kingdom of heaven should be alive in us now, and continues after the resurrection with the blessings of all broken trust having been destroyed, thus setting us free in redemptive power.

I will add a personal vignette. In 1987, when my second oldest son was six, and in the middle of building a Lego castle, he said to me: "Daddy, when we die, we go to live with Jesus forever in heaven, right?" And I said, "Yes Stuart." He continued: "But what will we do there? Forever is an awfully long time." The human time frame finding natural and early reference. As well, how many Lego castles can a boy build before he wants to move on to new and more challenging projects?

In the meantime, Stuart (now a pastor) and I have arrived at an answer that floods our souls with joy: Heaven is an eternity to explore the infinity of God's library, and put into practice what we learn. We will never but scratch the smallest corner of the creation, and be forever creative and growing. And it starts now, with the choices we make in the trajectory of our earthly lives.

In 2001, my wife and I stopped at a used bookstore in Door County, Michigan, en route to Washington Island (about 100 miles north of Green Bay), where my wife's parents are buried, where much of her extended family summered. The bookstore was beautifully organized (some 20,000+ titles I would guess), and at the end of one bookshelf this sign was posted: "So many books, so little time." Stuart and I know the resolution to this quandary. Childlike wonder, with ever growing maturity, learning and experimenting forever (cf. Matthew 18:1-4).

In this chapter, as Rob examines the interaction between earthly and heavenly life, he makes one passing reference to the Hebrew *olam habah* for "eternal life." But he leaves it there.

17. In looking at the question of heaven and hell, and thus the nature of eternity, does not the Hebrew understanding of *olam* take interpretive precedent, and thus require at a sufficient overview?

Rob spends more time with the New Testament Greek word *aion* (from which we derive the English, eon). He starts in Luke 18 with the rich young ruler and his quest for eternal life. Rob says: "*Aion* had multiple meanings – one we'll look at here, and another we'll explore later" (p. 31). He gives two free-standing references to its usage as he later encapsulates it: "The first meaning of this word *aion* refers to a period of time with a beginning and an end" (p. 32).

Now, we have already reviewed *aionios*, and mentioned its root word, *aion*. The former means without limit in terms of time, and the latter does sometimes. The word in question in the New Testament is *aionios*.

18. Why does Rob choose the non-applicable term over the applicable one?

19. Is this a matter of tendentious preselection?

20. Or in only looking at the root word, not its cognate as used?

From this vantage point he examines the very this-worldly, rich and down to earth Hebrew sense of life (but without reference to the Hebrew language in play), and of a tangible earthly "age" or "eon" to come. He is seeking to correct the folly of these doctrines and churches that disconnect how we live this life and how we will live eternal life. But I am also concerned that his starting point in the Preface – of reacting to false doctrines of heaven and hell – leads him to put too much weight on the present, as opposed to a full integration between the present and the full future.

21. In so doing, has he boomeranged too far?

Later Rob states: "Another meaning of *aion* is a bit more complex and nuanced, because it refers to a *particular intensity of experience that transcends time*" (p. 57). In this context, "eternal" can be used to describe what happens, say, when boredom makes time drag to a stop and escape is sought, or ecstasy so floods the soul that it fills time and does not want to be released.

22. What are the other meanings and usages of *aion* in classical Greek and the New Testament, and/or cognates, and why are they not explicitly brought into the picture here?

23. Why does he not thus identify and exegete *aionios*?

24. Is *aionios* the same as a *"particular intensity of experience that transcends time?"*

25. If so, is this not still a slanted representation of the word?

Rob then says *aion* is a different word than "forever."

26. Then what is the Greek term for "forever?"

27. Why is it not defined here?

28. Is Ron dancing around the language so as to avoid true definitions of terms?

29. Can any honest reviewer not pose this last question?

At this juncture, Rob gives a theological summation to this portion of his argument, and his thoughts are worth quoting in appropriate length (pp. 58-59):

"Let me be clear: heaven is not forever in the way we think of forever, as a uniform measurement of time, like days and years, marching endlessly into the future. That's not a category or concept we find in the Bible. That is why a lot of translators choose to translate *aion* as 'eternal.' By this they don't mean the literal passing of time; they mean transcending time, belonging to another realm altogether."

30. What is time?

31. In saying that time marches on is not a "category," is this very question not an imposition on the text?

32. "No literal passing of time," a different "realm altogether" as though such time is a negative, needing abolition not fulfillment?

33. Namely, is linear time absented in the kingdom of heaven where Jesus speaks about those who will rule cities (e.g. Luke 19:17-19)?

34. For fun, what about Revelation 8:1 where there is silence in heaven for about "half an hour?"

35. Is not the relation of humanly experienced time to the eternal nature of Yahweh Elohim far richer than this putative contrast?

Rob continues:

"To summarize, then, when Jesus used the word 'heaven,' he was simply referring to God, using the word as a substitute for God."

This is untrue. "Heaven" as a substitute word for God is miniscule. In Daniel 4:26, as the prophet speaks to King Nebuchadnezzar of Babylon, he says "Heaven rules." He is using Aramaic cross-culturally to a pagan king who does not confess Yahweh. And we know that Daniel knows that Yahweh Elohim rules the heavens. Heaven is his throne (e.g. Isaiah 66:1).

Now, in the gospels where Jesus speaks, "heaven" is used about 110 times, most always as the domain where God rules. This is most preponderant in Matthew as "the kingdom of the heavens"[1] (or "heaven"). And a few times in the gospels as the physical space beyond the earth. Maybe an exception can be carved out for the parable of the prodigal son who speaks of sinning again "heaven" in Luke 15. Even there, Luke knows who rules heaven.

> 36. Why such a feint to avoid the overwhelming reality of the biblical text?

To continue this long quote from Rob:

"Second, sometimes when Jesus spoke of heaven, he was referring to the future coming together of heaven and earth in what he and his contemporaries called life in the age to come."

> 37. "Sometimes?" What is the ratio?
>
> 38. Does this reflect the tyranny of the minority in terms of the use of biblical language?
>
> 39. When we speak of "the age to come," or "from age to age," that is, from "*aion* to *aion*" (Revelation 20:10), can we see the human perspective of using temporal terms that aim toward that which has no end?

Continuing again:

"And then third – and this is where things get really, really interesting – when Jesus talked about heaven, he was talking about our present *eternal, intense, real experiences* of joy, peace and love in this life, this side of

---

[1] Translation note: Across the Hebrew Bible and in much of the New Testament, "heaven" is in the plural, not singular. This distinguishes the transcending realms of God's domain (plural), from the lowest physical one we can look on (singular).

death *and* the age to come. Heaven for Jesus wasn't just 'someday"; it was a present reality. Jesus blurs the lines, inviting the rich man, and us, to the merging of heaven and earth, the future and present, *here* and *now*.

"To say it again, eternal life is less about a kind of time that starts when we die, and more about a quality and vitality of life now in connection to God." Thus:

40. What is the biblical language to which others appeal for a concept of "forever?"

41. Has he conflated *aion* with *aionios*?

42. To what extent is Rob being pre-selective in his review of the biblical language about heaven and eternity?

43. To what extent is his language so reactionary to truly false doctrine, that he mutes a proactive definition of the post-resurrection reality about the kingdom of heaven, where, e.g., he has to use a negative clause such as "eternal life is less about …"?

44. And in an argument about time and heaven, where does the dominating nature of heaven's biblical reality – the good rule of God – fit in?

In Chapter Three, Rob focuses on hell. And again, he zeroes in from a reactive perspective to problematic metaethics such as "Turn or burn" (p. 63). This two-word clause is cited as a summation of a nasty use of "hell" that overshadows the good news of "heaven."

Now certainly, the idea of hell can be and is terribly misused. But too, as we earlier quoted the "good news" in Mark 1:1, we can also note the first words of Jesus in Matthew's gospel following his temptation in the wilderness: "Repent, for the kingdom of the heavens is near." In the prior chapter, Rob does talk about the confrontational nature of "heaven."

45. But the subject of hell starts here with a reactive to the reactive, and the question arises: Can hell be first talked about in the proactive?

81

- This question hits the radical core of biblical theology.

So Rob says he will show "every single verse in the Bible in which we find the actual word 'hell' " (p. 64) He starts with the Hebrew term *sheol*, which describes a place of the dead. But this is not the same word or exact parallel to hell.

46. Is "hell" the only biblical term that refers to judgement, indeed, final judgment?

Next, he says that the Hebrew usage of "life" and "death" is used "in a different sense than we do" (p. 66), in a more "nuanced" way. For example, when Moses puts "life and death" as a choice before the sons of Israel in Deuteronomy 30, Rob says that "death" does not mean being killed on the spot. Yes, life and death are not mere references to being with or without the breath of life on earth, but all the same, the presence of breath or lack thereof is real.

47. Where does the biblical definition of life and death originate, here at the end of the life of Moses, or earlier?

48. And does the answer to this question matter?

49. Where is there any nuance in choosing life *or* death, at any juncture?

50. Has Rob yet found the "actual word 'hell' " as promised, thus far in the Hebrew scriptures?

From this point, he moves into New Testament usage, and notes how Jesus uses the term translated as "hell" in Matthew 5, 10, 18 and 23; Mark 9, Luke 12 and James 3 (as we have already reviewed).

Rob speaks of the word referring to the trash dump outside the walls of Jerusalem where it is always burning.

51. But why does he not also give the prior Hebrew context to its original usage as *ge'hinnom* in its various references, especially in the judgment on it in Jeremiah 7 and 19?

In other words, whereas he promises to cite every verse in the Bible that mentions hell, his Hebrew Bible references do not do so, and he does not cite the Hebrew contexts which are the source for the New Testament use of *gehenna*, the transliterated *ge'hinnom*, the word we translate as "hell."

In the balance of the New Testament, Rob cites two Greek words conflated with the idea of hell. First is *tarturus* (Greek for the underworld or even abyss), and second is *hades* (which in the Septuagint – the third century B.C. translation of the Hebrew Bible – is the translation for *sheol*, the place of the dead, even "the waiting dead").

52. Why are the Hebrew and Greek usages of the actual word "abyss" not referenced and defined?

Then Rob says: "And that's it." The metaethical sense of this summation is a mathematical one. Namely, hell has comparatively few references in the Bible.

53. Is mathematical superiority the measure of interpretive biblical authority for central concerns?

54. The language of the "image of God" is used much less often than the language of hell; thus, is the image of God less important or strategic a term?

From this point, Rob treats hell as he does heaven, in the sense that both terms are not just restricted to the "afterlife," but are fully linked with our earthy lives. And here we come to a juncture where Rob steps back from an overemphasis in one direction, and aims at some balance.

"... it is absolutely vital that we acknowledge that love, grace, and humanity can be rejected. From the most subtle rolling of the eyes to the most violent degradation of another human, we are terrifyingly free to do as we please.

"God gives us what we want, and if that's hell, we can have it.

"We have that kind of freedom, that kind of choice. We are that free" (p. 72).

But still, hell has not been defined as eternal, and his language leaves open the door for an "ultimate reconciliation" universalism.

55. Is this another feint where he knows the ethical nature of hell, a reality of freedom, but is trying to preclude its impingement on universalism?

56. What is Rob's biblical definition for human freedom?

Here, Rob does segue into the biblical content of the title of this book, *The Freedom to Choose Hell*. But only partially. His qualifications of language are always in the mix. He then says that "some words are strong for a reason" (ibid.), such as "sin." Then:

"And that's what we find in Jesus's teaching about hell – a volatile mixture of images, pictures, and metaphors that describe the very real experiences and consequences of rejecting our God given goodness and humanity. Something we are all free to do, anytime, anywhere, with anyone.

"He uses hyperbole often – telling people to gouge out their eyes and maim themselves rather than commit certain sins. It can sound a bit over the top at times, leading us to question just what he's so worked up about. Other times he sounds just plain violent" (p. 73).

One difficulty I have is this: Rob's "expansive love" interpretive leverage always shifts his readers in only one direction – toward his doctrine of an "ultimate reconciliation" universalism.

57. "Anytime, anywhere, with anyone" – a blurring of distinctions away from any sense of final Judgment?

58. To question what Jesus is "so worked up about," as if discrete evil is "over the top?"

59. Is the literary structure of the language of hell in fact serving hyperbole?

60. Is Jesus sometimes able, in word or deed, to be "just plain violent?"

In other words, Rob may technically not call "hell" hyperbole, but these two paragraphs are syntactically linked and almost demand that he does call it hyperbole. And to qualify the language of "hell" as sounding "a bit over the top at times," and even "violent" as with other language of Jesus, in Rob's estimation, it comes across as reacting to a certain generational demography.

61. Why not instead define the clarity of how the listeners to Jesus understand the language of hell, and then address the present church culture from such a foundation?

The Hebrew use of *ge'hinnom* by Jeremiah, just prior to the Babylonian exile in 586 B.C., proves key. The Jewish listeners to Jesus know with exacting and painful clarity his historical point of reference with the language of "hell" – children being burned alive to the false god *ba'al*, as the specter of Babylonian conquest draws ever nearer. They know it is not hyperbole. And too, at the very end of Isaiah, the concluding judgment looks over the Valley of Ben Hinnom, with undying worms and unquenchable fire consuming bodies.

Continuing in Chapter Three, Rob states that "Jesus did not use hell to try and compel 'heathens' and 'pagans' to believe in God, so they wouldn't burn forever. He talked about hell to very religious people to warn them about the consequences of straying from their God-given calling and identity to show the world God's love" (p. 82).

This hits the mark in that Jesus, nor any person faithful to biblical covenants, would employ coercion of the human will. But it also misses the mark in that Jesus first comes to the Jews to fulfill the Messianic promises, not himself to preach to the Gentiles, but entrusting that mission to his disciples and the church. In other words, Rob is so often in a reactionary mode, and squeezes in the Gospel to critique real problems, but without stated recourse to the foundation of how the Bible interprets itself. And here an enormous questions looms:

62. Is the language of hell the proper prism through which to understand the biblical teachings on judgment and final judgment?

- I say no. The church has erred greatly in making hell the primary prism, and Rob and others have reacted honestly to much of the problems inherent in using hell this way. Namely, judgment begins in the Garden of Eden, and there is a long history from there that sets the stage for the power of the language of *ge'hinnom* in the Hebrew Bible, and its transliterated *gehenna* in the New Testament. Without such a foundation defined for the readers, they are impoverished in grasping the true nature of hell, and they are thus more vulnerable to a reactive posture.

Indeed, in the title of this book, I need to use "hell" as opposed to "abyss" or "death" or "judgment," otherwise far fewer people will understand the subject I am addressing. It is that powerful of a term in our collective imagination. The real issue is defined by the interpretive leverage in Genesis 1-3. This structure will set things in an order that best addresses all questions from all angles.

In moving toward the end of this chapter, Rob talks briefly about Sodom and Gomorrah, raises good concerns, but again through his assumed theme of "expansive love." This is in a continued context of ranging away from the exact term of "hell," and probing into the larger theme of judgment.

63. What is the unifying reality about the nature of Sodom and Gomorrah across its 48 biblical references?

Rob then references Satan as an agent for redemption in one particular case, as it were. But there is no discourse on who Satan is biblically.

64. Who is Satan and what is his nature?

65. Is just a passing reference to him sufficient?

66. How can hell be biblically understood apart from knowing the theology of demonology?

He concludes the chapter with a reference to the parable in Matthew 25 of the sheep and the goats. The former go to "eternal life" and the latter to "eternal punishment," indeed "the eternal fire prepared for the devil and his angels" (v. 41). But Rob again says the idea of " 'forever' is not really a category the biblical writers used" (p. 92), referring to the Greek term *aion* as an example, along with the Hebrew term *olam*.

67. Why then has Rob not given us a full review of the Hebrew use of *olam*, and moreover, why has Rob only discussed the meaning of the root *aion*, and we were to look at the salient cognate of *aionios*, what would we learn about "forever?"

Chapter Four in *Love Wins* is titled: "Does God Get what God Wants?" A provocative and key question that raises many angles, especially in terms of human freedom.

68. If God does not get what he wants, and if he wants all people to be saved (e.g., explicitly in 1 Timothy 2:4; 2 Peter 3:9), has he "lost?"

• To answer this question is to answer the debate.

Here, Rob again starts with the reactive, citing several church statements of faith: "The unsaved will be separated forever from God in hell," and "those who don't believe in Jesus will be sent to eternal punishment in hell," and "The unsaved dead will be committed to an eternal conscious punishment" (pp. 95-96). These facile statements and their power to cause people to flee the church, is the demographic to which Rob is aiming. But a reactive to a reactive will not cut it. Biblical belief is not an atomized statement; it is loving God and neighbor with the whole heart, soul, mind and strength – as Jesus taught, the very One in whom we believe.

He then looks at church statements that focus on God's greatness, that he "is in control," and surveys various biblical passages that affirm the same.

69. What is the intrinsic nature of the sovereign power of God, and how does it relate to human freedom?

Rob thus writes: "God in the end doesn't get what God wants, it's declared, because some will turn, repent, and believe, and others won't. To explain this perspective, it's rightly pointed out that love, by its very nature, is freedom. For there to be love, there has to be the option, both now and then, not to love. To turn the other way. To reject the love extended. To say no. Although God is powerful and mighty, when it comes to the human heart God has to play by the same rules we do. God has to respect our freedom to choose to the very end, even at the risk of the relationship itself. If at any point God overrides, co-opts, or hijacks the human heart, robbing us of our freedom to choose, then God has violated the fundamental essence of what love even is" (pp. 103-104).

Here, with the clause "its declared," Rob addresses important questions in the theoretical of how these issues have been posed in the church, in defining love and freedom.

70. What does God want?

71. Would he ever resort to imposition against the human will to get it?

72. What is the biblical definition of the interface between love and freedom?

73. What interface does Rob share with any of these sentiments?

74. For those who so believe, if God "has to respect" or "has to play by" the human rules of freedom, does this mean freedom is somehow foreign to God's nature?

75. For those who so believe, and if God is love (1 John 4:8), and love is freedom, is then the "fundamental essence of" love somehow greater than God?

In other words, Rob is addressing some crucial questions in the church as he seeks to advance an "expansive love," and to wrestle with the nature of hell which seems to threaten such love.

He continues to set a sense of the freedom to choose hell against an expansive love. "We aren't fixed static beings – we change and morph as life unfolds" (p. 104). He then posits the deepening ruts of patterned choices to reject God's love and embrace evil, and asks: "Could a person reach the point of no longer bearing the image of God" (p. 105). This is a superb question.

76. When can humanity itself be forsaken, if at all?

Next, he posits the idea of a "second chance" after death, and whether there is "an endless amount of time for people to say yes to God. As long as it takes, in other words" (p. 107). The doctrine of "ultimate restoration."

"And so, beginning with the early church, there is a long tradition of Christians who believe God will ultimately restore everything and everybody" (ibid.), citing the language of "the renewal of all things" in Matthew 19:28, and when Peter says in Acts 3:21 that Jesus will "restore everything."

77. If God cannot convince someone of his love in this life, what changes in him or us, so that more time will do the trick?

78. What, for Rob, is the biblical use of "all?"

In this vein, Rob cites support for this in third century fathers Clement of Alexandria and Origin; then Gregory of Nyssa and Eusebius in the fourth; and comments by Jerome, Basil and Augustine that most people in the church believed in an "ultimate reconciliation."

79. Why does Rob not give some examples, in historical context, of the biblical arguments made by these church fathers?

"To be clear again, an untold number of serious disciples of Jesus across hundreds of years have assumed, affirmed and trusted that no one can resist

God's pursuit forever, because God's love will eventually melt even the hardest of hearts" (p. 108).

80. What is the relative authority and reality between Scripture on the one hand, and the sentiments of mass opinion, on the other?

Rob is setting different opinions side-by-side, as he does often, but what is his interpretive purpose in how he goes about it? For example, on the matter of "ultimate restoration," he keeps at it with repetitive paragraphs. "Which is stronger and more powerful, the hardness of the human heart or God's unrelenting, infinite, expansive love? Thousands through the years have answered that question with the resounding response, 'God's love, of course' " (p. 109). In other words, the metaethics of his language is an encouragement to those seeking to find a rationale for "ultimate restoration."

81. Is this matter reduceable to a mere dichotomy?

82. What is the definition of "stronger" relative to freedom?

83. If "love" is stronger, what is the nature of its strength?

84. Will love and freedom ultimately impose itself if love and freedom are rejected?

85. Is this the definition of strength?

Rob continues: "At the center of the Christian tradition since the first church have been a number who insist that history is not tragic, hell is not forever, and love, in the end, wins and all will be reconciled to God" (ibid.).

86. Is history tragic if the freedom to say no to God arrives at an endpoint?

87. What other option is there, in Rob's theology, but the genuine tragedy and oxymoron of an imposed "paradise?"

Then he moves into the Book of Revelation, citing its "apocalyptic, heavily symbolic nature," and aims toward an "ultimate restoration": "Will everybody be saved, or will some perish apart from God forever because of their choices?" (p. 115). At this point, Rob only continues to posit the same questions over and over.

88. What is the literary structure of Revelation?

89. How does the "restoration" of all, at the end of Revelation, aim to restore us to the original given goodness at the beginning of Genesis?

90. If there is freedom at the outset of Genesis, what does a restored freedom look at the end of Revelation?

91. At what point do we decide a matter and move on to the deeper or subsequent questions?

His answer: "Those are the questions, or more accurately, those are tensions we are free to leave fully intact. We don't need to resolve them or answer them because we can't, and so we simply respect them, creating space for the freedom that love requires" (ibid.).

Now we arrive at a troubling juncture.

92. With all the open-endedness Rob celebrates throughout his book, how does he now merely state that we have neither need nor ability to arrive at an answer to the question of his assumed universalism?

93. Are the powers of freedom and an expansive love insufficient in this regard?

94. How does love "require" something without violating freedom?

Troubling, because Rob is syntactically strategic. He does not use the word "universalism" (it carries much baggage in the evangelical world). But he relentlessly aims for it as hopefully as possible.

Troubling, because, immediately upon declaration of a non-answer, Rob then reverts to the pursuit of an answer he dare not forthrightly claim – an "ultimate restoration" universalism. "God announces 'I am making everything new' " (p. 116). "That's what God's love does; it speaks new words into the world and into us. Potentials, possibilities, and the promise that God has an imagination and is not afraid to use it" (ibid.).

95. What is the nature of God's "imagination," and how does it relate to his will?

Rob concludes the chapter with "Does God get what God wants?" (ibid.), does not answer it, and says there is a better question, "Do we get what we want?" (ibid.), and says yes: "God is that loving" (p. 117). Again, this quandary continually inches it way toward an undeclared form of universalism ... "because love wins" (p. 119).

96. Has Rob taken a simple and proactive thought, "love wins," sought to squeeze Scripture into it, and in the end, all that is left is a muddled theology of a declared non-declaration that declares a form of universalism?

97. Am I able to measure up to the trajectory of these tough questions and give some clear biblical answers?

In Chapter Five, "Dying to Live," Rob looks at the purpose of the cross and resurrection. His trajectory further selects those elements which serve an "ultimate reconciliation" universalism.

"Paul writes to the Colossians that through the cross God was reconciling 'to himself all things, whether things on earth or things in heaven, by making peace through his blood, shed on the cross.' 'Reconciliation' is a word from the world of relationships. It's what happens when two people or groups have something come between them, some argument or difference or wrong or injustice, and now they've found a way to work it out and come back together. Peace has been made" (p. 125).

98. With the Greek terms for "all" (*pas, pasa, pan)*, as already noted, there is a wide variety of how these words are used in various

contexts – why has Rob not alerted us to this fact and investigated it?

99. When Rob speaks of people having "something come between them" in need of reconciliation, is this a suitable analogy to the gravity of sin and evil introduced in the Garden that requires the cross?

100. Rob concludes in Chapter Four that we all ultimately "get what we want" – is this a form of "reconciliation" that includes the freedom to eternally choose hell?

101. How does this relate to C.S. Lewis and his observation that if we do not say "Your will be done" to our heavenly Father, he will say, "your will be done" in reply?

102. What is the biblical definition of "peace" – the absence of conflict, or something proactively deeper?

Rob posits a conflict of interpretations: "So when Jesus died on the cross, was it the end of the sacrificial system or was it the reconciling of all things?" (p. 126).

103. Is this a real conflict, or two angles on the deeper reality (which the biblical writers reflect repeatedly), or a posited conflict to serve the presupposition of an ultimate universalism?

In Chapter Six, Rob continues pressing toward "ultimate reconciliation." In speaking of the good Creator and his good creation, he posits a conflict: "Is [the universe] limited to what we can conceive of and understand, or are there realities beyond the human mind? Are we the ultimate orbiter of what can, and cannot, exist?

"Or is the universe open, wondrous, unexpected, and far beyond anything we can comprehend?

"Are you open or closed?" (p. 147).

- This question is the anvil of decision for Rob's book, designed to hammer all others on the unstated presupposition of an "ultimate reconciliation" universalism.

I honor Rob in his pastoral love for all people equally, and I honor why he protests the facile theology that only an arbitrary "select few" are "saved." But too, his book is a relentless and unidirectional push, and via a unique hortatory employment of questions. And here, this question is meant to corner people into an either/or, where if they disagree with his trajectory, they must be "closed" to God and the universe. Most able to shame vulnerable people into thinking otherwise, whether intentionally or not. Instead of going directly for the potential answers to good questions as they arise, he so often leaves them "open" to a further rewrite of the same questions.

104. Is this "openness" thus a potential means to close off the discussion?

There are two major doctrines in church history he is addressing, oftentimes at the opposite end of the spectrum, predestination and universalism. Yet he never identifies each, using instead language evasive of what any biblically trained person knows he is talking about.

105. What Christian person believes that he or she can be the "ultimate orbiter of what can, or cannot, exist?"

106. [Orbiter or arbiter?]

107. A straw figure question?

108. If one were "open" to the Creator and his good creation, does that therefore require an "ultimate reconciliation" universalism?

109. Are therefore those who believe in the freedom to choose hell – which Rob seems to ethically approach – "closed" to the good universe?

110. Is Rob thus presenting opposite sentiments as though he is being balanced, while aiming in only one direction?

Rob also writes in this chapter about the question of exclusivity and inclusivity. In the former, "Jesus is the only way" and "You're either in, or you're going to hell" (p. 154). In the latter, there is the idea that all paths lead to the same (G)od. Then he posits a third way where "there is an exclusivity on the other side of inclusivity. This kind insists that Jesus is the way" (p. 155). Though he does not say so here, it is the doctrine of an "ultimate reconciliation" universalism that makes this third option possible. Also here, there is great opportunity to quote John 14:6 in the words of Jesus to Thomas: "I am the way, the truth and the life. No one comes to the Father except through me."

111. Why does not Rob quote and exegete this very central passage, known widely in the evangelical church, as he addresses its very content?

For myself, I have two perspectives here: 1) when the biblical history of redemption is known from Genesis on forward, and in contrast with pagan and secular reality, for Jesus to say he is the only way, life and truth, it is the most inclusive statement in history; and 2) all paths do not lead to the same God; from all paths, the one true God draws people to himself (e.g., Acts 17:23).

In this chapter, Rob continues to affirm his definition of openness and concludes with two observations. First: "[N]one of us have cornered the market on Jesus, and none of us ever will" (p. 159).

112. Is this notion of "cornering the market" a reaction to people with facile theologies on heaven and hell, to others as well, and how does Rob apply it to himself in his relentless argument for his unstated but hugely presupposed doctrine of "ultimate reconciliation" universalism?

And second here, he states: "[I]t is our responsibility to be extremely careful about making negative, decisive, lasting judgments about people's eternal destinies" (p. 160). Most certainly yes, if we are talking about human judgments about a given person or group of people. And I understand Rob's reactionary posture to false judgments.

113. But, if the Scriptures are clear in stating there is the Judgment Day, and even though Rob has eschewed looking at so much in this context, is he not using such a pronouncement, again, only in a one-way service to his presupposed doctrinal assumptions?

In his final two chapters Rob focuses on saying there is something better than hell, and uses Tim Keller's review of Luke 15 and the two sons. In this context, Rob says: "Hell is our refusal to trust God's retelling of our story" (p. 170), and "Hell is refusing to trust, and refusing to trust is often rooted in a distorted view of God" (p. 175). Yes, but preliminarily:

114. What is the biblical origin of trust, and how did it come to be broken?

115. What is the original source for the distortion of seeing God?

Rob is comfortable in speaking in generalizations, then jumping to prescriptive judgments, but too often sans specific biblical explanation. He is comfortable in speaking about the ethics of hell, but not as a final destination. In his "Further Reading" section at the end of the book, he recommends C.S. Lewis's allegory, *The Great Divorce*, which profoundly profiles the ethics of choosing hell. But Rob does not embrace Lewis further to the conviction that there is a real and final judgment.

And so Rob meanders to his conclusion the same way, doing all to tendentiously arrive at an unspoken but very real embrace of an "ultimate reconciliation" universalism. And he returns again to where he began – a reaction to an evangelical milieu he knows so well where a facile theology of heaven and hell is taught:

"I have sat with many Christian leaders over the years who are burned out, washed up, fried, whose marriages are barely hanging on, whose kids are home while the parents are out at church meetings, who haven't taken a vacation in forever – all because, like the older brother [in Luke 15], they have seen themselves as 'slaving all these years' " (p. 180). Ron describes a broken church culture.

116. Is the healing found in a reactive universalism, or in the depths of biblical truth and beauty?

In sum, Rob 1) starts with a reactive experiential posture, a visceral repulsion against a doctrine that believes God sends people to hell arbitrarily; 2) is highly selective in how he cites Scripture; 3) minimizes the nature of the whole inspiration of Scripture; 4) minimizes the question of God's judgment; 5) does not give a biblical interpretive structure; and 6) minimally addresses the underlying question of biblical freedom.

♦ ♦ ♦

Chapter Four

Questions for Paul Young

Paul Young has sought God and wrestled free from the sexual molestation he suffered as a boy, as he testifies publicly and boldly – first by tribal people in Papua New Guinea, and second, by upper classmen in a missionary boarding school. It took him decades, and it was painful, indeed explosive, to escape such imposed evil. His book, *The Shack*, was written in this process, and in his 2017 *Lies We Believe About God*, he seeks to give theological explanation.

Underneath the hell of his sexual molestation is the question of a prior theological molestation. As we have already cited, Rob Bell, in *Love Wins* (p. 7), quotes the opening words of *Renee Altson* in her book, *Stumbling Toward Faith*:

"I grew up in an abusive household. Much of my abuse was spiritual ... my father raped me while reciting the Lord's Prayer ... I mean that my father molested me while singing Christian hymns."

1.   To what degree does Paul share the same hellish reality, in that it is a theological molestation that precedes and opens the door for the sexual molestation?

2.   Having overcome the latter across many years, what now is needful to overcome the former?

I trust we can all understand the pain of reaction to evil, as we seek to escape it. But too, reactions to reactions only beget further reactions. So, I have some concerns about Paul's reactions to perceived theological lies he comes to diagnose.

At the outset, Paul states: "The world I grew up in did not place a high value on questions. At best, questions were a sign of ignorance and, at the worst, were deemed evidence of rebellion. Anyone who disagreed with our theology, science, or even opinion was an enemy or target. What mattered was certainty (p. 16).

Now, whereas all non-biblical institutions resist being questioned, biblical faith celebrates our given freedom to ask the toughest questions of God, leaders and one another. Questions serve our learning curve as image-bearers of God. Thus, in *Lies*, Paul's self-defined starting point is in reactionary pain to a non-biblical censorship of the childlike freedom to ask any and all questions.

3. Is the prohibition of honest questions the starting point for theological molestation, no matter where, how and to whom?

Paul also testifies about what I call the "theological molestation" of his father, who converted dramatically from a broken background. After Bible School, he and Paul's mother went on the mission field to Papua New Guinea. But he physically and verbally abused Paul, letting loose on him the unreconciled anger from his own abusive upbringing.

4. How does the experience of such a cycle of abuse inform Paul's instinct toward others, in wishing them not to suffer the same?

5. And how might this sow seed in his soul for the putative comfort of a possible universal salvation in order to reconcile justice and mercy?

In the book, Paul identifies twenty-eight "lies." This is a concern for all of us.

6. But do we address our concerns proactively or reactively?

7. As Paul titles his book by diagnosing "lies we believe," to what extent does it put readers on the defensive and hinder communication on the deeper substance?

Accordingly, here are at six concerns I have.

8. First, who is the "we" in the book title?

This proves to be Paul's autobiographical angst of the "missionary kid" world in which he grew up. The twenty-eights questions he formally poses aim at deficiencies he experienced in such a world.

9. Well and good, but too, how many of his questions are needlessly provocative?

For example, in various chapter headings he defines some of the "lies" as: "God is in control," "You need to get saved," "Hell is separation from God," and "Sin separates us from God." The metaethics of these chapter titles are clear:

10. If it is a "lie" that God is in control, then is it the "truth" that God is not in control?

11. If it is a "lie" that we need to be saved, is the truth that we do not need to be saved?

12. If it is a "lie" that sin and hell do not separate us from God, then do sin and hell reconcile us to God?

And I think that all of Paul's questions, most of which do not directly address our subject here, are part of the subterranean groans of an unhealthy church culture. We cannot diagnose and address the up-front questions without knowing the milieu which produces them.

13. Do these questions open the door for a doctrine of an "ultimate reconciliation" universalism?

14. Now, in these chapters, as elsewhere, Paul Young pulls back some of these provocations, but why start in such a manner?

Young frames these issues in deep visceral and honest pain to the theological violations in his formative identity, one where he was taught that God, salvation, hell and sin are all arbitrary, that they operate apart from justice, love and mercy. But in many of his answers, there is no biblical exegesis present, only some proof-texting and a few atomistic observations, mixed in with free-standing opinions.

Second, Young says: "There is a common appeal, whether in the New Testament, the Hebrew Scriptures, the Koran, the Bhagavad Gita, the Analects of Confucius, etc., to what many of us would recognize as the Golden Rule" (pp. 46-47). The Golden Rule is the proactive of treating all others as we wish to be treated, loving all our neighbors, and is highlighted by Jesus in the Sermon on the Mount (Matthew 6:12) and the parable of the Good Samaritan (Luke 10:25-37). To be raised without the Golden Rule is to be theologically molested.

15. To what extent does this perspective set the stage for an ultimate universalism?

16. Does Paul know that the Golden Rule cannot be located outside the Bible?

Outside the Bible there is only what is known as a reactionary "silver rule" of "don't do to others what you don't want them to do to you."

17. Thus, what are Paul's sources for this statement?

18. For example, does he know how the Sira of Ibn Ishaq interprets the Qur'an, and the only "golden rule" located there is for fellow Muslims, and not for Jews, Christians and pagans?

From the seventh century on forward, non-Muslims in Muslim nations were subject to Islamic domination or death as inferior peoples.

Third, Paul says: "The image of God in us (*imago dei*) is not less feminine than masculine. The feminist/masculine nature of God is a circle of relationship, a spectrum, not a polarity" (p. 73).

19. Where does this "spectrum" of sexual theology finds its biblical warrant?

20. Is this reactionary language against a violent fatherhood he experienced as a boy?

If so, a boomerang ensues where Paul feminizes God in *The Shack* and *Lies*, against those who masculinize God.

21. Is this "inclusiveness" another reactive predicate along the path to universalism?

22. Does this feminization of God, and Young's quasi-androgynous rendering of the image of God, provide a safe space away from male violence?

Neither will do, for in both cases, people are viewing God in the image of their own broken human sexualities. The biblical understanding is that man and woman are equals and complements as joint image-bearers of God, where the Fatherhood of God is greater than male and female. As well, the power of God the Father is to give blessings, as modeled in him to Adam for Eve, then reciprocated.

Fourth, Young's reactionary posture is evident as he says: "Government is not instituted by or originated by God" (p. 103). His reference is rooted in a reactionary definition of human governments poisoned by sinful nature, reacting to the reactions of the socio-cultural "religious right" (with the "religious left" found at the other end of the reactionary spectrum).

23. So, when he makes a subsequent passing reference to the kingdom of God, does he not know that he has identified the original and enduring government of God?

24. Is final judgement the domain of God's government, and what part will human agency play in it as image bearers of God (e.g., 1 Corinthians 6:2-3)?

25. How does the kingdom of God affect human government in matters of judgment?

26. And how much of the human experience in fallen government resorts to the exercise of male chauvinistic top-down power "over"?

Fifth, Young argues that hell is not separation from God (pp. 131ff.), some important questions are raised, but in his answers, no biblical texts are cited in this regard.

Now, since Paul's book is not only concerned with the possibility of an unspoken universalism, these select issues and questions serve to give background to the territory of the issue which now arrives. The 28 "lies" Paul raises receive only the briefest theological treatment each.

27. Why the provocation of saying that it is a "lie" to say that hell does not equal separation from God?

28. Why does Paul not define what hell is in biblical terms?

29. Is he satisfied in raising the subject sans any biblical references?

30. What is its place in the midst of broader biblical language concerning final judgment?

31. If hell does not equal separation from God, does it, in some capacity, equal "reconciliation" with God instead?

32. Or are there mid-stations between separation and "reconciliation?"

Sixth, Paul further opens the door to a "universal salvation" in Chapter 21 (pp. 181ff.), and does not close it. Here, the "lie" is stated as "Death is more powerful than God." This "lie" is posited in an answer to a friend where Paul says: "God would never say, "I'm sorry you died. There is nothing I can do for you now. Death wins' " (p. 181). His friend believes our choices are sealed at death, period.

Now, we need to be careful when we paraphrase a hypothetical of what we think God would or would not say in a given context.

As the conversation continues, Young says to his friend: "To be clear, you don't think we should have any choice postmortem, after we die? You don't think we can change our minds?" (p. 183). He continues a little later:

"Is it possible that the intent of judgment is to help us clear away the lies that are keeping us from making a clear choice?" (p. 184).

Both of these are reasonable questions, and need address – biblically not just anecdotely. But their trajectory also puts the conversation into a one-way pursuit of a possible ultimate universalism.

33. What does Paul know about this debate biblically and in church history?

Then he says a little later: "Personally, I believe that the idea that we lose our ability to choose at the event of physical death is a significant lie and needs to be exposed; its implications are myriad and far reaching" (pp. 185-186). Thus, as Paul says hell is not separation from God, and choices made at death are not final, not settled, his direction and agenda is clear.

34. If some form of an "ultimate reconciliation" universalism is in view, why not simply say so?

35. Or why not say it is in view, there are questions outstanding, and then address the questions?

36. What is the difference between a personal belief and the nature of Scripture?

The implications need to be reviewed, but Paul does not do so in his book. Historically, the implications lead to a form of ultimate universalism, whether via purgatory in classical Roman Catholicism, or some of the present views we are reviewing.

I think a full biblical review yields far more dynamic realities. And I also think Paul has excellent reasons for raising the question in the face of some genuinely facile fundamentalist or "missionary kid" theologies.

37. How well thought out is his theology?

In sum, Paul 1) starts with a reactive experiential posture, a visceral repulsion against bad theology that includes a doctrine that believes God sends people to hell arbitrarily; 2) makes very minimal and selective use of Scripture; 3) does allow questions about the nature of Scripture to enter in; 4) does not address the question of God's judgment; 5) does not give a biblical interpretive structure; and 6) barely glances at the underlying question of biblical freedom.

♦ ♦ ♦

Chapter Five

Questions for George Sarris

In his book, *Heaven's Doors: Wider Than You Ever Believed!*, George Sarris argues up front for an "ultimate reconciliation" universalism. In the Preface, he begins by saying: "For the first 500 years after Christ, most Christians believed that God would ultimately redeem *all* of his creation," (p. 1), namely, all will be in heaven.

1. Is the historical reference to popular belief the starting hermeneutic for George?

2. Does George trace the Hebrew Bible and New Testament usage of "all" in its three categorical applications, apply it here and elsewhere to sustain his argument?

He says: "During the first five centuries after Christ, many of the most prominent Christian leaders believed that hell was real, but it had a positive purpose. And it didn't last forever!" (p. 2). George then cites Origen and Gregory of Nyssa. He attends to church history in Chapter Four.

"They and others believed that God doesn't defeat evil by shutting it up in a corner of His creation and leaving it there forever, like some kind of cosmic graveyard keeping sinners imprisoned for all eternity. Instead they were convinced that God will destroy evil by transforming the hearts of evildoers, ultimately making them into those who love goodness" (pp. 2-3).

3. What are good and evil?

4. "Making them into ...?"

5. Does this belie a metaethics of arm twisting?

6. How is this accomplished, and what are the mechanisms that work after the grave that did not work before?

7. Is this mechanism the eternal plan all along?

8. If so, what is its sense and purpose in contrast to a plan of a simple mechanism that works the first time it is tried?

9. Did God fail in his first attempt, thus requiring another?

George then posits that this doctrine has been supported by certain luminaries across the darkness of the past 1500 years, but "where most of Christendom has been told that the majority of the billions of people who have lived on this earth will remain separated from the love and mercy of God for all eternity. The moms and dads, grandmas and grandpas, sons and daughters, relatives and friends who have not exhibited the 'right kind' of faith here in this life will be shut up in a place called hell to suffer forever" (p. 1).

Again, this is his starting hermeneutic, with an emotional and intrinsic reaction to a damning doctrine.

10. Is it possible to articulate a proactive starting point instead?

George credits the origins of deceit about hell to the force of a "power-hungry" Roman emperor, and "supported by a highly respected but misinformed cleric" (p. 2), referring to Justinian and Augustine.

In Chapter One, George says, "This is not a safe book" (p. 10), because of how it challenges the status quo.

11. But why be concerned about "safety" or controversy since everyone will be saved anyhow?

George gives reference to a loving father in his upbringing, and thus his sense of self-worth. He separates his doctrine from that of "cheap grace," and insists that repentance and faith are necessary. "Does the book teach that everyone God has created will eventually be in heaven? Yes! Evil will not remain a part of God's creation forever. At the end of time, all those who God's created will experience the peace and joy of being in His presence" (p. 13).

12. When is the "end of time?"

13. Is it at the Final Judgment in Revelation 20, or does time continue thereafter until all choose heaven, and then time ends?

14. Is hell thus a part of the creation for its duration?

15. Will Satan and his demons also be liberated from hell and rejoin the heavenly angels?

16. What is the original biblical understanding of "the abyss" and its relationship to the creation?

17. What is the biblical source, definition and nature of evil?

18. Why would God allow evil to begin with if ultimate salvation is pre-ordained?

19. What would be the purpose?

20. Could not some call this a charade, asking how a loving God could make us endure all this pointless suffering?

21. Why did God not just prohibit evil from ever entering the scene?

In Chapter Two, George starts with a hypothetical story of a child who interacts with his friend Johnny, who does not attend church: "I told him that if he didn't believe in God, he would go to hell!" (p. 15). Thus, an anecdote rooted in a visceral reaction to an unpleasant church milieu. Then George talks briefly about Sunday School, predestination, free will and how preachers like Jonathan Edwards and Charles Spurgeon preached hell.

In Chapter Three, George addresses the source for the idea of "endless punishment." He begins by saying that the Old Testament does not refer to a spirit world or a future state.

22. Really?

23. Are not Adam and Eve created to live forever, and how does this assumption interpret all the Hebrew Scriptures in preparing the way for the Messiah and his redeemed promise of eternal life, the

restoration of the same at the end of Revelation as it ties up all the issues introduced in Genesis 1-3?

24. What is the reality of the relentless profile of angels across the Hebrew Bible, and their interface with humans as messengers of Yahweh Elohim?

25. What is the reality of Saul's pursuit of a medium in 1 Samuel 28?

George immediately says: "For example, the first instance of punishment mentioned in the Bible, pronounced on Adam and Eve in the Garden of Eden, was natural death. God told Adam not to eat fruit from the forbidden tree. If he did, he would die. Adam disobeyed. He ate from the forbidden tree. And he died" (p. 26).

He is referring to Genesis 2:17, and his interpretation has no basis. If it were only referring to a "natural death," Adam would have died on the spot, but he lived another 930 years. This wrong assumption from the limits of a standard English translation is common. And George compounds this error as he states: "The punishment was physical death. It occurred in this life. The consequences lasted until they returned to the ground. The same is true throughout Scripture" (p. 26).

26. In this argument, is there not a non-sequitur between the past tense that "he died," and the future reality "until they returned to the ground?"

27. Which is it?

28. Does George know the nature of the forbidden fruit in the Hebrew text?

29. Does he know the Hebrew words, parallelistic structure and syntax involved that frame this verse?

30. If he does not, how can he say that his stated understanding remains true throughout Scripture?

31. Does George know how Genesis 2:16-17 defines freedom for the whole Bible?

- As George here references 2:17, he has landed on the most important text in this debate. But he needs first to know how v. 16 modifies v. 17, and how they both sum up the context beginning in v. 7.

- The biblical understanding of Genesis 2:16-17 is so central to an interpretive leverage for the whole Bible, that we need to look at it thoroughly. If we err here, we err across all Scripture and church history.

Based on his assumption, he also says: "So, what does the Old Testament teach about hell? In the words of one contemporary scholar, 'Very little' "? (p. 27).

32. But if George's understanding of Genesis 2:16 proves erroneous, is it possible the opposite is true?

Namely, by starting with an accurate translation of Genesis 2:16-17, the Hebrew Scriptures are utterly foundational for grasping the language of judgment, and the specific language of "hell" employed by Jesus.

In this chapter, George says simply: "The Sadducees didn't believe in a resurrection to heaven or future punishment in hell. The Pharisees believed in both" (p. 32).

33. Is George thus siding with the Sadducees (who also did not believe in angels, in the spirit world), over and against the Pharisees?

In Chapter Four, George delves into church history, and says there were six major centers of Christianity in the early church.

The first two are Alexandria and Caesarea, which "favored the doctrine of ultimate restoration" (p. 39), and he cites three writers from the former and none from the latter. The second two are Antioch and Eastern Syria, which "favored ultimate restoration on the principles of Theodore of Mopsuestia" (ibid.). Theodore is from Antioch, and as well, George cites another writer from Antioch. But he cites none from Eastern Syria.

The fifth school, of Asia Minor, "following Irenaeus – held to the annihilation of the wicked" (ibid). But he does note quote him. And the sixth school, Northern Africa, following Tertullian, believed in "future endless punishment" (ibid.).

Concerning the Alexandrian school, George begins by noting: "For either the Lord does not care for all men; and this is the case either because He is unable (which is not to be thought, for it would be a proof of weakness), or because He is unwilling, which is not the attitude of a good being ... Or does He care for all ...?" (p. 42).

34. Is the dichotomy of inability versus unwillingness sufficient?

35. Likewise, in terms of the latter, for the dichotomy of not caring versus caring?

36. What therefore is the definition of good and evil?

37. What is the definition of "ability?"

38. What about the possibility that God cares for all equally, but willingly in a way that does not impose his will and thus dehumanize us?

Then, George cites Origen, who "was convinced that the absolute goodness of God, coupled with the persuasive power of his love, would ultimately result in all rational creatures submitting voluntarily to Him through persuasion, not constraint" (p. 44).

39. What is the definition of "absolute," how would a Hebrew person approach the concept, and how would a Greek person do so?

40. What, in the persuasion of God's love, after the grave, changes from beforehand?

41. How many people are "rational creatures" when suffering?

42. Does Origen need God to make people sufficiently rational before he can save them?

43. If Origen posits the untenable concern of God being "unable" to save everyone, why is he "unable" before the grave?

44. Why does God not employ such persuasive love so powerfully in the here and now, that the possibility of hell is cut short from the outset, and thus, we do not have to be dragged into such a debate about it?

45. If all will be "persuaded," with no other ultimate option, is freedom vitiated in the end?

Now, George argues that the purpose of temporal punishment is to purify the soul, but these questions still remain. He then notes how the Emperor Justinian, in the sixth century, shuts down Origen's "ultimate restoration" universalism.

The third Alexandrian father George references is Gregory of Nyssa, in the late fourth century: "Gregory believed that those who had expressed their faith in this life and had humbled themselves before God through baptism did not need any further purification. However, those who would not repent needed to be purified in the succeeding ages by fire" (p. 51).

This seems to address the question about what changes after the grave, but still:

46. Why does "purification" need to take so long?

47. Is there a lack on God's part, namely, that he is unable to do all the purifying in this age?

48. Is there a lack on God's part, namely, that the power of the fire is insufficient to consume sin faster, whether in this age or past the grace?

49. Or is there a lack on man's part, namely, that it takes a long time of suffering past the grave to "induce" willingness?

- Now crucially here, there is a biblical text George never addresses, and its applicability to the who debate has great interpretive leverage. Namely, in Hebrews 9:27-28a, Barnabas says: "For as man is certain to die once, and after this, to face judgment; accordingly, Christ was sacrificed once for all, to take away the sins of many." In the comparison between man facing judgment once, and Christ paying its penalty once, the language is clear. There is no room for intermediate judgments, nor for George's idea that there is more than one judgment, all in a theoretical process that eventually manipulates all into heaven.

50. How does George interpret this central and otherwise unaddressed and text?

51. If hell is an imaginable suffering, how can anyone withstand even a few moments?

52. Is this persuasion, or does this make George's God the cosmic wife-beater where hatred sells itself as love?

Another important issue is broached here. Prior to Constantine becoming emperor in the early fourth century, baptism was overwhelming a "believer baptism," an active embrace of the faith. But as Constantine begins to employ the power of the state to enforce doctrinal orthodoxy, he starts a trajectory that leads to Emperor Theodosius (a contemporary of Gregory), and to Emperor Justinian, born a century later. This brings about the passivity of infant baptism as the de facto necessity for the church, since citizenship records come to depend on it.

53. As George thus cites Gregory of Nyssa, how does the baptism question affect the doctrine of an ultimate universalism?

54. Namely, for Gregory, is purification dependent on passive or active faith?

55. And, is George embracing the formal doctrine of a post-death purgatory?

George now cites a key concern, as Gregory mentions *"the introducer of evil* – the devil" (p. 52).

56. Thus, do the devil and his demons qualify for "ultimate restoration?"

57. What about God's sovereign power in creating Lucifer (before he became Satan) to begin with?

58. What responsibility does God therefore have for evil?

59. And if he has any, is he in some sense obligated to an "ultimate reconciliation" according to Gregory of Nyssa, et al.?

Concerning Antioch, George first cites Diodorus of Tarsus, where "punishments" are not "perpetual" (p. 53). Then his student, Theodore of Mopsuestia is cited. George says of him, with sustaining citation: "Being great, God was not taken by surprise at the entrance of sin into His creation. Being good, He incorporated it into His plan in order to ultimately benefit mankind" (p. 54). The issues of God's sovereignty and human freedom percolate everywhere, but:

60. Why does George not address this question fully, and in its tensions and depths?

So, these five writers, from the schools of Alexandria and Antioch, equal George's quoted substance of the early church witness. And the greatest weight of authority George gives is to Origen, who, as we have noted, does not even examine the Greek *aionios* in his writings on the subject.

61. Is this all?

There are at least thirty-six ante-Nicene fathers whose writings survive, in part or greatly, not to mention dozens of other church writings from this era.

In Chapter Five, George looks at the Apostles and Nicene creeds. In the former, he notes that though it speaks about Christ descending into hell, of the resurrection of the body and life everlasting: "... not a word is written about the endless, conscious suffering of the wicked" (p. 66).

62. An argument from silence, as we see so often in this debate?

63. And how much is George fishing for a certain predetermined language, and in not finding it, dismisses it as a larger concern?

64. For example, as we have already noted, and will note again, when *aionios* is paired in Matthew 25:41 for describing the destiny of both the righteous and wicked, does not the reference to the one include the other?

65. Also, to what extent is the clause "endless, conscious" reflect a reactionary starting point in his whole review, thus clouding the prism of exegetical observations?

In terms of the latter creed, he notes the same absence. But too:

66. What is the ratio in early church debate concerning universalism compared with the Trinity?

The latter hugely eclipses the former, and the Nicene Creed has the matter of the Trinity at its heartbeat.

In Chapter Six, George addresses Augustine as the culprit in church history: "... but many more are left under punishment than are delivered from it, in order that it thus be shown what was due to all" (p. 78).

Now Augustine, following his conversion, was more libertine in these and certain similar matters, but only later comes to the point here quoted by George. And central to his turn, in my estimation, is his embrace of the Constantinian to Theodosian to Justinian arc of having state power ordained to "protect the church," the *raison d'etre* for Christendom. This takes us through the end of the sixth century, past the birth of Muhammad. Namely, not only does infant baptism determine when legal rights begin, but hell also becomes a demarcation – both for the purpose of judging who is in and who is out.

But as erroneous as Augustine may be, it is ultimately Scripture to which we who are professing believers have accountability. George continues:
"Which presented with the dilemma of whether God would save all but *couldn't* – which would place a limit on His power. Or that He *could* save all but *wouldn't* – which would place a limit on His love. Augustine chose the latter.

"He was convinced that God is sovereign and could save all. But in fact, He will only save some" (p. 78). This is a facile antithesis, through the church history to the present.

    67. Is there no vision for understanding God to be greater than to be placed in such a box?

Only the foundation of a self-interpreting biblical structure will suffice.

Rounding out this chapter, as George traces the debate, he assigns his own position to Clement of Ireland in the eighth century; John Scotus Erigena in the ninth; the Albigenses in the eleventh; Raynold, Abbot of St. Martin's in France, in the twelfth; Solomon, Bishop of Bassorah, in the thirteenth; the Lollards in Bohemia and Austria, in the fourteenth; a sect called *Men of Understanding*, in the early fifteenth; and one Giovanni Pico della Mirandola in Rome, in the late fifteenth. In this list, George gives two quotes, first of Raynold, "that all men will eventually be saved" (p. 81), and second of Mirandola, "mortal sin of finite duration not deserving of eternal but only of temporal punishment" (ibid).

    68. How selective are these references, and how representative – a total of eight men over some 700 years of church history – and in view of the totality of other minority opinions and sects?

    69. Or, if they are a remnant of the wise, what in their lives commends them accordingly?

This list, and the quotes, are compiled from an 1884 publication, *Universalism in America*, and George does not dig deeper into the material to give us a sense of context. For example, the Albigenses in France were anti-sacerdotalists (opposed to the Roman Church), and most of what is known about them is through their opponents, and their surviving texts are rare and few. As well, Raynold's writing on predestination was steeped in Gnosticism, and in his dispute with Augustine on the matter of double-predestination, he seems to appeal to a neo-Platonic idea that evil does not exist.

70. Why not the primary sources, and thus, why not the texture of these debates?

In Chapter Seven, George begins by noting his internet search for a book "that had first given me hope for ultimate restoration" (p. 83).

71. If we look for a presupposition, can we not always find it, regardless of the source?

The book is by Edward Beecher in 1878, *History of Opinions on the Scriptural Doctrine of Retribution*.

George says: "I discovered that the internet offered access to information that previously could only be found in a theological library. As I sat in front of my computer, I realized there were search engines to put me in contact with many websites. The internet provided a treasure trove of documents, books and articles from around the whole world that I could never have accessed before!

"I felt like the proverbial kid in a candy store. I felt like I was about to embark on an exciting journey" (p. 84).

Now, in my own experience in research, I know the value of the more recent arrival of the internet. But too, in a library with the real books, periodicals, articles and such, and their shelving order and categories, there is a learning culture to consult, and also the irreplaceable value of leafing through a book that I might chance upon. Thus, the internet with its academic research engines provided through a given university or

117

collaborative of many schools, serves me best in directing me back to a real library, which for me, is usually Gordon-Conwell, Harvard, Hartford Seminary, or Oxford University when I am in England.

And when the internet becomes the major resource, the question of methodology comes into play. Just how do we do our research? George's book would face so very many and devastating critiques if reviewed by a colloquy of scholars who are familiar with his subject matter.

Now, my book here is not academic research in the formal sense. That would be far too large a project for my priorities. I am not footnoting what speaks for itself, but sourcing in context what is needful. And I have no esoteric knowledge to find or prove. This book is a modest reply to a request, where my purpose is to review these five writers for a wider audience. However, what I always write is subject to the most exacting critique of the appropriate scholars, to see if I am honest and competent within the limits I set for myself, in what I cite, and how I cite it. And when I arrive at my own proactive theological structure, it is the result of decades of scholarship and application, and continues to be. And specifically here, it serves the background for the questions I raise.

72. To what degree does George open himself up to scholarly ire when he writes the book as a research project, and yet it does not come close to the requisite criteria?

Thus, in this chapter, George sails through a summation of fellow universalist travelers as he sees it – William Law, Andrew Jukes, George MacDonald, F.W. Farrar, Charles Chauncy, Thomas Fessenden, Benjamin Rush, Elhanan Winchester, Edward Beecher and J.W. Hanson. Some noted persons, some less known. Then he touches on Eastern Orthodoxy, Roman Catholicism and Protestantism.

73. How representative are all these writers in the life of the church, and do they add anything new to the debate?

In Chapter Eight, now halfway through the book, George finally arrives at a review of the Bible.

74. As an evangelical Protestant, why does George not start with the Bible?

75. Does George affirm the Wesleyan quadrilateral of Scripture, tradition, reason and experience?

His purposes here are to review the nature of *sheol* in the Hebrew Bible and *hades* in the New Testament. And this is material we have already reviewed.

"*Sheol* is used 65 times in the Old Testament. The King James Version translates it to the word *hell* 31 times, *grave* 31 times and *pit* 3 times.

"*Sheol* is actually a general term meaning the realm of the dead. It's used in the Bible to refer to both the righteous and the wicked. The only distinction between the two is that the righteous will not be abandoned to it" (p. 106).

George gives a plethora of examples. *Hades* is used likewise in the New Testament, and gives up its dead to the final judgment in Revelation 20. He then looks at its use in the parable of the rich man and Lazarus, where it is not referencing hell or final judgment.

But Proverbs 27:20 reads: "*Sheol* and *Abaddon* are not sated." We will touch on *Abaddon* as a word for "destruction" or "the destroyer" (Satan).

76. If the grave and destruction have an unending hunger, what becomes of the idea of their supposed limited nature of existence?

In Chapter Nine, George address *gehenna* and *tartarus* in the New Testament. The latter is located in 2 Peter 2:4, and it is rooted in Greek mythology as the deepest abyss of Hades.

In terms of *gehenna*, George adds to the discussion:

"*Gehenna* is derived from the Hebrew words referring to a valley, the Valley of Hinnom. That valley is mentioned a total of 13 times in the Old

Testament, always as a literal valley located outside the ancient city of Jerusalem.

"The first time it takes on a negative meaning is when we're told that it was the place where two Old Testament kings burned their children alive as part of their idolatrous worship rituals" (p. 117).

77. Why does George not mention its very specific usage in Jeremiah 7 and 19 – which proves to be the exact basis for how Jesus employs the term – and the judgment of Yahweh upon it?

78. And too, given how it is a turning point that leads to the Babylonian captivity and exile, and thus the seared image it has in the first century Jewish imagination, why not explore this so as to get a sense of what *gehenna* means to the hearers of Jesus?

Instead, George updates its meaning in terms of the image of Auschwitz, and this is dynamically and hellishly true. He concludes this section:

"*Gehenna* was definitely a reference to God's judgment. But it was a judgment on earth. It was considered a temporary place of punishment. It never meant endless punishment beyond the grave" (p. 119).

Now, the Law of Moses – for which Jerusalem is being judged in 586 B.C. for her failure to obey – is a "tutor" or "guardian" of the faith until the coming of Jesus (Galatians 3:24-25). And Jesus fulfills the Law of Moses (Matthew 5:17).

79. Thus, how suitable is it to judge the fulfillment of the Law by the prior Law itself?

80. In other words, as with all antetypes to Christ in the Hebrew Bible, how can the partial judge the complete, how can a shadow judge the reality (Hebrews 8:5)?

81. Which is to ask, how can the temporal judge the eternal, how can Jeremiah's use of the term be used to judge how Jesus uses it?

82. Thus, how can George reduce its usage only to the temporal?

83. Does not Jesus define the fulfillment of the temporal judgment of *ge'hinnom* with the final judgment of *gehenna*?

Now George again returns to Origen, who says *gehenna* refers to a purification, not a final judgment (p.120). Then finally he gets to the texts themselves.

One key use of *gehenna* by Jesus is in Mark 9:43-48, where he uses it three times relative to those who cause little children to sin. As *ge'hinnom* is the place of child sacrifice, Jesus is warning those who would do so will meet the same fire their forefathers gave to such children. This text concludes as George quotes it: their "worm does not die and the fire is not quenched" (p. 123). And this ratchets up the fate of those in Jesus's day.

84. This is a quote by Jesus of the last verse in the prophet Isaiah (66:24), so why does George not tell us this and look at how it is first used in Isaiah?

This verse says in full: "And they will go out and see the corpses of the men who rebelled against me, and their worms do not die and their fire is not quenched, and they become an abhorrence to all flesh." The imperfect tense used here for death can be related to the interpretive grammar we will see in Genesis 2:17, robustly rendered, "a dying that keeps on dying."

85. As Isaiah says they will "go out and see," does George know that this is a picture of the people leaving the walled city of Jerusalem to literally look upon *ge'hinnom*, and that this is the point of reference for Jesus in quoting *gehenna* in Mark 9?

George here goes in for special pleading:

"Doesn't *unquenchable* fire refer to fire that continues on forever, and never goes out?

"No.

"The real meaning of unquenchable fire is not that it keeps burning forever. The real meaning is that the fire doesn't go out until it does what its intended to do. It is not put out or quenched until is purpose is accomplished" (pp. 123-124).

86. Where is this "real meaning" found?

87. Is it in Isaiah, which George does not quote?

88. Why does George neither define nor explain the language about the worm not dying, and the fire not being quenched?

89. Where, in George's review, do we have the biblical language that unquenchable fire is ultimately quenched?

90. Does Jesus add in the idea of "until it does what it is intended to do?"

91. Or is this an example of eisegesis?

92. Why is George spending so much time in a reactive posture explaining away clear meanings of a given text, meanings that have exegetical and historical review at a prior depth that George does not explore?

What George does is to say how centuries later Eusebius uses it for the "inextinguishable fire" of martyrs being burned to death, and says the fire is done within an hour. Now, Eusebius is writing a church history that serves the coming of Constantine as a "Christian emperor," often in service to his romanticized purposes.

93. Is Eusebius perhaps referring to the fire of hell in the theological sense as it is used to burn the martyrs?

Then George cites Josephus relative to the *unquenchable and always burning* fire in the temple, although it had already been quenched when the Romans destroyed the temple in A.D. 66. But this fire was purposed to be unquenchable in Jewish stewardship until the coming of the Messiah, and

Jesus fulfills it in the baptism with the Holy Spirit and fire for his disciples on outward (e.g., Matthew 3:11-12).

94. Why here does George ignore a) the actual use of the language, b) its precedence in Isaiah, and c) resort to arguments after the fact?

George reviews the other uses of *gehenna* in the same presuppositional light.

In Chapter Ten, he addresses the concept of "forever" in examining *aion*, *olam* and *kolasis* – and in stated reaction to the idea of endless punishment.

He opens by saying: "*Olam* and *aion* are relative terms – words where the meaning is determined by the things they relate to" (p. 133). He cites a German scholar from the 1884 *Universalist Quarterly*.

95. Instead of source shopping from an old Universalist argument, why not look directly at the Hebrew and Greek through the best present grammars and lexicons, those that have resources which far exceed what was available in 1884?

As an example, the scholarly work in Hebrew, especially, has made enormous strides in this period. First, we can note the rediscovery of parallelism as the nature of Hebrew poetic structure, accounting for over thirty-five percent of the Hebrew Bible. And second, we can observe how the 900 root words in Hebrew compare with thousands in classical and *koine* Greek. Out of this reality we see a general rule in Hebrew where the context modifies the word, but in Greek the word modifies the context.

In Hebrew, for example, *yadha*, the verb "to know" is used some 830 times. In about 800 occurrences, it refers to cognitive knowledge in a range of contexts. But in thirty instances, the context of the exact same word refers to sexual knowledge, for example, in Genesis 4:1: "And Adam knew his wife Eve, and she conceived ..." But, as we have already reviewed, the many Greek words for love each define their own context. Including *eros* versus, e.g., *philos* and *agape* in classical Greek.

From this point, George looks at English translations that use the word "forever." But he does no work with the Hebrew term *olam* itself.

96. With *olam* in the chapter title, why not give us its etymology?

97. How can this glancing secondary reference suffice for a whisper of scholarship, especially given the centrality of the term in question?

We have reviewed *olam* already, but it is good here to return to it. *Olam*, as the main word in the Hebrew for "forever," is not a word of strictly linear quality – a human grasp of time without end, as it were. It aims for that which is greater than space, time and number. In its 300 or so uses in the Hebrew Bible, it touches on the remote past as well as the distant future, and with certain prepositional uses in the Hebrew Bible, it means unlimited, incalculable, continuance, eternity.

It is likely rooted in the word *alam*, which means something "hidden" from human comprehension. In the prior Ugaritic, of which Hebrew is a cognate, the word *lm* means "eternity." In Ecclesiastes 3:11, Solomon states: "He has also set eternity (*olam*) in the hearts of men; yet they cannot fathom what God has done from beginning to end." The last three words here would be literally "upon the days."

98. Can we take what is "hidden" from human comprehension and comprehend it?

99. How central is this reality in the difficulty of trying to grasp hell experientially?

100. Is an ethical approach wiser?

Also, in Isaiah 44:6, Yahweh compares himself with finite idols, saying: "I am the first and the last, and apart from me there is no God." The use of "first and last" is a classic Hebrew merism describing all there is to know between polar opposites.

101. Now, we are finite, so how does Yahweh connote his eternity to us?

Yahweh Elohim is greater than space, time and number, as his name indicates in the Hebrew etymology; thus, he is intrinsically before the first and after the last. Adam and Eve are to live forever, not to die. And the language of *olam*, along with other Hebrew constructions, aims beyond the limits of human understanding to relate to Yahweh Elohim. This bears the need for in-depth review.

Now George does face a conundrum here, and this is how he puts it.

"What about God? Doesn't he exist outside of time? Isn't he the *eternal God*? Doesn't he exist from *everlasting to everlasting*?

"Absolutely.

"God is truly eternal. He did not have a beginning. Nor will He have an end. However, when speaking of God, the term translated *forever* or *everlasting* takes it meaning from him. The praises in the Psalms tell of His greatness not because the word used necessarily meant eternal or never-ending, but because he is the eternal, never-ending God" (p. 136).

    102. Does God exist "outside of time" as though it were a foreign domain to him?

    103. Or is Yahweh Elohim greater than the good time he has created, and into which he incarnates himself?

On the one hand, George is saying that the word means one thing when it refers to God (forever) but on the other, it means something different when the reference is to any other subject (limited duration).

    104. Is Hebrew lexigraphy, grammar and syntax consistent or not?

    105. Is not George simply making a statement of faith apart from any concern for consistent Hebrew usage?

George then says: "In the New Testament, the word *aion* always carries with it the notion of time, and not eternity" … We often use age in a way similar to how the New Testament uses *aion*" (p. 136). But, as we have already noted here, "always" is not always.

125

In crafting his major example relative to endless punishment, George addresses a crucial issue: "In my experience, the passage most pointed to as the clearest example in the entire Bible that punishment in hell is endless, is Matthew 25:46. In that verse, Jesus Himself says that the wicked 'will go away to eternal (aion) punishment, but the righteous to eternal (aion) life.'

"Remember that *aion*, the Greek word Jesus used here, is the same word we've been talking about. And it's used to refer to both the punishment of the wicked and the life of the righteous" (p. 138).

106. As an important aside to George's argument, is *aion* the specific word in use here?

- This is a huge error on George's part, and seems to belie the use of an interlinear translation, not the Greek text. The noun in use in Matthew 25:26 is not *aion*, but a cognate noun, *aionion*. In *Liddell and Scott*, and in *Bauer*, we note that *aion* sometimes refers to a limited time frame, other times without duration. But always *aionion* (or *aionios*) means "without beginning and end." Never in classical or New Testament Greek does it refer to a limited time frame. And, indeed, the verbal form is *aionizo*, and its only meaning is "to be eternal." In fact, in the thirty major English translations of the noun in Matthew 25, it is only translated as "eternal," "forever" or "everlasting."

107. Does George do his work simply by looking in an interlinear, finding the place where one related noun refers to a limited time frame, and then adopt it for his own preselected purposes, ignoring the actual noun in use?

Back to the line of George's argument, this is also a conundrum. For, in the grammar of this text, if punishment is not everlasting, then life cannot also be everlasting. But in an act of tendentious jujitsu, George now finds a scapegoat in Augustine (nearly four centuries later), whom he claims "didn't read Greek" (ibid.), and who argues in this text that punishment is everlasting.

126

108. Does the biblical text judge Augustine (and all of us), or does Augustine judge the biblical text?

109. How well does George read and translate Greek?

110. And why jump to Augustine instead of first dealing with the very text Augustine is addressing?

111. And where, specifically, is Augustine deficient in the segue from the Greek text to the Latin Vulgate?

Next, George says: "We often use relative terms more than once in the same sentence with a different meaning each time" (p. 139), and then cites an analogy by an NBA basketball player.

112. If, thus, *aionios/aionion* is a relative term, what is the ground for the bedrock certainty of life everlasting?

113. How, in the Greek text at hand, can the real word in use, *aionion*, mean something different back to back?

114. What are the rules of grammar that make this possible, including the use of *merismus*, as well as parallelisms of the opposite, since Jesus spoke in Aramaic, a cognate of Hebrew?

115. And too, whereas *aion* can refer to a limited duration of time, allowing George to insert his preference, and then he uses ex post facto sources and unrelated analogies accordingly, what about the actual word used in the text, *aionion*?

George now steps into it again with an eisegetical prism:

"So what kind of punishment is Jesus actually referring to in this passage if it's not endless?

"The Greek word for *punishment* in Matthew 25:46 is *kolasis*. It was originally used to mean pruning trees to make them grow better. In fact, in all Greek literature outside the Bible, it's never used for anything but remedial punishment" (p. 141).

This is simply untrue.

116. What is George's source for this utterly comprehensive claim? In turns out to be William Barclay's 1977 *A Spiritual Autobiography*.

117. Seriously? Does this pass muster for such an academic conclusion?

118. Why not cite exactly Barclay's argument and sources?

Barclay 1) believes the New Testament makes no claim that Jesus is God incarnate, 2) believes in the macroevolution of man from lower animals, with Jesus being the highest form of evolved man, and 3) believes in universal salvation.

119. Does George also believe that Jesus is not *Yahweh Elohim* in the flesh, and too, in Darwinian macroevolution?

120. If not, why use Barclay as his only source here?

121. Is it because George cherry picks universalist sources?

In *Liddell and Scott*, there is one single reference from Plato's student, philosopher and botanist, Theophrastus. Here, in the classical Greek, he uses the noun *kolasis* for "checking the growth of trees," especially almond-trees. Then, in all other references, *Liddell and Scott* speaks of *kolasis* as "chastisement," "correction," "punishment" or "divine retribution."

Then, the verbal form is also referenced, *kolasteira*. It first means "to be chastised," "to be punished," and then, with the tertiary possibility of "one must prune." Grammatically, a noun identifies what a verb accomplishes in action.

122. Is not George's first responsibility to exegete the use of the word in question?

123. Why does he not explain here why he takes a tertiary meaning of the word – which is only used once in classical Greek – and make it not only primary, but singular?

124. Why does George ignore the prior and major translation history of *kolasis*?

125. Thus, how does George take one botanical reference – which has nothing to do with judgment on sin – in classical Greek literature, extrapolate through the wider Platonic context, and somehow modify the *koine* or New Testament Greek context on the whole language of judgment?

Then, *Bauer's Lexicon* notes that in Hippocrates, Diodorus Siculus, Aclian, Maccabees, Philo, Josephus and Oracula Sibyllina, that *kolasis* simply means "punishment." There is no reference to this idea of "remedial pruning" anywhere in *Bauer*'s review. George only gives us the interpretive lens of one man, Barclay, who is a de facto Unitarian, Universalist and macro-evolutionist, and thus outside historical Christianity.

126. Is not George's work here but an example of classical eisegesis, where the meaning of the actual biblical text is changed to fit his presuppositions?

127. Is not George merely scholar-shopping in order to buttress his presuppositions?

128. How can we not observe at this point that George's whole book is only a case of special pleading, lacking in the critical points being sustainable?

In Chapter Eleven, George looks at the question of judgment based on his presuppositions, and it is brief and selective. It does not scratch the surface of the rich biblical territory, whether, for example, its origins, Noah's flood,

Sodom and Gomorrah, the Canaanites, the Babylonian exile, Matthew 23, Romans 1 or the trajectory in the Book of Revelation.

In Chapter Twelve, George looks at arguments, "honest questions" that thus challenge his position. He touches on the blasphemy against the Holy Spirit (which assigns the work of the devil to the Holy Spirit), forfeiture of the soul, the narrow door, Jacob and Esau, the hardening of Pharaoh's heart, anathema, the impossibility of repentance (which we have reviewed), the lake of fire and the book of life, Judas, and "what about missions?"

These are all dynamic texts or concerns, but he works with his same presuppositions for each. Of interest is Revelation 20:10 when the devil, the beast and the false prophet are cast into the "lake of fire and brimstone" and "tormented day and night, from *aion* to *aion*." Now here, George's use of *aion* is in place, but too, both *Liddell and Scott*, and *Bauer*, cite its use as either limited or not limited in scope. It depends on the prepositional usage, and here it combines with the definite article: *eis tous*, "into the." Namely, being deposited into "the" (chosen) destiny. From the chosen destiny, again and again, with no designation of limit. Unending finality.

129. Since this text applies to the devil and his sycophants, why has George curiously left this question unattended?

130. Will Satan also gain "ultimate restoration?"

With the language of burning sulfur, or brimstone, George again says it is purifying in nature, but not with biblical reference.

131. But what about the fire and brimstone of Sodom and Gomorrah, the archetypical biblical source for this language?

Their culture was completely sold out to chosen evil, and as a result, their destruction was complete, never to be resuscitated.

132. Why does George not reference and define Sodom and Gomorrah, here or elsewhere?

133. Is not destruction without rebirth for Sodom the ethical forerunner to an eschatological damnation rooted in settled choices?

Also, at the conclusion of Revelation 20, the text speaks of "death and *hades* being cast into the lake of fire," as well as calling it the "second death." In George's chronology, he only speaks of physical death, then a period of subsequent time in which all people in hell eventually choose God's love and gain escape.

134. Why has George not addressed the chronology of the judgment on death and *hades*, i.e., as places of death before the resurrection?

135. Or do death and *hades* eventually gain heaven?

136. Why has George not addressed the "second death" and its image of finality?

In sum, George 1) is rooted in a reactive experiential posture, a visceral repulsion against bad theology that includes a doctrine that believes God sends people to hell arbitrarily; 2) is selective in his use of Scripture; 3) whereas he keeps the primacy of Scripture in view, he also allows secondary sources to strategically take precedence; 4) is selective in addressing the question of God's judgment; 5) does not give a biblical interpretive structure; and 6) hardly attempts an address of the underlying question of biblical freedom.

And in sum for all five writers, key issues that need address include: 1) the stated dichotomy between God's love and power; 2) the relationship between God's desire and will; 3) the relationship between God's justice and mercy; 4) the nature of good and evil; 5) the nature of freedom and slavery, including the question of predestination; and 6) the nature of life and death.

◆ ◆ ◆

Chapter Six

Biblical Theology 101 and the Freedom to Choose Hell

With the contours of the present debate reviewed, concerns affirmed, questions posed and critiques made, my purpose here is to step back and seek to gain perspective. Thus, I will review what I call Biblical Theology 101, my best grasp on how the Bible understands and interprets itself on its own terms. And from within this structure, whenever issues in the current debate find a natural home to address, I will do so.

The structure for all biblical theology, its storyline and teachings (doctrines), is rooted and interpreted by an understanding of creation, sin and redemption as introduced in Genesis 1-3. This assumption and reality has never ceased to percolate across all church history.

1. Would any of our five writers disagree?

Simply:

Creation → sin → redemption.

The word "fall" can be inserted in place of "sin," as it describes what the first sin does to man and woman – we fell from God's original place, and need to be lifted back. But too, the word "sin" describes both the original fall and its consequences, so I use it as the primary term. "Sin" is a word that is easily misunderstood. It essentially means brokenness of trust, and we all know that from one or many angles.

2. Is not the starting point of each writer a reaction to tangible broken trust?

3. Thus, are they not handicapped in not starting with creation?

4. What would change for each if they were to start with creation?

There are two ways we can describe these doctrines. The first is directional in nature:

The order of creation → the reversal → the reversal of the reversal.

The second is organic in nature:

The wholeness of creation → the brokenness of trust → the restoration to wholeness.

The order of creation is the root of all truth and reality in time and space:

From the beginning, God establishes the order of creation, and our lives, according to a set plan that is intended for our greatest joy as his image-bearers. But through a disobedient act of the will, Adam and Eve and the whole human race have submitted to a reversal of that order, and we reap the painful consequences. Sin can thus be understood as a reversal, as brokenness. It is a reversal in that it goes in the wrong direction. It is brokenness in that it breaks relationship with God, with one another and the wholeness of his creation, i.e., broken trust. Following the inception of human sin, God institutes the reversal of the reversal, the redemptive process designed to purchase us back from the slavery of sin, and to restore to us the original purposes, trajectory and wholeness of the order of creation.

The word "redemption" means to buy back out of slavery (e.g., the whole purpose of the exodus from Egypt, cf. Exodus 20:2). Slavery, by definition, is the loss of an original freedom. Thus, we can also define the doctrines of creation, sin and redemption a third way:

Freedom → slavery → return to freedom.

• Freedom is our defining thesis.

A Biblical Theology 101 begins with the biblical order of creation, what I call "Only Genesis," and there are eleven positive assumptions:

Only Genesis has a positive view of 1) God's nature (the power to give); 2) the heavenly court; 3) communication (the power to live in the light); 4) human nature; 5) human freedom (the power of informed choice); 6) hard questions (the power to love hard questions); 7) human sexuality; 8) science and the scientific method; 9) verifiable history; 10) covenantal law; and 11) unalienable rights.

These eleven positive assumptions reflect the integrity of the biblical content introduced in the order of creation of Genesis 1-2, and define virtually every subject in the universe. They also equal the basis for a fully genuine and rigorous liberal arts education.

Then there are six pillars of biblical power distilled from the eleven positive assumptions. Both these assumptions and the six pillars of biblical power are unique, and in their essence and wholeness, they are not found in any pagan origin text or secular construct. These assumptions and pillars are at the core of all that is good in human civilization.

These pillars are ethical in nature, which we have defined briefly already. "Ethics" comes from the Greek terms *ethos* and *ethikos*, for "social customs or habits," for how we treat people. And depending on context, "ethics" can be used either as a singular or plural term. "Ethics" as a term, apart from context, and is by definition neutral – there are good ethics and there are evil ethics.

The six pillars equal the basis for the most Spirit-filled doctrine possible, doctrine that leads to transformed lives and a transformable world. In fact, these pillars, as believed and lived, lead to the highest standards and accountability to the work of the Holy Spirit in our lives, and in the presence of skeptics.

The first four pillars are distilled from the eleven positive assumptions, and are placed in parentheses in the listing of the eleven assumptions above. The last two pillars are drawn from the order of redemption (specifically rooted in the Sermon on the Mount), which is to say, as a remedy for the broken trust of sin that assaults the goodness of the first four pillars.

Thus, the six pillars literally sum up the whole Bible ethically. Jesus repeatedly says that the whole Law is summed up in loving God with all our heart, soul, mind and strength, and thus, in loving our neighbors as ourselves. And as the rabbis say across the millennia, all else is commentary. The six pillars are my commentary, distilled through my studies and experiences of sharing the Gospel in the face of a skeptical age.

These six are the powers to give, to live in the light, of informed choice, to love hard questions, to love enemies and to forgive.

5. Are any of these assumptions and ethics not intrinsically biblical and attractive to our five writers, and do not their demonstrable reality serve well as a proactive against the reactive doctrines that view God and hell as arbitrary?

Here, we will review these eleven positive assumptions for an overall biblical literacy 101, and hone in where applicable to the debate at hand.

The first assumption **is** Gods' nature.

Bereshith bara elohim eth ha'shamayim w'eth ha'eretz are the first words in Genesis – 1) in the beginning; 2) the unique verb for God's creating power; 3) God; and 4) his creation, the heavens and the earth. In Hebrew, the verb precedes the noun, thus we translate it: "In the beginning God created the heavens and the earth." The object is *Elohim*, God, and hence God is the first assumption in the Bible. The nature of God is that he creates, he is the Creator. And to create is the essence of goodness.

When pagan religious texts are read, no such assumption is in place. In fact, the gods and goddesses are finite and petty, and what is assumed is a preceding undefined yet hostile cosmos.

Next, we turn to the compound Name for God in Genesis 1-2

The Hebrew word for God in the first sentence in the Bible is *Elohim*. The English word "God" comes from the proto-Germanic *gott* which refers to the act of giving a blessing.

In Genesis 1, we have the grand design of creation, and in Genesis 2 we have the first covenant between the Creator and man. Genesis 2 actually takes place within the theological structure of Genesis 1, on the sixth day.

In Genesis 1:

Elohim as the Creator of all mankind is used as a title.

Across the Hebrew Bible:

The use of *Elohim* carries with it this assumption, namely, the one true Creator that all people recognize, including polytheistic Gentiles.

In Genesis 2:

The compound *Yahweh Elohim* is introduced, where *Yahweh* is the personal name of the covenant keeping Creator.

Across the Hebrew Bible:

The stand-alone personal name of *Yahweh* refers to his specific covenant-keeping identity, as the Hebrew people recognize, but not by the Gentiles as they migrate away from the assumptions of Genesis 1-2.

Across the Hebrew Bible:

With the great frequency of the compound name, *Yahweh Elohim*, in the minds of the Hebrew peoples, both factors combine – personal name and title.

This leads us to the question of space, time and number.

- Here we embrace the right foundation to define and interpret *olam*, *aionios* and other terms and questions that relate to the "duration" of hell.

Yahweh is the third person form of the verb for "I am," thus translated, "He is." That is, *Yahweh* is the I AM, which in the first person is *Ehyeh* (HE IS), the original Existence and Presence who is greater to and prior to, and thus defines, space and time.

Elohim is grammatically a unique term. It is a masculine plural (known also as the honorific plural in contrast to the singular *el*). But *Elohim* is overwhelmingly used with the singular case. This means the singular *Elohim* is greater than the concept of number. In the few cases when the singular case is not used, the reference is to the plurality of pagan gods.

Thus, the name *Yahweh Elohim* in totality means the One who is greater than space, time and number – a concept found nowhere else in history. And this is exactly what Yahweh reveals to Moses in Exodus 3:14-15 at the burning bush.

6. To what extent have our five writers started looking at the question of hell through a human prism of time, thus missing altogether the ✸ truly eternal perspective of Yahweh Elohim?

7. Where and how might this perspective change the whole debate?

8. Namely, are not *aion* and *aionios* human proximate terms to approach eternity?

9. And thus, when *aionios* always means "eternal," "forever" and "everlasting" in *Liddell and Scott*, as well as *Bauer*, and is the term used as such in the New Testament, is this not the best proximate language to approach the domain of Yahweh Elohim who is greater than space, time and number?

In sum, God's nature and person, as Yahweh Elohim who is greater than space, time and number, is rooted in unlimited power and goodness, and his purpose is to bless all people equally. His nature is the power to give – the first pillar. This is the starting assumption in Genesis 1-2, where all is declared good (*tov*).

This is also where the "Gospel" is rooted (the Greek term here is *euangelion* for "good news," from whence "evangelical" comes). Namely, Genesis 1-2 is good news, and Jesus in preaching the Good News restores us to its promises.

- This starting point addresses and rebukes the idea of God being arbitrary.

10. If we grasp the reality that Yahweh Elohim is greater than space, time and number, how best can the question of hell and its duration be biblically addressed?

The second assumption is the heavenly court.

In Genesis 1:1, as we have already noted, it reads: "In the beginning Elohim created the heavens and the earth." These are two domains, with the heavens being the domain of Yahweh Elohim, and the earth being the given stewardship for man and woman.

- Thus, before we arrive at the question of heaven and hell as possible destinies, we need to understand the huge use of "the heavens" (*shamayim* in the Hebrew and *ouranois* in the Greek) across the Bible, and the relentless assumption that the text is speaking of God's domain of government, the domain of given human government, and hence, the nature and domain of the Intruder.

Then, in Genesis 2:1, the text reads: "Thus the heavens and the earth were completed in all their armies." Genesis 1:1 and 2:1 thus equal a unit of thought. Many translations render the end of this sentence as "in their vast array" or "in all their hosts." Why, in a statement of the summary goodness of the created order do we have armies? It is a noun rooted in the Hebrew verb *tsaba* for making warfare.

The term "host" refers to armies, but it is so antiquated in usage for many, that it loses its accurate edge. In English Bible translations, we see at least 250 times where the words are translated as the "LORD Almighty." In Hebrew, it literally means "*Yahweh* of armies," and the soldiers in Yahweh's armies are the holy angels.

The heavenly court is a positive assumption, that which includes the idea of a guarding army, even before the rebellion of the angel Lucifer, which is a subject too large for these pages. When Adam is made, his first charge is to "to work and guard (*shamar*)" the garden from the Intruder (genesis 2:15).

Thus, and perhaps more properly, this positive assumption of the armies of Yahweh is part of the domain of the heavens in Genesis 1:1, being a principal reference to his heavenly court, or assembly.

- This is also the original locale of Yahweh Elohim's freedom, a freedom given first to the heavenly host, and especially then to man and woman as his image-bearers to govern the domain of the earth, and to whom the heavenly armies are to be Adam and Eve's servants. And given the rebellion of a high-ranking cherub in the heavenly court, Lucifer, who thus transmogrifies into Satan or the devil, Adam and Eve are called to guard the Garden from the devil's intrusion.

- Ultimately, hell is the anti-domain of forfeited freedom.

The use of *shamar*, to guard, is strategically found across the Hebrew Bible, usually in this context, in both Genesis 3 and 4, later in Genesis 17, Exodus 20 and 23, Leviticus 25, Deuteronomy 11, Judges 6, Joshua 23, early in the book of Job, Psalms 91 and 121, the end of David's life, the end of Ecclesiastes, Malachi 2 and elsewhere.

The original freedom Yahweh Elohim gives to man is the language of informed choice, predicated on an honest definition of terms. And this is exactly how the Bible views itself – true in all it describes and affirms. The devil hates informed choice at the deepest level of his perverted soul, for he tries to destroy it in his narcissism and solipsism (his origins is a larger question, addressed elsewhere), and in the end it destroys him. Which is to say, the original positive freedom in the order of creation given to the angels is the underlying reality, and in the end slavery cannot conquer freedom.

Also, the names for *Satan* in the Hebrew (*ha'satan*), and in the Greek (*tou diabolos*), the devil, mean the same – "the *satan*" (but usually used as a proper name) and "the devil," both which mean "the accuser," "the slanderer." And in Revelation 9:11, we read: "They had as their king the angel whose name is the Hebrew Abaddon and in the Greek he holds the name Apollyon." Both *abaddon* and *apollyon* mean the "destroyer," or "destruction," and here as a most likely reference to the quintessential fallen angel, Satan. In Psalm 88:11-12, the language of *abaddon* and the darkness (*hoshek*) are in parallel construct.

11. Do we thus grasp how the issue of freedom is up front in Scripture, and its violation in the chosen rebellion of Satan?

Genesis 1:2 reads: "Now the earth was formless and empty, darkness was over the surface of the abyss, and the Spirit of Elohim brooded over the waters." The Hebrew translated here as "formless and empty" is *tohu w'bohu*, a description of non-existence. And darkness over the "abyss" describes the same – non-existence.

12. Do we see at the outset how Scripture defines for us the question of existence and non-existence?

Namely, the Spirit of Elohim, the I AM of existence, is present in a discernible way before anything can be discerned in human existence.

The Hebrew word here for "abyss" is *t'hom*, also translated as the "deep" or the "seas." One reason is because of the use of "waters" (*mayim*) at the end of the verse, and thus the thought of a great physical ocean. But this is not contextually possible, since the text is addressing what is happening before Elohim speaks light (v. 3) into the abyss, before the earth with its oceans are formed. The *mayim* is modified by the *t'hom* – an unorganized designation. And "abyss" is the definition of something that has no definition, boundaries and gravity – that of a bottomless non-existence. In the Septuagint, the Greek root for this term is *abussos*, which transliterates into English as the "abyss." This is the very abyss the demons fear (Luke 8:31), and used eight times in Revelation as a place of judgment, full of fire, the smoke of a great furnace, and the reality of destruction. In the biblical language of judgment, the abyss and hell have great interface. They are used independently of each other, while describing the same ultimate reality all rooted in the original abyss.

13. Accordingly, what is the linkage between the abyss (*t'hom*) before the good creation, and the abyss (*abussos*) at the end of a broken creation?

14. Does the reversal of creation → sin → redemption = the abyss → creation in God's image → rejection of such humanity → the return to the abyss?

15. Within the bottomless non-existence of the abyss, named for the angel of destruction (*abaddon* in the Hebrew and *apollyon* in the Greek) in Revelation 9:11, what is the possibility, by definition, for the reconsideration of God's love?

16. In the biblical language of hell and the abyss, and their interface and/or sequence and/or overlap and/or co-extensivity, does hell offer anything less dehumanizing than the abyss, and thus, anything more of a place for reconsideration?

17. How does the question of existence thus relate?

18. Is the abyss the starting point in understanding judgment as a place where those who refuse to live in the light, then return of their own accord, as per John 3:16-21?

19. If so, is not hell a subsequent term that needs to be understood accordingly?

20. Also, do we see how precise Genesis is in using our limited human language to press beyond the limits of our abilities?

• Indeed, the truly mysterious sphere in Scripture – that which is beyond human comprehension – is whatever presses us into the domain that is greater than time, space and number, that presses us into the nature of Yahweh Elohim. Thus, we need to know how human language – through which Yahweh reveals himself – can only reflect a shadow of the eternal substance.

- The original abyss describes the opposite of the good creation, and those who in the end choose the final abyss are those who hate the good creation, and exile themselves accordingly.

21. To what degree is this whole debate vulnerable to the imposition of human categories – such as thinking in terms of linear time – upon the divine?

22. Namely, how vulnerable are we to playing with language such as *olam* and *aionios* for shortsighted purposes?

23. Rather, is not ethics, the relational, the wiser prism of understanding?

The third assumption is communication.

In two sequentially parallel texts, Genesis 1:1-5 and John 1:1-5, we see the immediate assumption of communication:

> In the beginning Elohim created the heavens and the earth. Now the earth was formless and empty, darkness was over the surface of the abyss, and the Spirit of Elohim brooded over the waters. And Elohim said, "Let there be light," and there was light. Elohim saw that the light was good, and Elohim separated the light from the darkness. Elohim called the light "day," and the darkness he called "night." And there was evening, and there was morning – the first day.

> In the beginning was the Word, and the Word was with God, and the Word was God. He was with God in the beginning. All things were made through him, without him nothing was made that has been made.

> In him was life, and that life was the light of men. And the light shines in the darkness, but the darkness cannot understand and overcome it.

The apostle John deliberately makes the opening words of his gospel parallel to and building upon the opening words of Genesis. The presence of the Father, Son and Holy Spirit infuse these two texts together. Jesus is the one true Creator in human form – and the epitome of communication in the face of a darkened world.

At the simplest threshold, the language of light defines the nature of honest communication. Light reveals what is truly there: "Let there be light." And prior to that is sound: "Elohim said." Sound is also essential to communication. And light is the language of revelation, of God's nature and purposes.

24. In the face of our present debate, how well do we each honor the ethics of honest communication, one where the light shines on and illuminates all issues and questions equally?

- Which means no selective proof texting.

To ponder, for a moment, the scientific theory of the Hot Big Bang – sound and light define it. Who or what put the mass there to being with, and who or what prepared the fuse and ignited it? Intellectually, logically, aesthetically and in the joy of sheer wonder, only the One who is greater than space, time and number. Sound and light are the most basic elements in the universe. "And Elohim *said*, let there be *light*." Think of the language of observation and discovery – it starts with light. Biblical theology is the queen of all the sciences.

The biblical theme of light versus darkness is a commanding one across all Scripture, and its interpretive leverage is already noted in the side-by-side of Genesis 1:1-5 and John 1:1-5. Light, full communication and honesty are co-extensive, on the one hand; and on the other hand, darkness, broken communication and deceit are likewise co-extensive.

There are three domains.

First is that of physics. Wherever light is present, by definition darkness cannot exist. Light has an atomic weight, and darkness has none, which means darkness does not exist. We are speaking of absolute darkness, just as with absolute cold (-459 Fahrenheit) where life cannot exist because no chemical reactions can occur. Darkness it is the absence of light. So when the light appears, darkness immediately dissipates.

This observational reality is assumed throughout the Bible. Not in terms of modern calculations, but that modern calculations are made possible because of biblical assumptions about the inanimate and observable nature of the physical universe.

- The language of hell includes the physics of darkness.

Second is that of ethics. Consider the averted gaze where Cain looks away from the face of Yahweh, in his anger for not being able to deceive him (Genesis 4:1-7). Whereas Abel's offering is from the best of his livestock, Cain's offering from his grains is not said to be of the best – rather, almost as a grudging afterthought.

And as well, we can look at a contrast between two responses to the coming of the kingdom of God. In Luke 21:25-28, the words of Jesus point past the destruction of the temple and Jerusalem in A.D. 66, to his Second Coming. He commends his disciples to stand up and lift their heads – alluding to the Jewish posture of prayer – eyes fixed heavenward with arms outstretched to God. Jesus refers to an eyeball-to-eyeball yearning for the soon coming King.

In Revelation 6:15-17, as we have already noted, in response to the opening of the sixth seal, the peoples of the earth call on the mountains and rocks to fall on them and "conceal us from the face of him who sits on the throne and from the wrath of the Lamb!"

These two snapshots reflect a constant theme in the Bible, where those who choose to live in the light see God as a Friend who rescues them from judgment; and those who choose to live in the darkness see God as an enemy, the one who puts on them a wrath they have chosen. The eyeball language is again in place – unrepentant persons fear the face of God, and would rather be crushed to dust under the weight of the mountains than to look at Jesus, seek and receive forgiveness.

25. Is this not the ethics of a settled choice for hell?

To believe in Jesus is to live in the light. Here the language of John 1:1-5 links with Genesis 1:1-5. Jesus is the Word (from the Greek *logos* for word, thought, expression, idea, communication), the very communication of Yahweh in our midst. He is also the light and the life. And when we consider the reality in physics that darkness and absolute zero have no existence, we see the contrast dramatically. Jesus calls himself "the light of the world" in John 8:12, and in the Sermon on the Mount he calls his disciples the same (Matthew 5:14-16), where we have nothing to hide. Jesus calls himself the "life" in John 14:6, and he comes to give us that life (John 10:10).

- And here we naturally arrive at a crucially important text already raised in the debate at hand.

In John 3:19-21, as Jesus addresses Nicodemus, he concludes:

This is the judgment: Light has come into the cosmos, but men loved darkness instead of light because their deeds were evil. Everyone who does what is bad hates the light, and will not come into the light for fear that his deeds will be revealed. But whoever does the truth embraces the light, so that it may be manifest that what he has done has been done through God.

John further addresses the ethics of living in the darkness versus the light in 1 John 1:5-10. Here there is no darkness in God, we lie if we walk in the darkness, but we can live in the light through the candor of confessing our sins.

- The language of hell includes the ethics of darkness.

The third domain, spiritual territory, leads us back to John 1:1-5, and the parallel to Genesis 1:1-5. It is also a cognate to the reality of the heavenly court.

Thus, just as Elohim's first words in Scripture are "Let there be light," and the light is separated from darkness, here we see that Jesus as the Word is the "light" – defining John's constant theme of light versus darkness. The physics and ethics are in place in this parallel between Genesis and John, and now we gain introduction to the spiritual war between light and darkness.

In John 1:5, as the light shines into the darkness, the Greek term at the very end is *katalambano*. It is the metaethics of learning, of grasping – it most fully means to reach up, seize hold, pull down, dethrone and trample – to conquer. Thus, another translation here is that the darkness has not "overcome" the light.

Or to flesh it out a little more, we cannot overcome what we do not understand. Darkness cannot know or comprehend the light, and light knows darkness will flee its presence by definition. Satan is "the prince of darkness," in the words of Martin Luther as he reflects on biblical reality, and in the face of Jesus who is the Light of the world, the devil can neither understand nor overcome Jesus. Satan is, literally, the "prince of nothing." The power to live in the light resonates here in the language of James: "Accordingly, submit to God, resist the devil, and he will flee from you. Come near to God and he will come near to you" (4:7-8).

26. If darkness can neither comprehend nor overcome the light, how then can those in a "temporary" hell ever have resource to later embrace a light that by definition is neither present nor comprehensible?

27. So, what is the speed of darkness?

It has none, for it has no existence, atomically, ethically or spiritually, but only eviscerates in the presence of Light. Just as slavery has no power in the face of freedom.

• The language of hell includes the anti-domain of spiritual darkness.

28. If darkness eviscerates in the presence of light, does not hell eviscerate likewise?

29. What does that evisceration look like?

30. If the abyss is outside creation – where there is only the void of darkness – before and after the intrusion of sin, is that not coextensive with the language of hell?

31. And does not separation from creation also mean separation from space, time and number?

32. Thus, is not the question of the "duration" of hell moot?

33. And does not the question of "duration" this miss the much deeper ethical issues?

The assumption of communication in Genesis 1 and John 1 can be summed up in the power to live in the light – the second pillar. Light reveals what is there, reality, and along with sound, makes communication possible. If we embrace light in all of its permutations, and eschew darkness, we are a free people.

The fourth assumption is human nature.

In Genesis 1, the created order begins with the most remote up to the most accessible, from the lowest forms of life up to the highest. As creation reaches its apex with man and woman, we have descriptive reality defined. In Genesis 2, we encounter the storyline of exactly how Yahweh Elohim does this creation work. Genesis 1:26-28 defines man and woman being made in Yahweh Elohim's image. There are six elements here for what this all entails: 1) reflecting Yahweh Elohim's infinite character in our finite capacities; 2) being given the commission to govern the good creation under him; 3) man and woman are made after Yahweh Elohim's own kind, not after any animal or other species; 4) man and woman are male and female, equals and complements; and 5) they are called to fill and bring the earth under their stewardship and control.

- Then, 6) and central to our present focus, is that which is prior to the question of salvation – the Hebrew *nephesh* for "soul" or "personhood."

In Jewish history, the soul relates to the "breath" in Genesis 2:7, and thus there are two basic views: 1) the soul begins at "quickening" or movement in the womb that can be related to in utero "breathing," or 2) when born and breathes in the air. For Plato, and his influence on the Alexandrian school in the early church (Origen), the soul is pre-existent and "transmigrates" into the body.

34. With the doctrine of "ultimate restoration" universalism so deeply dependent on Origen, how does his Platonic idea of the soul affect his understanding of heaven and hell?

35. Namely, if the "soul" existed outside the body before the conception and birth of a child, what is its "eternal nature," as it were, to begin with?

36. If the soul existed prior to and apart from the body, thus having a pre-history, does its human embodiment somehow and intrinsically pollute it, and open up the possibility of a temporary hell?

37. Or if the pre-existent soul is "pure" in a Platonic and thus dualistic sense of the "idea" or "ideal," versus the body as intrinsically corrupted (classic early Gnosticism that polluted the early church) – why does not its purity prevent the possibility of lapse into sin and the danger of hell?

But when does this "embodiment" happen for others? The Eastern Church (e.g., Jerome) believes that God creates a new soul at the birth of each individual ("creationism"). The Western Church (e.g., Turtullian) are Traducianists, believing that the soul is inherited from the parents. Again, the question of the time of ensoulment. The debate continues between these last two positions until the Reformation, then splits between Luther (Traducianist) and John Calvin ("creationist").

- I believe all these ideas are completely off the mark, and thus lead to much confusion, including Origen's view of heaven and hell.

Only an exegesis of the Hebrew in Genesis 2:7, where the term nephesh first and interpretively appears, can ground us in biblical and scientific reality. The text reads: "Yahweh Elohim formed the man from the dust of the ground and breathed into his nostrils the breath of life, and the man became a living soul."

The Hebrew for "the man" is *ha'adam*, from which Adam derives his name. He is made directly from the dust, or dry earth, but he is not merely material stuff. Yahweh Elohim sets him apart as he breathes his own Spirit into him, and thus he comes alive.

The words translated "living soul" are *nephesh hayyah* in the Hebrew, or "soul alive," where in the Hebrew the adjective follows the noun. *Nephesh* is the biblical term for human nature and personhood.

There are two principal sources that define the term – Edmund Jacob's article in the *Theological Dictionary of the New Testament* (TDNT), where he examines the Hebrew background for the Greek parallel term *psuche*; and Hans Walter Wolff in *The Anthropology of the Old Testament*. *Psuche* is our root for the "psyche," for psychological wholeness.

Jacob says, "*Nephesh* is the usual term for a man's total nature, for what he is and not just what he has. This gives the term priority in the anthropological vocabulary ... The classical text in Gn. 2:7 clearly expresses this when it calls man in his totality a *nephesh hayyah* ... The *nephesh* is almost always connected with a form. It has no existence apart from a body. Hence the best translation in many instances is "person" comprised in corporeal reality (IX:620, Hebrew transliterated). There are six elements to understanding the usage of *nephesh*.

In the first place concerning *nephesh*, Adam is created as a whole, mature male adult, and the same is true for Eve as a female adult, as Yahweh draws her out of Adam's mature body. The idea of wholeness is rooted in the Hebrew *shalom*, where the common translation of "peace" is rooted in a prior integrity of the soul.

- *Shalom* is the proactive opposite to the reactive hell.

The language here is clear in terms of Yahweh Elohim*'s* active work in creation. Every form of life is made by him, mature and ready to procreate.

And likewise with man and woman in his image – they are mature and ready to govern the creation, to have children and build civilization.

All the assumptions and statements in Genesis 1-2 are by definition proactive. There is no brokenness of the body, trust or the environment in place – there is nothing negative present, so there is no reactive language. This is interpretively central. Namely, living in a broken world, millennia later, it is easy to put certain assumptions into the Genesis text that are not there.

In the second place concerning *nephesh* is the nature of breathing. I am daily thankful for every breath I take – it is the gift of God. And I think too that any of us who acknowledge the same, regardless of theological or cultural background, are reflecting the image of God, and are open to the work of the Spirit in our lives.

- This touches on true missiology – seeing who is open to every breath as a gift from above. They do not need a condemning and wooden doctrinal formulation, but the lived life of Jesus through us by way of introduction to the true storyline.

As *nephesh* is introduced, it is Yahweh*'s* breath that is primary, not that of *ha'adam*. It is Yahweh who breathes the breath of life into Adam's nostrils, this creation who takes on life from the dust. Man is not sufficient to himself, he is not his own creator, he is not something that derives from nothing. Yahweh Elohim gives and man receives. The text presents to us a fully formed man, but lifeless, nothing more than beautifully organized material stuff – until the breath of Yahweh Elohim is given.

Once Adam and Eve receive Yahweh Elohim's breath, being made after his own kind, they are set to pass on that breath to their children. This we see in Genesis 5:1-3 where man and woman are in the image of Yahweh Elohim, and Seth is born in the image of Adam (representing both man and woman in the Hebrew use of his name).

In the third place concerning *nephesh* is the question of essence versus achievement. As Jacob points out, *nephesh* is a matter of what we are, not what we have. We do not possess soul or personhood – we are souls, we are persons. We are what God has given us to be, not what we achieve by some other means (e.g. a godless and chance driven macroevolution). Essence not achievement is thus central to a universal humanity, with an assumption of equality of worth.

Adam and Eve, created as mature adults, then have children, and pass along the same humanity. This assumes that the whole procreative process – along with the human intellect and moral sense to steward the creation and build civilization – is not one of a secular achievement ethic. It is not where a definition of personhood is "achieved" somewhere in the process, by human effort, but rather, is there from the outset.

- The kingdom of heaven is a gift, able to be received by those who acknowledge *nephesh*, and not a doctrinal "achievement."

In the fourth place concerning *nephesh* is the unity of body and soul. Since *nephesh* does not exist apart from the corporeal (bodily) reality, we do not possess our bodies; rather, our bodies are good and integral parts of our whole identities. "Soul" sums it all up – heart, mind, spirit, body. Not just one aspect or another. Adam and Eve are created to live forever, and thus the resurrection body is assumed in redemption.

The nature of *nephesh* and its uniqueness in Genesis 1-2 stands in stark contrast to Gnostic dualisms – a Greek manner of thought that eventually traces back to Babylonian dualisms.

- Origen, though trained in Hebrew, falls prey at this juncture.

Most simply, Gnostic dualism sets up a war between the body and the spirit, where the body is evil and the spirit is good. When it infects the early church, it leads to asceticism on the one hand (hatred of the body and human sexuality) and sexual licentiousness on the other (since the body is viewed as evil, just let loose). In Hindu and Buddhist dualisms (which are historically derivative), there is no understanding of Genesis 1-2 and the goodness of the human body, being entrapped in the samsara struggle of karma and dharma, with no hope of a resurrection body and identity.

In the fifth place concerning *nephesh*, Jacob concludes with the observation that *nephesh* in its primary sense is best translated as "person," rooted in bodily reality. Yahweh Elohim makes us corporeal beings – we have no identity, no existence, no *nephesh* apart from the human body.

Thus, in grasping *nephesh*, we see that the body is good as defined by the biblical order of creation, meant to live forever until sin intrudes, and remedy is needed.

And in the sixth place concerning *nephesh*, the nature of *nephesh* involves needfulness or dependency. Wolff says that *nephesh*:

> stands for needy man per se … *nephesh* therefore does not say what a man has, but who the person is who receives life (*hayyim*): "person," "individual," "being" … If we survey the wide context in which the *nephesh* of man and man as *nephesh* can be observed, we see above all man marked out as the individual being who has neither acquired, nor can preserve, life by himself, but who is eager for life, spurred on by vital desire, as the throat (the organ for receiving the nourishment and for breathing) and the neck (as the part of the body which is especially at risk) make clear. Although in this way *nephesh* shows man primarily in his need and desire, that includes his emotional excitability and vulnerability …" (pp. 21, 24-25; Hebrew transliteration my own).

Wolff's chapter on *nephesh* focuses on the etymology, or word history, of the term. It is rooted in proto-Semitic languages concerning the anatomy of the throat and neck. It denotes a physical vulnerability, or needfulness, around the capacity to breathe. *Nephesh* is found some 700 primary times, with 350 cognates, in the Hebrew Bible, where this "corporeal needfulness" is always in place. Adam's breath and ability to continue breathing is dependent on Yahweh Elohim's original breath and the ecosphere he creates for us.

And as breathing is incessant, so our moral character is created and purposed to be continually eager and passionate for life. As well, the area of the neck and throat involves hunger and thirst. This assumption is in place as Genesis 2:8-9 identifies the pleasing nature of the fruit to the eye (artistic elements too), and the goodness of food. It is also in place when Jesus speaks of those who hunger and thirst after righteousness (Matthew 5:6), and at the end of Revelation where the restored tree of life is provided along with drinking from the water of life (19:7-9; 22:1-2, 14, 17).

Thus, the vulnerability of *nephesh*, prior to sin, is strength. Only when we acknowledge our need for God's good nature and his power to give, are we able to be nourished and have strength.

38. What therefore is the doctrine of salvation in Genesis 1-2?

- Well, there is none, and this is the point. All is whole, all is *shalom*, all is good, and all human needs are met. But on the other side of the brokenness of sin, of broken freedom, the nature of salvation returns us to the freedom, purposes and trajectory of the order of creation. It returns us to *nephesh.*

- Salvation is simply the return to the *shalom* of *nephesh*, the mere thankfulness in the sight of the Creator and his creation for every breath we take. Thus, any effort we make to serve *shalom* and *nephesh* in all image-bearers of God, thus advances the Gospel of salvation, and we become able to lift up the Name of Jesus in a way that can be truly understood.

- Ultimately, salvation is the chosen return to *nephesh*.

39. What does this look like for people of all backgrounds?

40. In the "missionary kid" theology of certain church subcultures, is there any grasp of this biblical reality?

41. How much "missionary strategy" in the church overrides *nephesh*, as it is rooted in an arbitrary either/or dichotomy, in belief that a stated doctrinal belief determines heaven or hell?

42. Is the mission of the Gospel to pigeon hole people, or to see where they acknowledge the needfulness of *nephesh*, and serve that need in the Name of Jesus?

The fifth assumption is informed choice, the nature of human freedom and our crux concern.

In the Bible, the first words Adam hears are in Genesis 2:16 when Yahweh Elohim "commanded the man, saying: 'In feasting you shall continually feast …' " The most important verb in the Bible is "to eat," at least when it comes to defining human nature. This metaphor is also the basis for human freedom as "an unlimited menu of good choices." This menu is protected when we do not eat poison and die.

The first words in history are when Elohim creates the universe and says, "Let there be light." These words reflect Yahweh Elohim's sovereign power, and that power is the power to give, leading to the power to live in the light, all of which reflects his freedom to do the good. Therefore, on the Bible's own terms, the sovereignty of God's nature is the starting point for all true doctrine, and the root for our human story.

There is nothing that precedes Yahweh Elohim's sovereignty, for apart from his sovereignty nothing else can exist. This means that the sovereign Yahweh Elohim provides human freedom, and the relationship between God's sovereignty and our freedom is the most important relationship in all Scripture and life. Thus, sovereignty equals the biblical starting point for describing Yahweh Elohim's nature, and freedom equals the biblical starting point for describing human nature. And as we have already noted, within his sovereignty is also freedom.

- Thus, we enter the great debate of God's sovereignty and human freedom, that which is also definitive concerning heaven and hell.

The text of Genesis 2:16-17 is predicated on the assumptions in 2:7-15. In 2:7 we have the soul, *nephesh*, and then we are given the context of the Garden of Eden. In v. 9, the subject of good and evil is introduced, and in v. 15 is the need to "guard" the garden (*shamar*) from evil. Then in vv. 16-17, we will see two opposites poles in the text --freedom versus slavery and life versus death.

Now, the Bible is not organized according to statements of propositional truth. That is an Enlightenment myopia in organizing knowledge. Rather,

154

and well prior, truth is grasped in learning the biblical storyline first, then we can organize it different ways. And as we get inside the story of Adam and Eve's creation, three all-defining opposites jump off the page:

- Good versus evil, freedom versus slavery, and life versus death; or to put it otherwise: good, freedom and life versus evil, slavery and death. One set of parallels against another. Do we choose the former or the latter? We are empowered to choose the former since here we have true definitions of all the terms.

This brings us to the look at the text of 2:16-17, the first recorded words of *Yahweh* to Adam:

And Yahweh Elohim commanded the man, "In feasting you shall continually feast from any tree in the garden; but from the tree of the knowledge of good and evil you must not eat, for in the day you eat of it, in dying you shall continually die."

The language in most translations here, "You are free to eat," or "You may freely eat" do reflect a reality, but there are far greater depths. We need to understand the Hebrew idiom in use. The Hebrew words *akol tokel* are fully translated this way: "In feasting you shall continually feast." The grammatical idea is more powerful than an active particle in Romance languages – the sequential use of the infinitive absolute and imperfect tenses for the verb "to eat," a feast that never stops feasting. It is the idea of an unlimited menu of good choices – not only in terms of food options in the Garden of Eden, but also in the application of this metaphor to all practical, moral and aesthetic choices in life.

This language of eating and feasting, with implicit drink, permeates the rest of the Bible. Worship in the Law of Moses revolves around a series of feasts, the Messianic prophecy in Isaiah gives invitation to eat and drink without cost, Jesus celebrates the wedding supper at Cana, gives invitation to the wedding supper of the Lamb, institutes the Eucharist or Lord's Supper, prophesies that he will again drink wine in the kingdom of heaven, eats fish as proof of his resurrection body, and the Holy Spirit beckons us to the wedding supper of the Lamb in Revelation as well. The final act of redemption, in the last chapter of Revelation, is the provision for the river

155

of the water of life (22:1) and the tree of life (22:2). In Jesus's final words, he invites us to partake of the tree of life (22:14), and after the Spirit gives his final invitation of "Come!", the apostle John adds, "Whoever is thirsty let him come; and whoever wishes, let him take the free gift of the water of life" (22:17).

Feasting permeates Scripture from beginning to end, it is celebrated as the essence of the mountain of Yahweh in the *eschaton* (times of the end; see Isaiah 25:5-9); it is the metaphor of human freedom (*akol tokel*). This is the freedom to feast from an unlimited menu of good choices – to satisfy our eagerness, hunger and thirst for life (*nephesh*). Or to sum it up theologically: "Taste and see that Yahweh is good" (Psalm 34:8).

But access to this feast requires a moral understanding of the freedom to choose between good and evil, and the feast of Genesis 2:16 carries with it the caveat, boundaries and structures for the power of human freedom. All humanity knows protective boundaries in daily life, from gravity to a highway median strip to a thousand other examples.

In Genesis 2:17 we see the "but." The unlimited menu of good choices has a restriction that is in reality a boundary of protection. Namely, freedom cannot exist without boundaries. Thus, Yahweh defines the power of informed choice. The protection of an unlimited menu of good choices requires the prohibition of a singular evil choice – do not eat poison.

To understand the trees of Genesis 2:16-17, we must return to Genesis 2:9:

> And Yahweh Elohim made all kinds of trees grow out of the
> ground – trees that were desirable in appearance and good for food.
> The tree of life was in the middle of the garden, along with the tree
> of the knowledge of good and evil.

This phrase, "the knowledge of good and evil," refers to Adam's given authority on the one hand, and inclusive of a Hebrew idiom or *merism*, on the other. Adam and Eve are created to rule over the creation, under Yahweh Elohim, and thus in accordance with his definitions of good and evil. Their authority includes the power to name, for names carry identity,

156

and terms are defined. But then, to eat of the forbidden fruit perverts such authority. It is for man and woman to say a) Yahweh is not good, that he must be withholding something good from us in the prohibition, that is to ✳ say, calling Yahweh evil; thus b) to rationalize the will to disobey Yahweh; c) to redefine good and evil; and thus d) to lift ourselves up to the level of Yahweh Elohim, if not actually seeking to transcend him.

To challenge Yahweh's goodness is the basic nature of unbelief. In the letter to the Hebrews, Barnabas speaks of faith as the quality of believing that God rewards those who earnestly seek him (see 11:1-6). God is good and worthy of invested faith, of trust.

Being limited within the good boundaries of space, time and number, how can we think we can redefine Yahweh Elohim's terms and realities, and still live and prosper in his universe? To eat the forbidden fruit is to redefine good and evil over and against Yahweh Elohim. Instead, man is ordained to judge good and evil in the universe congruent with Yahweh's definition of terms, recognizing the forbidden fruit as a test and a boundary.

Another factor is a Hebrew *merism* for that which is comprehensive, covering the ends and means of the spectrum. Namely, the polar opposites of "good and evil" can refer literally to the knowledge of everything. Everything there is to know lies in the spectrum between good and evil. The polar opposites of beginning and end are likewise comprehensive in defining time (see Isaiah 44:6; 48:12; Revelation 1:8; 21:6; 22:16). The polar opposites of height and depth, of east and west, are likewise comprehensive in defining space (see Psalm 103:11-12).

Therefore, "the knowledge of good and evil" is a concept that equals a whole unit. It is knowledge only Yahweh Elohim as the uncreated Creator can possess. As well, only Yahweh can know the totality of intrinsic evil without being tempted or polluted by it. Evil is ethically the absence of Yahweh Elohim's holy presence, the absence of true ethics, which means the absence of true relationships. Just as darkness is the absence of light in physics, ethics and spiritual territory.

43. How does the descriptive language of hell comport with the original definition of evil?

To know good and evil is to define it, in the sense of this Hebrew idiom – something only Yahweh Elohim can do. Adam and Eve are called to judge between good and evil, but based on Yahweh's true definitions. People who seek to define good and evil differently than does Yahweh, have become their own gods, and only have themselves, as a resource, in order to escape evil in the final consequence.

44. To what extent might a doctrine of "ultimate restoration universalism" in fact seek to redefine good and evil?

45. For such universalists, what is the biblical understanding of evil?

Accordingly, as a creature made in God's image, there is nothing "good" withheld from Adam, as the *akol tokel* idiom of positive freedom already establishes. He is given the "tree of life" to eat from, a tree which is the source for life, for eternal life. A good assumption is that, metabolically, it contributes to the eternal renewal of all the cells in our bodies. Alongside that tree is the forbidden fruit – forbidden if we wish to live. Metabolically, it assaults the renewal of our bodily cells. Then morally, relationally, to eat of the tree of the knowledge of good and evil equals an attempt to digest what we cannot, as if we who are limited by space, time and number, can grasp or wrap ourselves around eternity. We will explode first.

The choice between good and evil is powerfully portrayed by a parallelism in vv. 16 and 17. The phrase in most translations, "you will surely die," is likewise better grasped by the power of the idiom in place. The Hebrew here reads *moth tamuth,* which literally means, "in dying you shall continually die." It is the exact parallel of *akol tokel* in terms of grammatical construct, but opposite on moral nature, with the sequential use of the infinitive absolute and imperfect tenses for "die," carrying with it a force greater than that of an active participle – always dying, yet to die. It is also opposite as is the abyss to the creation in Genesis 1:1-2.

Thus, if we partake in the eternal quality of death, which the forbidden fruit introduces, we will continually experience the taste of death. This is the biblical root for the language and metaphors of hell – a chosen death that never stops dying (C.S. Lewis plays with this theme dynamically in his story, *The Great Divorce*). What this also means is that the definition of death is principally theological in nature, and not just in reference to the physical termination of life. Theological death is the brokenness of relationship with Yahweh Elohim and one another. It is alienation from his presence.

Adam thus "dies," only to continue "dying." Adam and Eve have been given the tree of life to eat from continually, so as to live forever. Once they partake of the fruit of death, this alienation from Yahweh Elohim's full presence removes from their bodies the regenerative qualities of the tree of life, so they begin to die physically. Adam's life span is shortened from forever to 930 years, and the increase in sin's impact upon the body over the subsequent millennia brings the average life span to well under 100 years.

This contrast of choices in Genesis 2:16-17 is marked, and the reader who knows the Hebrew picks it up immediately:

> in feasting you shall continually feast (*akol tokel*), or
> in dying you shall continually die (*moth tamuth*).

Another way of putting it is:

> an unlimited menu of good choices, or
> a limited menu of only death.

With parallel idioms in place, signaling opposite choices, the power of informed choice is defined:

> feast or die.

The command to feast is Yahweh Elohim's will, but the warning against dying carries with it a power to disobey that will. The very language of "will," or "willpower," connotes the exercise of choice. Yahweh Elohim's choice is that we live forever (e.g. 1 Timothy 2:4; 2 Peter 3:9), but he does not force it on us.

- Thus, any attempt here to say "death" in Genesis 2:17 only refers to physical termination of life, shows ignorance of the text.

- This text also sets the stage to understand that Yahweh Elohim uses no coercive power to bring people into eternal life.

- *Moth tamuth,* "in dying you shall continually die" is the predicate language for Isaiah 66:24, as it looks across *ge'hinnom* (the predicate for hell), as the worms "will not die" (*lo tamuth*), and consonant with the ancient serpent's lie in Genesis 3:4: *lo moth tamuthon,* "in dying you shall not continually die."

But why would a loving God permit evil to happen? Outside the biblical worldview, the best attempts to understand the origin of evil are to assume it has always been there, in a dualistic tension and co-dependency with the good. And therefore, the highest aspirations of dualistic religions cannot see past a negative view of freedom – freedom from violation – which ultimately is an escape from suffering into a forfeiture of individual identity, and thus, into an anesthetized sea of collective loss of memory. The Hindu doctrine of *maya* means suffering is an illusion, and thus the highest goal known is its mere escape. The concept of *nephesh,* resurrection and continued individual identity in shared community, are thus not conceivable.

Such a negative view of freedom is the highest concept of freedom imaginable to cultures that know nothing of creation, sin and redemption. And it is in knowing these biblical doctrines that we find the key to knowing the origin of evil, for evil is a "reversal" of the order of creation. The simplicity of evil's origin may appear to some as a scandal; namely, the origin of evil lies in the goodness of Yahweh Elohim. Evil is a parasite, just as darkness is to light.

46. Therefore, to what degree do our five writers fall prey to a negative view of freedom?

47. Is it due to a faulty understanding of evil?

Therefore, true goodness involves the permission, the freedom to choose evil, as given by Yahweh. Evil does not allow the permission, it does not allow the freedom to choose the good.

Evil is a choice, and Yahweh Elohim's goodness necessarily allows this choice because goodness is not forced. Yahweh Elohim's perfect will, and his loving, giving and good nature, is never diminished by this freedom given. The power of informed choice stands above reproach in every measure, and any human attempt to equal or surpass this definition of justice only adds further suffering. *akol tokel* or *moth tamuth*. Feast or die – the choice is ours as the gift of the good and sovereign Yahweh Elohim.

Is this a scandal to say that the origin of evil comes as a direct result of the goodness of Yahweh Elohim? Only to those who have compromised the sovereignty and goodness of Yahweh Elohim.

In Genesis 2:9, the text defines the two trees in the middle of the Garden – one leads to life and the other leads to death. Yahweh therefore lays the basis for Adam and Eve to make their choice. This sets up a contrast of opposing ethical systems which highlight the power of informed choice:

Yahweh's good ethics = true definition of terms = human freedom = life;

Satan's evil ethics = false definition of terms = human slavery = death.

In Genesis 2:17, Yahweh tells Adam that if he disobeys and eats of the forbidden fruit, then *moth tamuth*, "in dying you shall continually die." In Genesis 3:1-5, we see how Satan, incarnate as the serpent, reverses the order of creation with false definition of terms, which leads to misinformed choice, which leads to death. In v. 4, the serpent says *lo moth t'muthon*, "In dying you shall not continually die" (or most literally: "Not in dying you shall continually die").

There are good ethics, and there are evil ethics. Telling the truth, indeed, "truth in advertising," is the same as living in the light, and it is the means for discerning the difference.

We can note how Satan's false definition of terms leads to misinformed choice and therefore to death; in contrast to God's true definition of terms which leads to the power of informed choice, and therefore to life. When

God says there is a tree of life, and a tree of death, he speaks accurately. On this basis, people can choose life.

We can note how:

Yahweh's true definition of terms leads to the power of informed choice and life;

Satan's false definition of terms leads to misinformed choice and death.

When Yahweh says there is a tree of life, and a tree of death, he speaks accurately. On this basis, people can choose life.

Here is an applied sequence: 1) If man and woman are free, and made in the image of Yahweh Elohim, must not Yahweh Elohim first be free? 2) If so, is Yahweh Elohim free do evil? 3) No, for freedom is the power to do the good; and to do evil is to be a slave to it. 4) And Yahweh Elohim is a slave to no thing. 5) Informed choice is predicated on a true definition of terms, as we see in Genesis 2:7-17: good versus evil, freedom versus slavery, life versus death. 6) Therefore, to be free, we must have a level playing field between these opposites to exercise the power of informed choice; Satan fiercely oppose the genuine level playing field.

Only Yahweh Elohim can get away with giving us this radical human freedom. Only Yahweh loves us enough to let us choose whether or not to accept his love. This is Yahweh Elohim's nature, which uniquely provides a level playing field to choose between good and evil.

48. Does not an "ultimate restoration" universalism thus abolish the idea of a level playing field? ✓

Yahweh Elohim does not force his love on us, for that would deny his very goodness. Goodness is the power to give, and to be forced into accepting his love is an oxymoron. Love is a gift, and human nature as given by Yahweh is predicated on the power to give. To be "forced to do the good" would be by definition evil, and thus not possible for goodness to remain good. Or to be more graphic, forced love equals rape. For Yahweh to force his love on us would be evil, it would be pagan – it would be the surrender of his sovereignty, it would be a dualistic condescension to the devil's ethics.

49. To what extent does an "ultimate restoration" universalism rape human freedom?

Here is another sequence: 1) Goodness equals the power to give; 2) evil equals the power to take; thus 3) goodness cannot be forced – it can only be a gift received by informed choice.

Thus, goodness can never be forced, and when attempted, the good that is envisioned turns into evil. By the same token, evil can never act like a gift – it is always something that is deceptive and/or impositional. Another way of putting it is in this couplet:

Love is a choice that cannot be faked; and
Hatred is a choice than cannot be hidden.

As image-bearers of Yahweh Elohim, if we were forced to accept his will, the qualities of responsibility ("ability to respond") and creativity would be moot – we would be no more than animals or puppets.

- This, we arrive at the title of this book: *The Freedom to Choose Hell*. Or to put it another way: *Hell is an object of God's love*. This is the surprisingly proactive, not reactive, theology at hand.

- Or as we started this book by interpolating the love of God in John 3:16 into the text of Genesis 2:16. In doing so, we come up with the following verse in the RSSV (the "Rankin Sub-Standard Version"): "For God so loved the world, that he gave us each the freedom to choose to go to hell if we damn well want to." I use the word "damn" with theological precision – a curse people choose.

The nature of Satan is the power to take and destroy, and therefore, he is in no frame of mind to give us freedom to say no to evil, he has no interest in a level playing field. No pagan religion or secular construct allows a level playing field where good and evil are honestly defined and presented

163

side by side, for they have no definitions of an original goodness. Thus, the best they can offer is a hope to overcome evil and distrust, but without any means. Thus, there is no informed choice, only one unhappy non-option.

Yahweh Elohim does not force his love on us, for that would deny his very goodness. Goodness is the power to give, and to be forced into accepting Yahweh Elohim's love is an oxymoron. Love is a gift, and human nature as given by Yahweh Elohim is predicated on the power to give. To be forced to do the good is evil, and thus not possible for goodness that remains good. Or to be more graphic, forced love equals rape. For Yahweh Elohim to force his love on us would be evil, it would be pagan – it would be the surrender of his sovereignty, it would be a dualistic condescension to the devil's ethics. Here is the sequence:

Goodness equals the power to give;
Evil equals the power to take; thus
Goodness cannot be forced – it can only be a gift received by
informed choice.

Thus, goodness can never be forced, and when attempted, the good that is envisioned turns into evil. By the same token, evil can never act like a gift – it is always something that is deceptive and/or impositional. Another way of putting it is to say that, in the final analysis, love is a choice that cannot be faked, and hatred is a choice than cannot be hidden.

The nature of human freedom comes from God's nature. God is free, and as image-bearers of God, we are made to be free. But what is freedom? It is the power to do the good. Is God free to do evil? No. To do evil is to be a slave to it, and God is a slave to no thing. And the Creator, if infected by any destruction (the grandest oxymoron imaginable), could not sustain the universe. To do the good is to be free. But since we are finite, we must make the choice between good and evil, with both realities possible.

As image-bearers of God, if we were forced to accept his will, the qualities of responsibility ("ability to respond") and creativity would be moot – we would be no more than animals or puppets. Love as a gift calls us to respond, and response involves the exercise of choice. Yahweh Elohim takes the cosmic risk, that for the sake of those who choose "yes" to his love, there are be those who choose "no." The giving of love always involves risk in this sense of the word – the risk that our desire for others to receive our love might be rejected. In 1 Timothy 2:4, Paul says God desires all people to be saved, and in 2 Peter 3:9, Peter says that God wants nobody to perish, yet Scripture also says that not all people will be saved. The dynamics of freedom.

50. What therefore is God's perfect will?

51. Desires to save, but will not, cannot …?

- Simply, God's will, consistent with his nature, is to give us the freedom to choose whether or not to accept his will. Freedom is his nature, freedom is our given nature, freedom is the power to do the good, freedom is not imposed, to impose freedom is evil and an oxymoron, and thus the flip side of true freedom is *the perverse freedom to choose to go to hell if we damn want to*, and apart from the perverse freedom, true freedom cannot be chosen. God's will is thus fulfilled in the coming of Jesus who pays the price for our salvation, if we want to receive it.

52. As we look at the ethics of hell, in all the language we have reviewed, to whom does Jesus rebuke with the promise of hell?

53. Is it not to the few who hate mercy for others?

54. And are not the many the throngs who are like sheep without a shepherd, whose *nephesh*, whose thirst for life is evident?

55. And if biblical ethics, whole in the order of creation, broken in sin, and restored in redemption, are the interpretive leverage in Scripture, and as we look across the whole biblical record – who embraces *nephesh* and who hates mercy?

56. And since in Scripture no one is ever judged apart from chosen deeds, how to we understand the yearnings of those trapped in totalitarian and enslaving pagan idolatries?

57. Those in the dungeons whom Jesus came to liberate (Luke 4:18)?

58. How does this help us understand Romans 1 where all people know God through creation, and that the wrath of God is revealed not against the groping and lost people, but against those who actively "hold back the truth" in their "unrighteousness" (v.18)?

59. Is this not a matter of ethics?

60. And thus, in Romans 2, Gentiles who do not know the Law of Moses formally, have it written in their hearts so that their consciences testify for or against them (v. 14-16), and thus, is this how they face the very Judgment itself?

- Accordingly, hell is that domain of the self-chosen few who choose wickedness and hate mercy.

- Thus, Paul can say to the Athenian pagan elitist philosophers that the people of Athens are worshiping an unknown God whom Paul now proclaims.

61. *Nephesh* on the part of the many people, but resisted by the few elitists?

- For in the rest of Paul's preaching, the few who "rule over" are those who resist *nephesh*, and the many who are suppressed by the few yearn for the Good News.

- Now for a tough question to myself. In the Sermon on the Mount (Matthew 7:13-14), Jesus says that the gate to life is narrow that leads to life, and few find it; and the gate to destruction is broad, and many follow it.

62. Is this not the opposite of what I am arguing?

- Very good question. The first observation concerns this metaphor as understood by the listeners to Jesus. The word for "gate" (*pule*) is immediately seen in the context of an entry way through the

walls into the city of Jerusalem. In other words, into the City of
Zion which is the light to the Gentiles; and then, as we see at the
end of Revelation, into the New Jerusalem as the capital of the
new earth. The gates are large, and yet, if 300,000 people are
pouring through them as during Passover week, it requires order.
But the gates are also narrow compared to an absence of walls to
begin with. When Jesus says he is the "gate" or the "door" in John
10:7-9 (*thura*; parallel term to *pule*), he is explicitly saying he is
the One through whom people enter the "sheepfold" (a parallel
metaphor) and are saved. In terms of the contrast between the
narrow and the wide, the only gate to the road which leads to
destruction is for those who reject the city. And of course, here,
Jesus is speaking to his Jewish disciples, the covenant people.
Those who are unbelievers in Jewish context, who reject Jesus as
Messiah, are those who choose to leave through the gate and into
the wild, wide and disordered realities outside. In both cases the
"gate" is Jesus, and there are two ways to use it in this metaphor –
going out or coming in. And being the one gate, the narrowness or
wideness is a matter of how the gate is used, a matter of the heart
and the will. All people here have access to move in either
direction. Now, in terms of the few and the many who choose
either, we can consider the end of John 6 where thousands leave
Jesus because of his words and the cost of discipleship, and only
the Twelve (at this juncture, pre-resurrection) remain with him.
And then we can consider the power of grace for those who may
enter the road to destruction and later turn back. Jesus is always
seeking to save the lost. In Isaiah 2:2, the prophecy is one of all the
pagan nations streaming toward the city of Jerusalem, as they
climb the mountain of Yahweh, to learn of him and walk in his
ways. This anticipates Revelation 21:24-25, where for the nations,
the gates to the New Jerusalem are not shut but open. Now, too,
this is after the abyss has been sealed with settled choices in place.
The very language here of "the nations" ill-serves a putative
doctrine of the few who are saved versus the many who are
damned. Which is to say, freedom requires boundaries, order, and
this ethic is understood by those who hear Jesus at the Sermon on
the Mount. The second observation is one of eschatology. The
gates to life and death focus toward the coming destruction of the

temple (which occurs in A.D. 70), and only then telescope toward eternal life. And indeed, only a few of the Jews found escape from the destruction of the temple and the city when crushed by the Romans. The third observation is that, also in the Sermon on the Mount, Jesus uses hyperbole to emphasize the cost of discipleship, e.g., Matthew 5:27-30). In sum, we are looking here at a rich texture of many levels, with the cost of discipleship being the point. And with classic hyperbole, as Jesus does elsewhere in the Sermon. To retrofit a doctrine of numerical contrast, between the saved and the damned, misses the point and violates the texture. Storyline defines doctrine, not vice versa.

As we have already noted, that hell is an object of God's love. Those who choose hell are those who accept God's loving provision not to have his love shoved down their throats. When the Jewish context of Jesus's language of hell is examined, we see that those who choose hell are uniquely a (limited) class of people who enjoy causing injury to others. They are those who hate mercy for themselves (out of their pride) and mercy for others (out of an impositional attitude that is rooted in their pride).

I think of its moral nature in these terms. Most of us as adults know the reality of anger and bitterness. Bitterness is rooted in "trust betrayed," and if allowed to grow, it deadens the human spirit toward love and friendship. If this downward cycle of sin's vortex is not arrested and reversed through repentance and forgiveness, then the human soul becomes more perversely self-justified in its anger and bitterness. Ultimately, this bitterness is expressed toward God. People with such a hardened attitude toward God would rather stew in their juices than become humble in his presence. They (perversely) enjoy bitterness more than humility. We all know of people who would rather die in bitterness, than forgive someone who has betrayed them.

Though betrayed, to hold onto revenge is to play God, and to be destroyed by the *moth tamuth* of such folly, disobedience and lack of trust. The Bible says that vengeance is God's alone – he will repay (see Deuteronomy 32:35; cf. Romans 12:19). He alone has the mercy and righteousness to judge all men and women fairly. And he alone has the power to forgive for those who choose mercy over judgment. Those who enjoy revenge are given its eternal and perverse enjoyment of its unending implosion. The redeemed forsake revenge forever. It is a question of which we yearn for – mercy that triumphs over judgment, or self-righteous judgment that dispenses with mercy (see James 2:12-13).

There are two ways of accomplishing revenge against someone – the "pagan way" and the so-called "sanctified way." The pagan method is simply to push the person in front of an oncoming Mack truck. The "sanctified" method is to pray that the person will trip and fall into the path of an oncoming Mack truck. When the disciples want to call fire from heaven upon a Samaritan village that does not welcome Jesus, he rebukes them – no "sanctified" human revenge is allowed (see Luke 9:51-56). Vengeance belongs only to God, for he alone is sovereign, and completely just and fair, consistent with the power of informed choice.

- Hell is that dark and therefore colorless community (which is really no community) of people who are satisfied in the fire of hate, unforgiveness, self-righteousness, bitterness and moral darkness. It is that domain where music cannot exist, for the very nature of music is predicated on order and harmony, whereas human irreconcilability equals the cacophony of discordant, sharp and abusive angles.

- God's will is to give us the freedom of settled choices.

63. What is the trajectory of human nature as we make choices and build on them throughout life?

64. What changes after the grave, internally, to change such a chosen trajectory?

65. Especially if, in seeing Jesus on the Last Day, hell is still self-chosen for the same people?

66. What in Scripture indicates any sense that the final Judgment is not actually final, but is instead the penultimate judgment?

The writer of the letter to the Hebrews (see 6:4-8), and the apostle Peter (see 2:2:17-22), both address this reality as they speak of leaders who by their own choices moved past the realm of forgiveness. The metaphor Jeremiah uses for the potter and the clay is also applicable (see 18:1-12). If we remain in the Potter's hands, we remain moist and moldable. If we excuse ourselves from the Potter's presence and influence, avoiding altogether or cutting short his work, we harden and crack. The more hardened we become, the more softening up we need for restoration. C.S. Lewis describes this in *The Great Divorce* as people who continually move away from each other, because they cannot stand friendship and the mutual trust and vulnerability it requires. There can come a point when a person becomes so far removed from God's presence that he sears his conscience.

On Judgment Day, those who are "yearning in love for his appearing" (2 Timothy 4:8), who come to Jesus on his own good terms (see Matthew 11:28-30), will rejoice as they are received into God's kingdom. *Akol tokel.* Those who do not love God detest his presence and wish to flee from it. They get what and whom they have loved. *Moth tamuth.* In John 3:16-21 we see how Jesus talks of those who love darkness more than light because they know their deeds are evil. Jesus comes not to condemn but to save, so those who are condemned are self-condemned.

God's love is to give us what and whom we choose to love. Evil people go to hell shaking their fists in defiance of God in the ultimate perversion of holding onto a self-righteousness that loves sin and pride more than truth and reality. They love such a defiant stand, for the true heaven is hell to them, and hell is their actual heaven. The moral dimensions of hell are remarkable, extraordinarily just, and understood as the necessary risk of God's love as evidenced in the power of informed choice.

This theology concerning the nature of hell is important, for the most common objection to the Gospel in our culture is "don't shove it down my throat." How often are people able to misinterpret the Gospel because they have not heard about the good order of creation, and the positive nature of human freedom? Namely, they have encountered preaching that up front seeks literally "to scare the hell out of them." That is, if we start with the condemnation of hell, absent its moral dimensions of informed choice, we pollute the Good News and it is seen as bad news.

- This is the starting point of objection to hell we have seen in our five writers.

The good order of creation must be first defined – so the depths of sin can be understood in contrast, not as a starting point – and then the height of redemption can be grasped. An opposite error is to speak only of the goodness of redemption without rooting it in the order of creation and reality of the fall.

In 1991, I was invited to address a group known as the Democratic and Secular Humanists (DASH) of Boston, meeting at the Phillips Brooks House at Harvard. The leader introduced me as "an evangelical minister who likes to be raked over the coals by skeptics." As part of my presentation I argued that any expression of order in the universe must come from a greater Order, and there is no evidence in all human knowledge for a lesser order producing a greater order – of nothing being able to produce something.

So, I asked what came before the beginning of the universe. One man said, "Eternal matter." I responded, "What then, in intellectual terms alone, is the difference between believing in eternal matter on the one hand, and an eternal God on the other? In both cases, we are accepting something greater than space, time and number, something beyond our finite capacity to grasp."

He paused, and said, "Theological baggage."

As we unpacked these two words, it was clear he did not want to admit the possibility of a personal God. He fears that "believers" would then take the license to "shove religion down his throat." In other words, his resistance to the Gospel is at the ethical level – "do not violate my person" – not at the intellectual level. The true definitions of terms concerning heaven and hell need to be known; and as well, concerning the biblical power of human freedom versus the pagan and secular ethos that equals slavery.

The undeniable justice of these ethics is profiled in Ezekiel 23, as rooted in the prior reality of Ezekiel 16, where the prophet ministers to the Hebrew

171

exiles in Babylon in 593ff B.C. In a parable of two adulterous sisters, representing Samaria and Jerusalem, Ezekiel portrays their lustings after the Assyrians and their idols, instead of loving Yahweh. Then v. 9 jumps out of the text: "Therefore I gave her into the hands of the sons of Assyria, upon whom she lusted."

In other words, Yahweh Elohim hands us over to what and whom we have loved. What could be more just? God does not force us into heaven or hell. The text continues in v. 10: "They uncovered her nakedness, took her sons and daughters and killed her with the sword. She became named among women, and judgment was done to her." Choices have consequences. We reap what we sow, we can choose idols if we please, but God warns us of the consequences.

- Those who deliberately reject the Savior will have an eternity of stewing in their juices, continually reaffirming their choices, growing more alienated and lonely, in greater darkness and the gnashing of their teeth in self-righteousness, yet with a fire raging in their breasts, in an ever-shrinking humanity – but never for an inch desiring the humility of reconciliation. They will increasingly want to slam their fists into the face of God, also into the face of one of his image-bearers, being aligned forever with the choice of the power to destroy. In this sense, heaven is hell for the unbeliever, as hell is their chosen heaven.

- We are not free to say yes to God, unless we are first free to say no. There is no commission in the Gospel to force, coerce, trick or deceive anyone into the faith. Those are the devil's ethics. If we honor human freedom as the gift of Yahweh Elohim to Adam and Eve and all their children equally, then those who say no to it will actually be receiving a gift, and thus confirming God's sovereign nature. They cannot then accuse God or his ambassadors of "shoving" it down their throats.

Those who hate God may shake their fists at him, but inside their souls they know they have no just cause for doing so. If there are those who receive this same freedom, and say no to the gift of saying no, which means saying yes, then the angels rejoice (see Luke 15:7,10). In all capacities, we as servants of the Gospel are always to be in the position of giving to others with no strings attached, based in the security of knowing God is sovereign and he alone judges the human heart. Accordingly, hell is an object of God's love, and those who choose residence in hell are still loved by God, in that he loves them enough to give them such a choice.

The gift of human freedom and therefore, its interpretive importance in defining human nature, is strategically restated as the Bible unfolds. We have it first in the words of Yahweh to Adam, then restated in the final public words of Moses, the final public words of Joshua, in the shortest sermon in the Bible, delivered by Elijah at the apex of prophetic witness against Israel's apostasy, and all assumed in the nature and content of the Gospel.

In Deuteronomy 30:11-20, Moses brings to a conclusion his series of final sermons, the final public words of his life before the Israelites enter the Promised Land. He declares the accessibility of the power of informed choice, setting before all of us "life and good, death and evil" (v. 15). This is the exact choice given Adam and Eve in the Garden, even now in the face of human sin – *akol tokel* or *moth tamuth*.

We do have the power to choose life, but to have such power does not mean our sinful nature has the ability to achieve salvation, to "ascend into the heavens" (v. 12) as it were; rather, there is within our fallen humanity the remains of Yahweh Elohim's image sufficient enough to say "help" (to acknowledge *nephesh*), and whether we say "help" is a matter of the human will.

Our human spirit as touched by the Holy Spirit can respond to God. In fact, this power of informed choice is fully in place for Cain before he murders Abel, one generation after the exile of his parents from the Garden. He could have overcome the sin "crouching at (his) door," but instead chooses to let it come in and rule him (Genesis 4:6-7). The Hebrew verb at play refers to a leopard preparing to spring on its prey, yet man and woman are originally given authority over the animal kingdom. Cain chooses to be ruled by Satan.

When the Israelites complete the conquest of Canaan, as much as they do, Joshua gives his final public address at Shechem. In 24:14-15, we read:

> Now fear Yahweh and serve him in soundness and faithfulness. Turn from the gods your fathers served beyond the River and in Egypt, and serve Yahweh. If it seems evil in your eyes to serve Yahweh, then choose for yourselves this day whom you will serve, whether the gods your fathers served beyond the River, or the gods of the Amorites in whose land you are dwelling. But as for me and my household, we will serve Yahweh.

This covenant on the plains of Shechem is the final gathering of the exodus community, and as this passage continues in vv. 16-24, Joshua uses a powerful form of dissuasion, requiring the Israelites to count the cost of discipleship before they say yes. Joshua presses them toward the freedom to choose "no" in order to ensure the integrity of their "yes." No games, no manipulations, no trickery. Joshua is basing his appeal on the power of informed choice.

The informed choice Joshua presents is simple. If serving Yahweh seems evil, choose to serve a) the Babylonian deities across the River (referring to the Euphrates), b) the Amorite deities of Canaan, or c) the gods of Egypt (where the chief deity, the sun god, can be transliterated as *ra* or *re*, likely a word-play on the Hebrew word for evil, *ra*). Who is good and who is evil? Yahweh Elohim on the one hand, or *Marduk* and *Ra* on the other?

With this predicate of informed choice, theocratic Israel is a "community of choice." ("Theocracy," a word coined by the first century Jewish historian Josephus, refers to the rule or laws of God.) Yahweh commands blessings for those who will obey. His theocratic rule is not a forcing of unwanted legislation down their throats. Rather, Yahweh tells the Israelites the exact boundaries of freedom, the power of informed choice. If they do not like or agree with these ethics, they are free to go to Babylonia, Egypt, among the Canaanites, or elsewhere.

They are free to leave anytime if they think anything Yahweh says or does is evil. But if they choose to stay in theocratic Israel, it is because they know and trust the goodness, justice and provisions of Yahweh Elohim, as demonstrated by the signs and wonders of the Exodus. Yahweh has earned their trust. They know Yahweh's goodness (e.g., Deuteronomy 29:2-6). They are free to choose to become part of the "chosen people."

There is also an interesting balance between the words of Moses and Joshua. Moses emphasizes the accessibility of making the right choice, and Joshua emphasizes its difficulty. This is part of the *merismus* of Scripture, "a little part here, a little part there" – when different elements are emphasized in different contexts, in a cooperative tension in the balance of the whole, in the very nature of a storyline. This reflects the balance between Yahweh Elohim's sovereignty and human choice. The right choice is accessible if we accept Yahweh Elohim's grace and admit our needs in his sight; it is inaccessible if we depend on the sinful nature. Joshua is pressing the Israelites to discern the difference.

When Israel is led by Ahab and Jezebel (ninth century B.C.), the prophet Elijah challenges the 450 prophets of *Ba'al* and the 400 prophetesses of *Asherah* to a contest on Mount Carmel (see 1 Kings 18:16-40). The devotees of *Ba'al* call on their god to answer with fire from heaven, but in spite of daylong prayer and self-flagellation, there is no response. But Yahweh answers Elijah dramatically the moment he prays. In his public address to the apostate Israelites beforehand, Elijah is succinct in assuming the power of informed choice:

> And Elijah drew near to all the people of Israel and said, "How long will you limp upon a divided opinion? If Yahweh is the Elohim, walk after him; if *Ba'al*, walk after him.' But the people answered not a word" (1 Kings 18:21).

The power of informed choice, the third of the six pillars, and as defined at these interpretively key junctures, continues through the balance of Scripture. Jeremiah says to Israel that if they want to go ahead and sin, they are free to do so (see 15:1-2). He knows they know the power of informed choice, and have chosen disobedience. The power of informed choice is the invitation to believe, reiterated and fulfilled in the gospels (see Matthew 11:28-30), all the way to the final invitation in the Book of Revelation (see 22:17).

175

- Now we can look at the question of sovereignty and choice, and the nature of predestination.

The balance between Yahweh Elohim's sovereignty and human choice has occasioned much debate in church history. Let's make a few observations, noting again that the first words in Scripture underscore Yahweh Elohim's sovereign power: "In the beginning Elohim created ..." And Yahweh Elohim's first words in human history underscore human freedom: "In feasting you shall continually feast ..." The sovereignty of Yahweh Elohim provides for the freedom of man.

There is a necessary and positive tension between sovereignty and choice, like a spring or coil calibrated to the exact tension needed to perform its task of maintaining the proper balance and integrity of a larger mechanism. Or like the tension between electrons and protons surrounding the neutrons, necessary for the integrity of molecular structure and the existence of the universe. Such tensions produce the freedom for man and woman to live and prosper. It produces the balance between worship and responsibility. We worship in gratefulness to Yahweh Elohim for who he is and his goodness to us; we take responsibility to make wise choices in the stewardship he gives us. The opposite is self-sufficiency, and thus, chosen irresponsibilities.

This tension and balance is seen in 2 Corinthians 4:7: "But we have this treasure in this earthen vessel to show that this all-surpassing power is from God and not from us." Another way of translating "earthen vessels" is by "jars of clay," or "cracked pots," that is, leaky vessels. We are called to acknowledge that we are cracked pots, and therefore not crackpots. By confessing our humanity and fallibility we embrace reality, whereas a crackpot flees reality. The reality is that we have this "treasure" of God – the gift of his Holy Spirit who seals the promised eternal life – in our human frame, to demonstrate God's power.

And what is God's power? He is so totally in control, that he can place his perfect gift in imperfect vessels, and achieve a perfect result (in the Hebrew, not Platonic sense). His sovereignty is not wooden, so that it has to condescend to manipulating the human will within the confines of space, time and number.

Rather, his sovereignty is so great, that he alone can afford to give genuine human freedom, and not be diminished in the process. If Yahweh Elohim is diminished by the act of giving human freedom, then he is not free to begin with, nor sovereign – having been reduced to a pagan deity. Pagan deities are limited creatures (literally demons), and they diminish their pretense if they attempt an act of giving. Giving and pretense cannot coexist peacefully. But, hallelujah, Yahweh Elohim is the true Creator, and thus he was, and is, and always will be sovereign and free.

- Nowhere in Scripture are people judged by God apart from the consequences of their chosen deeds. They are never judged for deeds they do not do, or do not choose to do. This language is found often, where the tension and balance between sovereignty and choice is obvious. We reap what we sow. Hell is that oxymoronic community of choice, populated by people who consciously choose to say no to God – whether no to his covenant revelation, or no to the revelation Paul speaks about in Romans 1-2. Heaven is that true community of choice, populated by people who choose yes to God and therefore yes to the completed work of Jesus Christ – whether yes to his covenant revelation, or yes to the universal revelation Paul speaks about in Romans 1-2.

67. So, what about those who have never heard?

In Romans 1, Paul begins his concerns with the order of creation, and how godlessness among all people will be judged, for all people "knew God." In Romans 2, Paul works with tightly constructed language emphasizing the inseparability of belief and action, saying:

> God will give back to each according to his deeds. To those who by steadfast endurance in doing good seek glory and honor and incorruptibility, he will give eternal life. But for those who are driven by ambition, who disbelieve the truth and are persuaded by unrighteousness, anger and wrath (vv. 6-8).

Everything Paul asserts in Romans 1-2 is consistent with the image of God in the order of creation, and the gift of human freedom. Without distinguishing between Jew and Gentile, he says we will gain what we seek

– eternal life for those who do good, and wrath for those who are self-seeking.

Then Paul speaks about how those who sin and will be judged by the law they know – either covenant revelation for the Jew who has been given the Law of Moses, or for the grace of the image of God resident in all people, including those who have not received the Law of Moses. They are judged according to what they know and do, not according to what they do not know and do not do: *Being judged according to one's own standard, I don't know Jesus. Being judged according to one's own standard, necessitating no matter what your culture. Not so no matter what we will all, fall short of every standard Christ, no matter what your culture.*

For, when Gentiles, who do not have the law, by nature do the law, they are a law for themselves, since they show that the works of the law are written on their hearts, their consciences also bearing witness, and their thoughts accusing, even defending them. This will take place on the day when God will judge men's secrets by the gospel of mine through Jesus Christ (vv. 14-16).

we all wrote this is true historical maybe but what about geography now?

Paul says that judgment for those who have not heard the Gospel will be revealed through (the completed work of) Jesus Christ at the Last Day. What this means is that Jesus has the power to save those who seek the good, acknowledge *nephesh* (needfulness) in the sight of creation, but whose historical situation precluded them from hearing and understanding the Gospel of Jesus. Their hearts cry out "Help me God!" A marvelous literary example of this theology is in the *Last Battle* by C.S. Lewis, the seventh and final in his Chronicles of Narnia series – in how the soldier of Tash (the devil figure) is received by Aslan (the Christ figure).

There is no salvation by any other means – only in the name of Jesus, and Jesus has the power to give ("grace") it to those who seek truth in spite of their sin. God's mercy trumps judgment for those who seek it.

The power of informed choice, vis-à-vis human lineages, is seen as Gentile nations derive from peoples who consciously choose dualistic evil, and the Jews derive from the singular man of his age, Abraham, who chooses yes to Yahweh and no to dualistic evil. Thus, Gentile nations are far more deeply mired in sin since they live and model it for generation after generation.

If people who never heard of Jesus can get into heaven, what can't others simply live "good lives' in reference to vague qualities of God but not believe completely in Jesus do so as well?

178

But in the final analysis, each person is judged according to what he has sought and done. Did he or she seek grace from the Creator, or self-sufficiency in his face? It is appointed for each of us to die once, then to face the judgment (see Hebrews 9:27); and then the content of our hearts will be made known. Will we love our Creator, and love who Jesus really is as we see him face to face, or will we choose the darkness of our own idolatries?

In his Olivet discourse in Matthew 24 and Mark 13, Jesus speaks in terms of the "elect" – those who receive the gift of salvation in the face of the coming tribulation. In Romans 11:28-29, Paul speaks of the Jews in terms of election, rooted in their nature as the chosen people through whom the Messiah comes.

This language of "the elect" begs the nature of "predestination." Jesus says to his disciples: "You did not choose me, but I chose you and placed you to go and bear fruit, fruit that will remain" (John 15:16). Yet they all actively choose to say yes when called, and this passage is specifically in reference to the twelve disciples. At that time, Jewish men who wanted to study the Torah chose which rabbi they wanted to learn under, if they were accepted. Here Jesus is doing the choosing up front. He is no ordinary rabbi, and his mission is no ordinary mission.

How do we grasp this balance? The idea of predestination is most thoroughly covered by Paul in Romans 8-9. It is based on a concern of how Christians deal with suffering, and Paul's encouragement that "we know that for those who love God, who have been according to his purpose, all things works together for the good" (8:28).

Paul boldly declares that nothing can separate the believer from the love of Christ – whether the present or the future, angels or demons, etc. Thus, Paul says, to paraphrase in an enlarged context, "Hang in there – you are going to make it. How do I know that? Because God is sovereign, he is in control, you belong to him, and there is no power in all creation that can thwart his purpose – a purpose he ordained for you ahead of time. He is already where you are going to be, and he tells you that you made it."

179

Paul is strengthening the resolve of believers to faithfully endure trials, by rooting them in God's sovereign power and love. It is God's sovereignty that strengthens their power to make the right choices.

In Romans 8, as Paul uses the terms for "predestine" and "mark out beforehand" (*proorizo*), and to "foreknow" and to "know beforehand" (*proginosko*), he is expressing his human perspective as a "earthen vessels." Neither he nor any of us can ever access God's sovereign vantage point. To think we can describe God's sovereignty from his perspective is what happens when we try to defend God's sovereignty.

- We cannot defend God's sovereignty – it defends our faith. We compromise God's sovereignty if we try to bring it down to the limitations of human understanding.

- To predestine is to operate within the limits of space, time and number. Paul uses the language of predestination to describe God's activity on our behalf, because it is incarnational. Jesus becomes a man in order to relate to us, because we cannot reach up and grasp God in his eternal nature. God relates to us in the use of predestination language because of its ethical purpose – to reflect God's power to give on our behalf, to encourage us to hang in there and be overcomers.

- But whereas God does operate within the limitations of a human time line, as Lord of all, he is not bound by it. To abolish the real gift of human freedom in the name of God's sovereignty is to bind God to a human time line and thus vitiate his sovereignty. Sovereignty is God's domain and language, whereas choice is our domain and language – as a gift of the sovereign God in whom full and true freedom resides.

C.S. Lewis defines an analogy that imagines a time line with God's universe around us. That line begins at the moment of biological origin, and ends at the moment of biological death. From whatever vantage point the present affords us, we can look back to our origins, and forward to our futures. Whereas we can remember some highlights of our past, and experience the present, we do not have any experiential knowledge of the future, only expectations. For myself, I can graph it this way:

1952/3 [conception/birth]	2017 [present]	2040 [future]

As a human being, I am finite and bound to the space-time-number continuum while in this mortal body. I have the power to make choices this day, influenced by the past and determinative for the present and future.

- Yahweh Elohim is greater than space, time and number, but the language of predestination is a creature of space, time and number. Yahweh Elohim is Present before my conception, Present at my conception, Present in my present, and Present in my future. It is all in his Presence, and as such the "pre" of predestination does not hold Yahweh hostage to the limitations of time. Since my future is in his Presence, Yahweh can speak out of that Presence into my present before I have experienced my future, encourage me to hang in there, declare I will make it, in service to and not in violation the gift of human freedom.

- Yahweh Elohim is no slave to the finite universe and it measurements, he is no slave to pagan finitudes, dualities and fatalisms, and heaven and hell are not arbitrary.

Since I am a creature of time, and my only presence is the time-bound present, with memory and hope, I cannot grasp the future as actual presence. But Yahweh is not bound, and he grasps all the past, present and future simultaneously as the I AM. When we as humans try to say that God predestines us apart from our full choice in the matter, we have made God into a creature of time, like a pagan deity; we have bound him to the limitations of human perspective, thus compromising his sovereignty.

To put it simply: God's sovereignty encompasses time, but time cannot grasp his sovereign nature. It is this perspective alone that can define predestination. In other words, here we are through no choice of our own, in the face of a beautiful creation, empowered to live, to love, to laugh and to learn. How can we but worship God?

- God is sovereign, so we worship him; and we are free, so we are responsible – the essence of godly character. If we know that God the Giver is sovereign, we will not become proud, thinking we can earn salvation. If we know that God the Giver has empowered us to make real choices with real consequences, we will be good stewards of his gifts.

This tension and balance provides the "no excuse" of Romans 1:20 on the one hand, and the "choose this day" of Joshua 24:15 on the other. One without the other will produce an unbalanced faith. I can state with full integrity this paradox: I chose to believe in Jesus the Messiah – I could not choose otherwise. I said yes to Jesus's call to repentance, and left my former life to follow him, as did his original disciples. But too, Jesus first chose me. *Merismus*. His grace is truly irresistible for truth seekers.

Well and good. But the question is often asked: What about Pharaoh? Does not the Scripture indicate that Yahweh's choice overrides Pharaoh's choice, and that God in effect predestines Pharaoh to go to hell?

In setting up this question in Romans 9, Paul first quotes Malachi 1:2-3, saying that God loved Jacob, but hated Esau. Some might ask: "Is this not a form of prejudice?" For God chooses Jacob, the younger of the twins, to take preeminence over Esau, before they are born, and before either of them does a good or bad deed. Again, if we grasp God's nature as being greater than space, time and number, then this language is clearly reflecting God's sovereign vantage point, which we cannot attain ourselves.

As well, Paul's point here is to articulate the just prerogatives of God in the face of human pretense. The "him who calls" (language in Romans 9) reflects the power to give. So also with "I will have mercy on whom I will have mercy." God gives mercy, and though we cannot grasp his eternal perspective, we can grasp the biblical reality where no one is ever judged apart from deeds they choose to do. Both Esau and Jacob fully experience the power of informed choice.

In Genesis 25:1-34, we see Jacob is conniving, but too, Esau the skillful hunter cannot wait an extra minute for a hot meal. As he comes in from the open country, and wants some of the stew Jacob is making, Jacob demands that Esau sell him his birthright. "Look, I am walking to death," Esau says, "What is the birthright to me?" Esau can find himself some other food easily – bread, vegetables, grains – without needing hot food. He has been sometime without hot food as it is. Instead, he "despised his birthright," a position of honor and privilege, in his momentary and lazy hyperbole.

He despises a birthright that is a gift of Yahweh Elohim, the blessing of his father as the firstborn, the largest inheritance in that culture, but especially the inheritance of the Messianic promise through his father Abraham. To despise it is to despise, or hate, not only his father, Isaac, but likewise hate God as his heavenly Father; to reject Yahweh Elohim's goodness. Esau takes a cavalier attitude toward Yahweh's blessings, similar to Cain's attitude toward Yahweh in Genesis 4. The use of the word "hate," in both the Hebrew and the Greek, literally means to "regard with less ✳ affection than" in the context of human relationships. It then leads to abhorrence. This is Esau's attitude – he regards Yahweh Elohim and his birthright with less affection than his belly in a moment of hunger. Thus, Yahweh Elohim regards Esau with less affection than Jacob, from Esau's perspective, and Esau knows he gets what he deserves, what he chooses.

As well, it is important to note that the "hate" of God toward Esau, recorded in Malachi, is contextually addressing the Edomites, the nation that comes from Esau, and hates the nation that comes from Jacob, that is, the Israelites, even cheering on their enemies from the Exodus to beyond the Babylonian exile. Too, this language says nothing about the ultimate recognition of *nephesh* by Esau as a person.

Paul anticipates the proper concern with the justice of God: "Is God unjust? Not at all!" The power to give defines all. Thus, Paul focuses on God's prerogative for mercy – his act of giving mercy to those of us who do not deserve it. To exemplify God's prerogative to show mercy, Paul cites Pharaoh.

The question is this: Is it fair to assume that the reference in Romans 9 to God's hardening of Pharaoh's heart means Pharaoh has no true choice in the matter? Once I tallied the number of clauses in Exodus 4-14 that refer to the hardening of Pharaoh's heart. There are various Hebrew verbs in use here, and they connote "strengthening," "hardening," "making heavy," and "yielding."

Depending on how clauses and references are calculated, the following balance emerges: 14 clauses where Yahweh takes responsibility for Pharaoh's decision; 4 clauses where the language does not tell us who takes responsibility; and 35 clauses where Pharaoh takes responsibility for his own decision. A 5-2 ratio emphasizing human accountability.

Of the 14 clauses where Yahweh takes responsibility, in 9 instances it specifically says he "hardened" Pharaoh's heart. Of the 35 clauses where Pharaoh takes responsibility, in 4 instances it specifically says Pharaoh "hardened" his own heart. Then in verses like 10:27, we read the balance that Yahweh "strengthened Pharaoh's will, and he was not willing to send them on their way."

In other words, Yahweh's sovereignty precedes and defines Pharaoh's fully owned choice – just as in the Garden of Eden with Adam. In Exodus 9:16-17, we read the passage that Paul quotes in Romans 9, as the balance is again in place:

> "But I have raised you up for this purpose, that I might show you
> my strength, and that my name might be recounted in all the earth.
> You still exalt yourself against my people and will not send them
> on their way."

Or we can note the balance in Paul's words on Mars Hill, where God "commanded the appointed times for them and their fixed dwelling places … so that men would seek and grope about for him …" (Acts 17:26-27). Sovereignty and choice, the latter made fully possible by the former. Pharaoh actively chooses to oppose freedom and justice for the Israelites.

The showing of Yahweh's power to Pharaoh is his power to give. Egypt has forgotten the deliverance it received 430 years earlier by the hand of Yahweh through Joseph, and the subsequent pharaohs enslave Joseph's descendants with cruelty. In Exodus 4-14, Yahweh again and again gives Pharaoh the chance to relent from such cruelty, but he does not do so – he owns the choice to resist Yahweh, to resist his mercy. The judgment that

Yahweh passes on Egypt is for their sin of despotic slaveholding, which is derivative of their idolatry. Egypt mocks Yahweh by forgetting Yahweh's servant (Joseph) who had brought them deliverance in an earlier time, and now they compound that sin by building their nation's wealth on the backs of Joseph's progeny.

Accordingly, when Paul alludes to Pharaoh in a context designed to emphasize the sovereign prerogative of God and his power to give, he is rooted in the text of Exodus 4-14, its antecedents, and the balance between sovereignty and choice found there. Pharaoh chooses to be judged by Yahweh rather than relent his position of self-aggrandizing power – he loves the darkness rather than the light.

Finally, in this abbreviated review of the content of Romans 8-9, we come to what I call the "cosmic risk" taken by God, as I brushed by earlier. That is, God loves us enough to allow us to reject his love, for he loves us enough to risk those who refuse to believe for the sake of those who do believe.

But too often we think of risk in strictly human terms, in the sense of an investment that might not bring in its expected return, or one in which the principal can be lost. Not so in theological terms. In Matthew 25:14-30, in the parable of the talents, Jesus says that those who invest in the kingdom of God will gain the return proportionate to their abilities and the risk they take. God is sovereign over his "markets."

In Romans 5:1-5, Paul speaks of a hope that has is honed by suffering, perseverance and character. It is a hope that "does not disappoint us" because of the reality of the Holy Spirit. Too often, we use the term "hope" not with its theological certainty, but in a sense of uncertain wishfulness.

The only risk we have in deciding to follow Jesus is that of losing worldly reputation, its material goods and therefore any false security they may bring. But if we know the Lord and the reality of the kingdom of God, this is no risk at all. In the parable of the man who finds a treasure buried in a field, Jesus says that he goes and sells all he has in order to buy the field (Matthew 13:44). He risks his whole material well-being in the certainty of knowing the treasure is there.

185

This is what we see reflected in Romans 9 (vv. 22-24) where God says he bears with patience "the objects of his wrath" for the sake of "his objects of mercy." He ethically treats all people the same – as Scripture says, he shows no favoritism (see Acts 10:34-35; Romans 2:9-11). He is willing that some are free to choose his wrath for the sake of those who choose his mercy. Satan and Pharaoh, even in their wickedness, remain servants of Yahweh (however unwillingly, in their exercise of the will to disobey). Yahweh is sovereign.

When we consider the balance between sovereignty and choice, the question of prayer and its nature is crucial. Do we pray for something we cannot change? That would be a passive and puppet-like faith. Or do we believe that Yahweh Elohim's character can change due to our influence? That would-be folly and idolatry.

Yahweh Elohim's character is that his sovereign goodness provides for our human freedom. As the Bible is examined across its pages, it is seen that all prayer involves spiritual warfare – as image-bearers of Yahweh Elohim, we are called to take our given authority over the demonic powers. We pray for their presence to be removed in the lives of people and nations, so that people can experience the level playing field to hear the Gospel, to choose between good and evil, as designed for Adam and Eve from the outset.

In reading Genesis 18:16-33, we enter a remarkable saga where Yahweh informs Abraham of the coming judgment on Sodom and Gomorrah. He is an image-bearer of Yahweh Elohim, called to judge between good and evil in Yahweh's sight. And yet Yahweh allows Abraham to challenge the propriety of the judgment, and to negotiate the threshold down to the point that Yahweh will withhold judgment if there are only ten righteous people in those cities. Here we see the power of informed choice, and the power to love hard questions (the substance of the next chapter), merge. We already noted the antithesis to Abraham with Bala'am in Numbers 22-24, where the same freedom of informed choice, grounded in reality, is given.

Yahweh Elohim does not change in his character (see 1 Samuel 15:29; Psalm 110:4; Malachi 3:6; Hebrews 7:21 and James 1:17); and Yahweh seeks people to repent and change, so that, consistent with his character, he can change prior outcomes they are enslaved by (see Jeremiah 18:7-10; Ezekiel 18:21-32).

The gift, the Good News, the assumption of human freedom, of the power of informed choice, the third of the six pillars of biblical power, as defined in the biblical order of creation, is without peer in comparison in its beauty, justice and mercy. It is a pure positive, attractive to all people of good will. Do we thus live *akol tokel*?

The sixth assumption is hard questions.

The level playing field provides space for the toughest questions to be posed of Yahweh Elohim, various leaders and one another. This is the fourth of the six pillars of biblical power – the power to love hard questions. It is a cognate to the power of informed choice, namely the freedom to ask questions of Yahweh in governing the good creation. The Hebrew Bible and New Testament are unique in that no questions are ever prohibited of Yahweh Elohim, the prophets, Jesus and one another. We can note some examples across the biblical text.

68. Do we really love hard questions that come our way, especially as they are demonstrably biblical in nature?

69. If questions upset what we think we know, or challenge how we live our lives, do we still embrace them willingly?

• For our five writers, I have asked some hard questions I believe should lead them to deep reconsiderations.

70. How willingly will they embrace them, and give response?

• I fully embrace any questions that come my way in response, no matter how hard or provocative.

71. How well will I respond?

Job's friends have an unrestricted freedom to question him about the source of his sufferings. Job poses questions in response, also to Yahweh, and then Yahweh answers with questions Job cannot answer. And Job is vindicated as a result.

In Genesis 18, Abraham is free to question Yahweh's plan of judgment on Sodom and Gomorrah, as he intercedes on their behalf. Jesus also says "if" Sodom and Gomorrah had seen the miracles he performed in Galilee, they would have been spared. The dynamics of the open-ended "what if" question.

In 1 Kings 10 (cf. 2 Chronicles 9) the Queen of Sheba travels 1,000 miles north to "test" King Solomon with "perplexing questions." He gives her the freedom to literally talk with him about "everything she had on her mind." Solomon answers her questions to the queen's satisfaction, and in conclusion, she praises Yahweh Elohim, and his anointing of Solomon to "maintain judgment and righteousness." And Jesus praises the Queen of Sheba for seeking out Solomon (Matthew 12).

The Book of Psalms highlights the power to love hard questions. One scholar has titled it *Out of the Depths* because of its focus on the reality of broken relationships, and the emotional, physical, spiritual and intellectual questions that result. The Psalms are widely loved, and especially Psalm 23 – they minister to the souls of all of us, for we all know heartache. In his painful depths, David is free to cry out to Elohim in Psalm 22, "My *Eli*, my *Eli*, why have you deserted me?" And Jesus presses these very words to his lips on the cross (Matthew 27 and Mark 15).

The Book of Ecclesiastes reflects the literary device of a man who knew better to begin with, who nonetheless indulges in folly, and emerges afterward knowing better what he knew better to begin with. The purpose of Ecclesiastes is to think aloud in retrospect, and to embrace hard questions in a conversational style. The reader, any reader, is invited to experience the process with the writer.

The prophet Jeremiah pours out his complaint to Yahweh following some unexpected suffering (chapter 20). He is free to complain to Yahweh for "opening" (Hebrew *patah*) him up to the mockery of his enemies, as it were. Then he praises Yahweh, and yet again, reverts and curses the day of his birth. He is free to lay open his emotions in suffering.

In the Book of Jonah, it concludes with a question of the prophet by Yahweh relative to justice and mercy. In the Book of Habakkuk, the prophet poses his toughest questions of Yahweh concerning justice, he is given answer, and then rejoices while still facing further suffering.

As the quintessential rabbi, Jesus's teaching style is such that he poses far more questions (188 separate examples in the four gospels) than he gives answers. He proactively goes into the wilderness to face the devil's false questions, gives true answers, and thus the devil is silenced. Jesus teaches in parables that leave open-ended freedom for his hearers to do more thinking, and to embrace further questions. And he celebrates the freedom of his enemies to question him during Passover week, gives answer, and in the end, they choose to silence themselves.

When the apostle Paul addresses the Stoic and Epicurean philosophers in Athens (Acts 17), on their turf, he does so in openness to their questions. And when addressing two deeply divisive debates in the early church, Paul insists that "each one in his own mind should be fully convinced" (Romans 14:5).

And with no restrictions on freedom of speech and questions, this also means the freedom to speak to and question political power. This the prophets do across Scripture, for example, with Moses to Pharaoh, Elijah to Ahab, Samuel to Saul, Nathan to David, Jeremiah to Zedekiah, and John the Baptist to Herod. Sometimes these questions yield changes in the political potentate, sometimes the prophet suffers or is killed. And Jesus does it in his own powerful and unique way as the Son of God, as we will see.

The seventh assumption is human sexuality.

Genesis 1-2 is the only text in human history that assumes the definition of healthy human sexuality to be one man and one woman in mutual fidelity, for a lifetime, as the basis for trust in human relationships, and thus for the building of a healthy social order. And it is a proactive assumption. After Yahweh makes the man, gives him the gift of freedom and shows him that he is lonely, he makes the woman to complete the image of Yahweh Elohim.

72. To what extent is the visceral reaction to the doctrine of an arbitrary hell rooted in violent men who mock true manhood and fatherhood?

All pagan texts and secular constructs move beyond this boundary of sexual freedom as located in faithful marriage as broken trust emerges and the reactive posture is assumed. The assumption of healthy human sexuality is thus relentlessly assaulted, and we witness this contest introduced in Genesis 1-19, then across the biblical text until final redemption.

In Genesis 1, the social order is created for male and female together as the image of God to govern his good creation.

In Genesis 2, man and woman become one in marriage as the foundation for the social order.

In Genesis 3, the ancient serpent divorces the decision making between the woman and man in order to destroy marriage and the social order.

In Genesis 4, this brokenness leads to murder and bigamy.

In Genesis 5, the equality and complementarity of male and female, and the goodness marriage and parenthood, are reiterated.

In Genesis 6, the judgment of the Flood is due to the reification (reduction to the status of property) of women in the building of harems – the very mockery of marriage.

In Genesis 9-11, the stage is set for the Canaanites and Babylonians to advance the triad of sorcery, sacred prostitution and child sacrifice, further degrading faithful marriage.

In Genesis 16, Abraham yields to taking a concubine, and this broken marriage yields endless wars between the nations.

In Genesis 19, the judgment on Sodom and Gomorrah is due to a sexual anarchy that morphs into social anarchy and the trampling of the poor and needy, as the biblical concept of marriage is but a distant memory.

- One consequence of all this becomes the pagan practice of child sacrifice (e.g., Leviticus 20:1-5), which indeed leads to the metaphor for hell in Jeremiah 19:1ff. (where in the Valley of Ben Hinnom, child sacrifice takes place within the ever-burning city trash dump; where the Hebrew *g'hinnom* is transliterated into Greek *gehenna* in the Septuagint, and is the New Testament word used for "hell" by Jesus). It is all male chauvinism.

- Thus, hell itself, is a consequence of broken marriage.

This assumption of biblical sexuality has been challenged afresh by the rise of pagan and secular feminism in the past half century. And the reactionary posture is evident.

Christine Overall, in her Introduction to *Ethics and Human Reproduction*, gives a succinct definition of feminism rooted in five essential components:

1. women's experience;
2. women's victimization by male dominance;
3. understanding the origins of male dominance;
4. rebellion against male dominance; and
5. the creation of structures to teach and reproduce a worldview that succeeds in such a rebellion.

In a review of Genesis 1-2, we can note its content this way:

God → Life → Choice → Sex.

In Genesis 1-2, the biblical order of creation begins with God, and his purpose is to make human life as the crown of his creation, then his first words to the man are words of the freedom of choice, and the most important choice to be made is that of marriage.

But with the advent of sin, the reversal of the order of creation equals:

Sex → Choice → Life →/ God.

Historically, sex outside of marriage employs atomistic choice to destroy life through sexually transmitted diseases, infant exposure, dehumanizing of children born in concubinary, adultery, prostitution etc., the unborn in the act of human abortion, and on outward to the economic privation of any who live outside of a healthy marriage and family unit.

Thus, we have the reversal order:

Sex → choice → life →/God, on the other.

The *sex → Choice → Life →/ God* agenda has had great success, to the detriment of society, but also in reaction to the prior evil of male chauvinisms that drive the abortion ethos. Overall's critique is rooted in a reaction to the broken trust between men and women, yet the only remedy is to become rooted in the prior and proactive biblical assumptions of trust.

73. How much of the reaction against judgment is due to those who have suffered false judgment that finds its experiential source in some form of male abuse or fatherly absence?

In Genesis 1:26-28, we read:

Then Elohim said, "Let us make man in our image and likeness, and let them rule among the fish of the sea and the creatures of the heavens, and the livestock, and all the earth, and all the ground creatures."

So Elohim created man in his image,
in the image of Elohim he created him;
male and female he created them.

Elohim blessed them and said to them, "Be fruitful and multiply; fill the earth and subdue it. Rule among the fish of the sea and the creatures of the heavens and over all the ground creatures."

The exact parallel vertical grammar in the Hebrew equals:

man = the image of God = male and female;

192

his own image = him = them.

When Elohim creates "man," the Hebrew word is *adam*, from whence Adam derives his name. The word *adam* does not mean "male" (like *ish* or *zakar*), but it is the principal word for "mankind" or "humankind" – specifically including both male and female, and/or in plural reference.

Thus, *adam* is gender inclusive, and its use throughout the Hebrew Bible in the generic sense means that mankind includes both male and female. Adam takes on the name of *adam* as a personal name representative of humanity, representative of the unity Elohim designs for male and female as his equal image-bearers.

In the restoration of the image of Yahweh Elohim in Genesis 5:1-2, this is explicit: "In the day Elohim created man, he made him in the likeness of Elohim. He created them male and female and blessed them. And when they were created, he named them man."

He calls them *adam*. Thus, the biblical language is poignantly specific from the outset in a) demonstrating the equality of man and woman, that together they equal "man," and b) that the use of the male pronoun when referring to "man" or "mankind" is inclusive of both male and female. Male and female both come from Yahweh Elohim, and the use of the "he" refers to his power to give.

This leads us to consider the use of the male pronoun, the "he" of Adam, or better yet, the "he" of Yahweh Elohim. In Genesis 1:27 we see the use of three sets of nouns in parallel equality at the beginning of each line, and three corresponding pronouns at the end, as cited above.

Thus, the parallels in Genesis 1:27 above are obvious to the Hebrew hearer and reader, and Genesis 5:2 reiterates the same prosaic clarity – male and female are "man."

God the Father is above male and female, for both male and female equally derive from his character, and he is at peace within himself in triune community. He is neither male nor female in the human sexual sense, in terms of a singular sexual identity. Jesus applies a female metaphor to himself (see Luke 13:34), but God is called "Father" (see the language of Deuteronomy 32:6; and especially of Jesus's use of "Father" for God), always uses the masculine pronoun, is never given the title "Mother," and never is described with female pronouns. Elohim is "he" and not "she."

So, whereas the Hebrew Bible is unique in describing men and women as equally sharing the image of Elohim, the description of Yahweh Elohim is in masculine terms. The masculine "man" is the designated term to include man and woman, as opposed to the feminine "woman" being the designated term. This is due to the simplicity of the power to give, and accordingly, the important question to ask is not why Yahweh Elohim is called "he," but why Adam is called "he." Or in other words, the "he" of Yahweh Elohim is not a designation of being male; and the "he" of Adam is a designation of the power to give as initially received from Yahweh Elohim.

Human sexuality, at its deepest core, is designed to be the epitome of where the power to give is expressed in human community, and is designed for the covenant of one man and one woman in marriage. If we make the mistake of looking at Yahweh Elohim through the prism of broken human sexuality, then we can end up making him a "male." This is what pagan religions do with male gods and female goddesses.

Adam as male derives the nature of his "he" from Yahweh Elohim, and not vice versa. God the Father employs all his power in the power to give, to bless and benefit we who are made in his image. And within the Trinity, we see the dynamics of this relationship as based on giving and receiving. God the Father, Son and Holy Spirit are consistently giving honor to each other (e.g., John 14:25; 17:1), and receiving it from each other, in his unified nature.

This is why Genesis 2:24 says a man will leave his father and mother, cleave to his wife and the two of them become one flesh. The two – male and female – became one because of the prior reality of Yahweh Elohim, in whom the three are one; and because the image of Yahweh Elohim requires both male and female in order to reflect the nature of the triune God, where unity and diversity exist together in unity, where diversity is in service to unity. This unity and diversity represented in the two becoming one in marriage reflects the unity and diversity within the triune God, the three who are One. True diversity in service to unity is rooted in man and woman in marriage as the purpose for the image of Yahweh Elohim.

In the biblical creation, God the Father initiates the power to give as he makes man and woman to receive such giving, and this reflects the dependent and needful nature of the human soul (*nephesh*). Receiving cannot happen without the prior reality of giving; thus, Yahweh Elohim is the Initiator of all giving. The "he" of Yahweh Elohim is best understood as reflecting this ethical dimension, and not to be seen as restricted to a human limitation of the male pronoun.

Adam takes on the designation of "he" because he is the first human to receive from Yahweh Elohim in Genesis 2, and thus empowered to be the first human to pass on the power to give. In the finitude of human nature, in order to catalyze the cycle of giving and receiving, Yahweh first demonstrates his giving to the one who receives the gift and that such a one naturally gives to another. The "he" of Adam. Giving and receiving is the true nature of all relationships as ordained by Yahweh; and in the sexual intimacy of marriage, it reaches the zenith, the most beautiful and complete nature.

All this equals the opposite of male chauvinism. There are three different equations for marriage. In a 1994 forum at Smith College, on *Feminism and the Bible* with the president of the National Organization for Women, I made a spontaneous observation that in life we have two possibilities: "give and it will be given, or take before you are taken." I also observed the three possibilities in human relationships, symbolized in three different types of marriage:

100-0;
50-50; or
100-100.

In the 100-0 option, male chauvinism is operative. Here the man demands 100 percent and gives nothing. This can also be described as "take before you are taken."

The 50-50 option can be described as "egalitarian," and is distinguished philosophically from "equality." In the philosophy of an egalitarian view, the equality of the sexes is defined by an appeal to "sameness." A woman can do anything a man can do, it is said. Accordingly, male and female roles in marriage are said to be interchangeable (apart from the inescapable reality of pregnancy, giving birth and natural succor).

In the "ideal" egalitarian marriage, each partner pursues career goals, defined not by service to the home as with a healthy marriage, but careers, which if push comes to shove, take precedence over the home. Thus, cooking and housework are split evenly if they cannot afford a cook or a maid. If and when they have children, maternity leave applies to the man as well as the woman, and they share 50-50 the work of child rearing. With or without daycare or a nanny, the husband is expected to make the same "sacrifice" of time away from his career, as does his wife. Such "sameness," as a definition for equality, is thus supposed to remove culturally imposed role distinctions between male and female – and lead to true equality.

Yet why is it that the language is one of "sacrificing" a career, and not that of "sacrificing" family? A boomerang against male chauvinisms – namely, where "career" is often the male idol to begin with. For a married man, unless his identify is first in the Gospel, then in his wife and family, it is his error that opens the Pandora's Box of human suffering. Which is the more enduring reality, for the individual and the social order? How many people on their deathbeds regret not having spent more time at their careers, or not having spent more time with their family members, especially children?

As the research makes clear, the upper middle-class ideal of egalitarianism is not only a myth, it is also a destroyer of families and children. As many feminists complain, when they enter such a 50-50 bargain, they discover that their workloads greatly increase, and their husband's workload remains roughly constant. As women, they are desirous or willing to pursue a career outside the home, but men are, as a rule, unwilling to share the domestic work anymore than was otherwise the case (though increasingly with a more "feminized" culture, things are more complex).

This leads to a warfare between one 50 and the other 50. Namely, 50-50 by definition is a taking proposition, with each party making an idol of career or identity outside of God and family. By putting such an idol ahead of relationship, each party clamors to protect his or her 50 percent. In other words, the arrangement is based on the "right to take" the 50 percent that belongs to him or her, and if one spouse takes 51 percent, there is war – the opposite of the power to give.

There is great freedom in a healthy marriage in terms of how income producing work and management of the home are shared, but only when the complementary nature of men and women is affirmed, not when distinctions are blurred. The irony is that the 50-50 proposition is no different than the 100-0 proposition. It too is "take before you are taken."

The Hebrew word for peace is *shalom*, as noted earlier, which primarily refers to integrity and wholeness. The only prescription for social peace is the original one of 100-100 in the Garden of Eden. This is the power to "give and it will be given," where Yahweh Elohim gives 100 percent of his divine best to the human Adam, Adam receives the 100 percent and gives 100 percent of his human best to Eve, she receives his 100 percent and returns 100 percent of her human best to Adam; then they together, in the integrity and wholeness as husband and wife, give their 100 percent of their human best in worship to Yahweh Elohim.

Hence, two choices – give and it will be given, or take before you are taken. I asked Patricia if she knew of any better arrangement for marriage or the human community. Neither of us could.

We see that Adam receives the "he" in his maleness because Yahweh designs him to also give to his wife. Or to put it another way, whoever is made first is by definition male, when male is understood in terms of the "he" of Yahweh's initiation of the power to give in the order of creation, and not in terms of the "he" of male chauvinisms, which does not happen until the reversal.

Having already noted the creation of Adam in Genesis 2:7, we can now note Genesis 2:18-25, where we are introduced to the specifics of the creation of Eve:

Yahweh Elohim said, "It is not good for the man to be alone. I will separate out a helper facing him."

Now Yahweh Elohim had formed out of the ground all the land creatures and all the creatures of the heavens. He brought them to the man to see what he would name them; and whatever the man called each living creature, that was its name. So the man gave names to all the livestock, the creatures of the heavens and all the beasts of the field. But for Adam no suitable helper was found.

So Yahweh Elohim caused the man to fall into a deep sleep; and while he was sleeping, he took one part out of the man's side and closed up the flesh underneath.

Then Yahweh Elohim built a woman from what he had taken from the side of the man, and brought the woman to the man.

And the man said,
  "This is now substance of my substance
    and flesh of my flesh;
  she shall be called 'woman,'
    for she was taken out of man."

Accordingly, a man will leave his father and mother and cling to his wife, and the two will become one flesh.

And the man and his wife were both naked, and felt no shame.

As Yahweh Elohim completes the stages of the creative progress defined in the days of creation, we see the idea repeated: "And Elohim saw it was good." Then on the sixth day, when man and woman are created, they are his goal, the crown of creation, and then the text says, "Elohim saw all he made, and it was very good." Thus, as Yahweh Elohim declares something "not good," we face a powerful disjunctive. How can something be "not good" in the order of creation? The answer is straightforward: Something is not yet complete, only "haploid" as it were.

In Genesis 2:18-25, we have the specifics of how and why the woman is made. Yahweh has already made Adam out of the dust, breathed the breath of life into him, and gives him the commandment of freedom. The *adam* of Genesis 2:7 is not referring to an androgynous creature, in the sense that *adam* here could be seen as being male and female in one nature and body. We know this because of the subsequent text that treats *adam* as the proper name for the first male, Adam, one in need of his female complement.

Part of Adam's freedom is his authority over and for the created order as Yahweh's vassal – the "why" of Adam's existence. So there Adam stands – naked, innocent and free in the presence of his Creator. Yet something is missing. Adam needs a "helper facing him." The Hebrew term for "helper" is *ezer*, and it has no sense of subordination. Indeed, the verb employed here (*neged*) says the "helper" is "facing" him, giving a visual of them both standing eyeball-to-eyeball as equals and complements. As well, whereas it refers to the act of giving assistance, it is more often used to specify the one who gives the help – to the power to give, which equals Yahweh Elohim's nature, and human nature in his image.

The most frequent use of *ezer* in the Hebrew Scriptures is in reference to Yahweh himself as the divine helper, and Eve reflects the image of Yahweh Elohim as she comes to help Adam. Here, *ezer* is a word for moral and relational equality, based on a mutual power to give and receive. Also, in the New Testament, the Holy Spirit is also called the "helper" or "advocate" (*parakletos* in John 14:16; 26; 15:26; 16:7).

In other words, Adam by himself does not fully bear the image of Yahweh Elohim. We already know this by the text in Genesis 1:27, where the language of mankind, and the inclusiveness of male and female, is descriptive of the image of Elohim. Here in Genesis 2, we see Yahweh Elohim demonstrating to Adam his need for a helper. Yahweh declares it is "not good" for the man to be alone, and then brings him various creatures in order for Adam to give them names.

What does the naming of the animals have to do with addressing Adam's loneliness? Yahweh is demonstrating to Adam the power to give, where the act of giving is intrinsically satisfying. In other words, we need to give – we need someone to whom to give, otherwise giving is not possible, and receiving is out of the question. The need to give and receive is provided for within the Trinity, and here Yahweh walks Adam through the steps of recognizing that as an image-bearer, he, too, is designed to give and receive.

Now that Adam has received, he is equipped to give, and at the same time is not complete without someone to whom to give, someone who is his equal. He can give back to God, but as a creature, not an equal. He cannot give to an animal and receive back with reciprocity, for he is not an animal. He needs a helper so that he can exercise the power to give, so that reciprocity in giving returns to him. His helper cannot be his mirror image – another man. He needs an equal who is also a complement, facing him as such, where between the two they complete each other, where they add unique dimensions the other does not possess.

He needs a woman. Adam needs Eve to give to and receive from in order for the image of Yahweh Elohim to be complete. He is made for communication, to share with an equal, not to be lonely. And giving must be initiated. Giving begets giving; but if taking is the initiative, then taking begets taking. The former is the prescription for peace. The latter is the prescription for war.

In the Garden, Yahweh initiates the power to give, and Adam needs to do the same in order to reflect his image as a male, to reflect the "he." Then Eve, as a female, receives, and is thus empowered to give and receive as "she." The cycle of giving and receiving is catalyzed, and either party can initiate the act of giving any time henceforth.

The Garden of Eden and all creation are before Adam, and he is given the power to name the creatures – the power to affirm the goodness of Yahweh Elohim's created order. This naming process is an initial exercise of his status as Yahweh Elohim's image-bearer. As Yahweh creates, now Adam is given the privilege to be procreative in the fullest sense of the term (to procreate is not only to have children; it is to be creative in all contexts with the resources Yahweh Elohim gives us in creation). Yahweh Elohim is the Creator, and Adam is now called to be the procreator. But his procreation is limited when his only relationship here is with the animals. Procreation comes as the gift of the Creator, the Father of us all.

Adam is alone, the giving of names is creative, and he also discovers first-hand the difference between man and animal. He does not smell like them or look like them; he notices the animals are in twos and he is in ones; he is lonely and does not want to (indeed, cannot) mate with any of them.

Yahweh Elohim teaches Adam in this exercise that:

1. he is made in Yahweh Elohim's image;
2. animals are not;
3. he is not an animal; and
4. his image-bearing status is not complete without "a helper facing him."

Most powerfully, Yahweh demonstrates to Adam, "You are not it." Adam alone is not the complete bearer of Yahweh Elohim's image, and he is in need of his equal who completes him, and whom he completes. Therefore, all power Adam exercises toward Eve is designed to be the power to give, not the power to take. And apart from woman, he is unable to give in a way that completely fulfills the image of Yahweh Elohim.

Among pagan feminists and other skeptics of the biblical worldview, rooted in real pain, their instinct is that the Bible is the source for male chauvinism, whereas it is quite otherwise. Such feminists often argue that Genesis 2:18-25 treats women as second-class, or even as an afterthought. But this is because post-biblical and current assumptions are brought to bear on the story. For example, the idea of "helper" can be wrongly viewed as subordinate and not equal.

74. To what extent is a feminist painful reaction to a misrepresented Scripture parallel to an "ultimate restoration" universalist's reaction to a misrepresented Scripture?

Such pagan feminists challenge the Genesis text, saying that since Eve is created last, she is therefore an inferior afterthought in the minds of the male chauvinists who are said to have written the story that assumes a male god. But this reading of the text has a foreign concept of chronology and moral order – that somehow the first is best, and the last is least.

In contrast, the whole thrust of Genesis 1 is that Elohim starts with the most remote and inanimate portions of the universe, then systematically orders everything as he moves up to more and more complex life forms, and when all is done, when the habitat is prepared for the crown of his creation, Elohim makes man and woman to govern and steward it all. But man is not fully male without woman, nor is woman fully female without man.

Paul says that man is "the image and glory of God; but the woman is the glory of man" (1 Corinthians 11:7). There is a symbiosis in place here. Man and woman together equal the image of God; yet in the making of man first, and showing his need for woman, she is his glory. And this is powerful language, since man is God's glory, the one in whom he delights, and woman's glory is that in which man delights. The power to give accrues and gives honor to the woman as the completion of the glory of the image of God.

As well, in the order of creation, Yahweh is always aiming at completion; thus, with the passing days of creation, he repeatedly states it is "good" as completion is achieved. With Adam in Genesis 2, Yahweh says it is "not good" for him to be alone – goodness is not achieved until the image of Yahweh Elohim is complete, until woman is made. Woman completes what lacks in man, so that together they equal mankind. When man and woman are finally standing side-by-side, as creation is complete, it is "very good."

Another concern raised by pagan feminists is the idea that the woman is made from one of Adam's "ribs." Thus, since woman is made from man, it is argued that she must be subordinate and of less worth in the eyes of the biblical writer. However, the language is otherwise. It can be looked at this way: If we had the choice, which would we prefer – to be made from human flesh and bone, or to be made from a pile of dry earth? After all, Eve is made from human tissue, and Adam comes directly from the dust.

In most translations, the word "rib" is used for what Yahweh takes out of Adam to make Eve. The Hebrew word is *tselah*, which means "an aspect of the personality." "Rib" is an accurate word for "an aspect" or "part" of Adam's person in physical terms, but I have chosen a more literal translation, "part." Eve is made from Adam to indicate her union with him,

202

her complementary equality, with no view toward a divisive understanding of woman at war with man that later comes with the fallout of human sin. Whether, in the case of Yahweh forming Adam out of the dust, or of Yahweh forming Eve out of her husband's body, in both cases it involves Yahweh's direct creative action.

Genesis 1:27 identifies their theological union as joint image-bearers, and Genesis 2 identifies their physical union as it shows us the order in which they are created to serve the initiative and reciprocity of the power to give. Genesis 2:7 gives us the explicit language of Yahweh Elohim breathing the breath of life into Adam; and though 2:21-22 does not explicitly say that of Eve, it is implicitly required by the structure of the text. And given the unity of man and woman in their creation in 1:26-28, this is further ratified.

Eve is an image-bearer, a needed helper for her otherwise incomplete husband, formed by Yahweh's direct work, and presented to Adam as a living breathing person. Yahweh Elohim breathes of his Spirit directly into Eve as he does with Adam. Also, the only difference between the dust of the ground and one of Adam's "ribs" or "parts" is that of molecular organization. Man and woman are both made from the same stuff of the universe, and we are distinguished from the rest of creation by the image of Elohim breathed into us.

When Adam awakes from his sleep and views Eve, we have the first poem in human history. Adam sees his helper, his complement, his equal. And as some like to say, a rough paraphrase of this poem is "Wow!" Adam has just named the animals, and in the process, realizes he is uniquely an image-bearer of Yahweh Elohim, and that all other creatures are not. The image of Yahweh Elohim within him – with the gifts of creativity, intelligence, choice, aesthetics and dexterity – need an equal and complementary partner with whom he also shares these gifts.

In the Genesis 1:26-28 passage, Adam and Eve are called to "rule" the work of creation together, under Elohim and for their joy. In the words "fill and subdue," we see a phrase that defines the inclusive spheres of rule for Adam and Eve. "Inclusive" means that Elohim gives to Adam and Eve unique dimensions not replicated in each other, so that true complementarity is possible.

By the same token, there is much overlap in gifts and nature between the man and woman, so that the spheres of rule are not "exclusive" domains. Men and women are equally human, men and women are different, and men and women need each other for a shared humanity. This balance is uniquely provided for in the biblical language.

"Filling and subduing" the earth refers to the dimensions of procreation and to the cultivating of the Garden of Eden to enjoy its fruit, and hence, to cultivate the planet, to build civilization. An inclusive and mutually submissive reality can be seen by the comparison of the muscular strengths between man and woman. The woman's greatest exertion of strength is in her uterine and thigh muscles, and this strength is taxed most in pregnancy and childbirth, in need for the critical moments. The man's greatest exertion of strength is in his shoulders and biceps, this strength is taxed most in heavy labor such as moving boulders, and built for endurance. A man cannot give birth or natural succor to a child; and a woman qua woman cannot lift nearly as much weight as can a man. But a man can hold an infant close in comfort – as a man. And a woman can do hard and diligent physical labor – as a woman. The distinctives remain.

This complementarity is seen in Genesis 2:7 and 2:22. In 2:7, when Yahweh Elohim "formed" the man from the dust, the verb employed is *yetzer*. The idea reflects Yahweh as the divine Potter, forming Adam literally from the clay, the red earth, or from the raw materials as it were. In 2:22, when Yahweh builds the woman from the man's substance, the verb employed is *banah*. It does not begin with the raw materials, but begins with the formed substance already in place. A suitable analogy is to compare the outward building of a house, beginning with the hewing of the lumber from the trees, in the forming of Adam, on the one hand; with the inner finishing of the house, as with beautification details such as furnishings and artwork, in the forming of Eve, on the other.

As we have already seen in *nephesh*, the human soul is by definition needful of Yahweh Elohim's original and continued provisions. His breath provides Adam with his original breath. Also, it means that the human body is a good gift, meant to live forever. Thus, human strength starts with the power to receive and be needful of Yahweh Elohim's power to give.

In reflecting on *nephesh*, we see the mutual dependency as designed by Yahweh Elohim. In the order of creation, it is the strength of the man to do the heavy labor, to work as the provider who builds the house and shelters his family from climatic extremes. In the order of creation, it is the strength of the woman in pregnancy, childbirth and succor to build the family that lives in the house. These are inclusive spheres of rule – to "fill and subdue" is a whole unit that requires a whole marriage unit to accomplish it. And when these spheres are honored, all subsequent blessings come. Men work inside the home and women work outside the home in many overlapping functions, but according to their God-given natures, not in contrast to them, and always in service to the home. No atomistic exclusivity.

In the Greek, the word for "household" is *oikos*, and the "rule of the household" is *oikonomos*, from whence we derive the word "economics." The married household with children is the original economic engine, where both husband and wife are joint partners in the true economy. Before the Industrial Revolution, more proximity and interface was possible; since then, it is a different and ever complicating matter as the nuclear and extended family units are increasingly fractured.

This is important to understand, if we want to change the language of the abortion debate. When I was studying for my Th.M. in Ethics and Public Policy at Harvard Divinity School, I interacted with many feminists who believed in abortion rights. And they thought that the God of the Bible was a male chauvinist, and such a wrong view of the text needs to be remedied.

Harvard psychologist Carol Gilligan published her influential book in 1982, *In a Different Voice*. It changed the feminist movement with her clinical observations that women think differently than men, and accordingly, models for healthy psychologies cannot be made to apply to girls if the only studies were done on boys – as the reigning psychological paradigm of Lawrence Kohlberg then assumed. She thus addresses the abortion question from the woman's relational priority, opposite male insensitivity.

But Gilligan, despite some good analysis, and in view of Kohlberg's imbalance, says that the problem "all goes back, of course, to Adam and Eve – a story which shows, among other things, that if you make a woman out of a man, you are bound to get into trouble. In the life cycle, as in the Garden of Eden, the woman has become the deviant" (p. 6).

Gilligan's comment about the nature of Adam and Eve and the Garden of Eden is unfortunately the norm among many scholars. Such an assumption then influences those who read these scholars, which translates into the influencing of the cultural elite who determine so much of what assumptions are filtered for the rest of society to hear. Thus, public perception and public policy are affected – many times against the better instincts and common sense of the population at large.

Somewhere in her training, Gilligan accepted an item of biblical "eisegesis" (a word that refers to placing something into the source, pretending it was there all along, then discovering it later; it is the opposite of "exegesis," which refers to discovering what is truly in the source to begin with). That is, this reflects some woman's interpretation of the text that comes not from an understanding of the Bible on its own terms, but from refracting the Bible through the myopia of sin and brokenness. And the chief sin here is that of male chauvinism, where too many girls grow up not seeing the power to give in their father (or father-figure when need be), and thus they cannot see the power to give in God the Father in the biblical witness.

Another way to sum up this balance is to say that the man naturally leads in task-orientation, and the woman naturally leads in relationship-building. A mutual submission to this reality leads to healthy marriages and a healthy society. A mutual submission to the power to give.

Earlier we noted the four definitive subjects in Genesis 1-2:

> The order of creation = God → life → choice → sex;
> The reversal = sex → choice → life →/God.

And as Satan, the ancient serpent, seeks to reverse the order of creation, we see his agenda. There is also another order and reversal in place:

> The order of creation = Yahweh → (Adam & Eve) → serpent;
> The reversal = serpent → (Eve → Adam) →/Yahweh.

Genesis 3:1-7 reads:

> Now the serpent was craftier than any of the living land creatures
> Yahweh Elohim had made. And he said angrily to the woman, "Did
> Elohim really say, 'You must not eat from any tree in the garden'?"
>
> The woman said to the serpent, "We may eat fruit from the trees in
> the garden, but Elohim did say, 'You must not eat fruit from the tree
> that is in the middle of the garden, and you must not touch it, or you
> shall die.' "
>
> So the serpent said to the woman, "In dying you shall not
> continually die, for Elohim knows that in the day you eat of it your
> eyes will be opened, and you will be like Elohim, knowing good and
> evil."
>
> When the woman saw the fruit of the tree was good for food and
> desirable to the eye, and desirable for gaining wisdom, she took some
> some and ate it. She also gave some to her husband, who was with
> her, and he ate it. Then the eyes of the two of them were opened, and
> they knew they were naked; so they sewed leaves of a fig tree
> together and made loin coverings for themselves.

The ancient serpent approaches Eve alone, a deliberate strategy to divorce her unity with Adam in making decisions. In other words, it is a calculated assault on marriage. The devil is also masquerading as a member of the animal kingdom, thus assaulting the governing authority of the image of Yahweh Elohim.

His question is perverse and angry. Anger always has a history, but that begs a deeper discussion on the origins of the devil, about which I write elsewhere. In the literal Hebrew, the word for nose (*nagap*) is also the word for anger. The serpent "gets in Eve's face" as it were. He is challenging Yahweh Elohim with a false question ("Did Elohim really say …?"), followed by a deliberate misquote of what Yahweh Elohim actually did say. The devil is marking out a false prohibition, trying to get the woman to agree with the prohibition of the good (!) and its freedom, thus agreeing with the evil (the earliest form of syncretism and dualism in history), in saying that Elohim is prohibiting Eve from eating from "any tree in the garden." No, it is only the one tree that is prohibited, the poisonous one, in order that Adam and Eve can live free.

In the gospels, many religious elitists who oppose Jesus are said by him to have as their "father, the devil," with the devil also being called "the father of lies" (John 8:44). So the devil is a liar in the Garden, and in Matthew 19:1-9, a group of Pharisees does the same. They seek to trap Jesus on the matter of divorce, asking: "Is it lawful for a man to release his wife for any reason?" They know this is a false question, just as the ancient serpent uses the word "any" for the purpose of distortion:

> He answered them, "Haven't you read that at the beginning the Creator made them male and female? And for this reason, a man will leave his father and mother and cleave to his wife, and the two will become one flesh? So they are no longer two, but one. Therefore, what God has joined together, let man not separate."

In his answer, Jesus unites the language of the grand design of male and female in Genesis 1, with the specific covenant of marriage in Genesis 2. The devil and this group of Pharisees use the same tactics to avoid a proper definition of terms, and Jesus says no to any attempt to divide a married couple, whether by the ancient serpent or by the Pharisees.

Yet the Pharisees persist:

> They said to him, "Why then did Moses command that a man give his wife a certificate of divorce and release her?"

> Jesus replied, "Moses permitted you, in the hardness of your hearts, to release your wives. But from the beginning it was not so. I tell you that anyone who releases his wife, except for fornication, and marries another woman, commits adultery."

Again, they lie in a slippery way. Moses makes no such command, but only allows divorce in the case of fornication (*porneia* in the Greek, any sexual encounter outside of marriage, or broken trust relating to emotional or physical violence). In the Sermon on the Mount, Jesus intensifies this reality of *porneia* with stronger language yet: "But I tell you that anyone who looks at a woman lustfully has already committed adultery with her in his heart" (Matthew 5:28). As we return momentarily to the reversal in Genesis 3, we will see how the original definition of sin is that of broken trust. The word in Matthew for lust is *epithumeo*, "to sexually desire" a woman, thus broken trust, broken union in marriage is the essence. The English word for "pornography" comes from the Greek roots of *porneia* and *graphe* (writing), namely, words or pictures that incite lust. Porn destroys marriage, and dehumanizes and reifies people at the same time, no matter what form it takes. It causes immense suffering for the innocent as well as the guilty parties.

And before the Pharisees persist in their deceit with Jesus, so had the ancient serpent beforehand – their very model. The woman gives an honest answer about her freedom to eat the good fruit, alongside the prohibition of the poisonous fruit, even intensifying the prohibition, "and you must not touch it." Eve learns the original words of the prohibition, in communication with Adam, since they were spoken before she was created, and also in communication with Yahweh thereafter.

There is a season when they are one flesh, thus being mature enough to give answer and rule over the ancient serpent when he comes calling. Eve is free to add her own words faithfully reflecting the truth, or the intensifier was spoken by Yahweh to them at another time. This is an assumption the text virtually requires, and as we read the Bible, we will see this often, where Yahweh Elohim invests in us as his image-bearers the ability to read the storyline and understand deeper assumptions and connections.

So, the ancient serpent again lies, and here is the reversal:

> In Genesis 2:17, Yahweh says *moth tamuth*, "in dying you shall continually die."

> In Genesis 3:4, the ancient serpent says *lo moth t'muthon*, "in dying you shall not continually die."

The ancient serpent calls the words of Yahweh Elohim a lie, and quite transparently and brashly so (the nature of anger). He simply places a negative in front of Yahweh's words (*lo*). Thus, the grammatical power of the infinitive absolute imperfect tense rendered "in dying you shall continually die" is literalistically "not in dying you shall continually die"! Quite the oxymoron.

How then does Eve succumb? The ancient serpent strategically succeeds in getting her to respond to him without consulting Yahweh or her husband. She is somehow isolated in her attention, and thus without the wisdom that communication within God-given unity and checks and balances of a healthy marriage brings. Then an unchecked desire enters her soul and she eats of the forbidden fruit.

Where is Adam? He is "with her." So how does it happen? In consideration of the "in your face" anger (*nagap*) reality in the serpent's original approach to Eve (verse 1), my best plausibility is to imagine a hushed anger of the devil, trying not to be overheard, and perhaps using natural noise distraction as well, timing it just right in the presence of rushing water or a rushing wind, or maybe something in the Garden is positively distracting Adam's attention. Or perhaps Adam does hear something, is uncurious, or in some fashion proactively fails simultaneously in not guarding (*shamar*) the garden and his wife.

Regardless, what should Eve have done? She could have, consciously in the presence of the living Yahweh Elohim, and in the strength of union with her husband, given Adam a pre-lapsarian nudge, and said: "Honey, there is something fishy going on here [pardon an import of a later metaphor]. There is a talking snake calling Yahweh Elohim a liar, and telling me to disobey him and eat the forbidden fruit."

If we grasp the power to give as the nature of true authority, and what it means to "rule" the animal kingdom, Adam's response would have been simple. He should have interrogated the serpent, and then judged it by crushing its head, his heel coming down in force, for rebelling against Yahweh and man. And since Adam would not have eaten the fruit, the sin could be atoned for by simple repentance on Eve's part, and the unity of man and woman would have remained unbroken. But instead, Adam acts independently of Yahweh and his wife by not asking him or her about the source of the fruit. And given the proximity they have to the tree of the knowledge of good and evil, and their experience in eating other fruit, Adam knows better. The fault is fully mutual.

The net result is this:

The woman acts independently of Yahweh and of Adam;
The man acts independently of Yahweh and Eve.

Trust is broken vertically between both of them and their Creator, and horizontally between themselves as husband and wife, fellow image-bearers of Yahweh Elohim. Jesus, in summing up as the Law of Moses, heals the broken trust by empowering us to love God and one another, reversing the reversal both vertically and laterally as cause and effect necessitate.

Thus, we see the original definition of "sin" (a word not used here but later): namely, broken trust.

The seriousness of this broken trust is seen in understanding the Hebrew language in vv. 8-10.

And they heard the thunder of Yahweh Elohim marching into the garden in the Spirit-driven storm of the moment, and the man and the woman hid from Yahweh Elohim in the trees of the garden.

But Yahweh Elohim called to the man and said, "Where do you belong?" He answered, "I heard your thunder in the garden, and I was afraid because I was naked; so I hid."

- All this material on man and woman sets the stage for us grasping, in appropriate depth, the beginning point for the judgment of Yahweh Elohim on sin. And from here, we can see it across Scripture, as *moth tamuth* metastasizes, from Noah's flood to Sodom and Gomorrah to the Canaanites to the Babylonian exile to the woes pronounced by Jesus upon his unrepentant elitist enemies to the summation by Paul in Romans 1 to the trajectory in the Book of Revelation.

- Broken marriage is hell – in both man and woman, and in the eschatological refusal to attend the wedding supper of the Lamb, as the church is his bride.

75. How can any "ultimate restoration" universalist speak of hell, in even the smallest sense, apart from understanding the depth and seriousness of this biblical storyline?

In so many translations, verse 8 is rendered something like: "The man and his wife heard the sound of the LORD God as walking in the garden in the cool of the day." This leads to all sorts of silliness. As though the Creator of the universe were out for his morning or evening stroll, and just happens to casually call out to the man to see where he is.

The Hebrew text tells a very different story. The word for "sound" is *qol*, and it can mean anything from a whisper to a thunderclap, depending on context, and often translated as "voice."

The word for "walking" is from *halak*, an act of going that can mean anything from a tiptoe to a military march, depending on context.

There is no word "cool" in the Hebrew text, and much speculation as to how it got there. The word for "breeze" is *ruach*, it is the term for wind or spirit (including the Holy Spirit), and can range in meaning from a breeze to a hurricane or tornado. Perhaps some translator, many centuries past, first had in mind a pristine Garden of Eden, and took the *ruach* as a "cool breeze."

Finally, the word for "day" is *yom*, a word marking time that can range in meaning from a moment to eons, but most commonly as a "day."

Thus, a wooden and sterile translation could be, "And they heard the sound of Yahweh Elohim as he was going in the garden in the wind of the time." In Hebrew, context determines how best to translate a given word.

So, what is the context here? Yahweh promises in Genesis 2:17 that in the *yom* (the day, even the very moment) Adam eats of the forbidden fruit, death will enter the creation. This is the largest possible disruption, as the ancient serpent lies about the very language. So Yahweh is not caught off guard, rather he is completely aware of what has just happened. Nor is Adam caught off guard – he and Eve are hiding from the thunderous approach of Yahweh who promised immediate judgment on what they know they have just done. And as evidenced in how they are now ashamed of their prior naked freedom, and seek to cover it up. Yet still, Yahweh uses the power to ask a hard question of Adam, as questions produce ownership of the answers.

Thus, I have translated it: "And the man and his wife heard the thunder of Yahweh Elohim marching into the garden in the Spirit-driven storm of the moment."

- The judgment is thunderous and echoes across Scripture until it is finally sealed in the abyss.

Translation matters, and thus we grasp why Adam and Eve are hiding, why Adam is afraid. The wrath of Yahweh Elohim is upon them like a freight train of enormous proportion, a category 5 tornado. They are no longer free in their nakedness in the sight of Yahweh Elohim and one another. The ancient serpent succeeds in causing the great rift, the great divorce. And he gains the driver's seat through dishonest language, just as does the pro-abortion advocacy today.

This rift is immediately seen in the subsequent text as Adam answers Yahweh by dishonestly blaming Eve (he knew the fruit he was eating), and then Eve honestly answers the Lord by confessing that she was deceived by the serpent. Then the devil, in his serpent masquerade, is cursed by Yahweh to live like such an animal, and the prophecy of the devil's demise follows:

And I will put an imposition between you and the woman,
  and between your seed and hers;
  he will crush your head, and you will bruise his heel (3:15).

This is the first Messianic prophecy, and is fulfilled on the cross as Jesus brings his heel down on the devil's head, his very authority (see Colossians 2:15) while also, just before the crushing, the ancient serpent strikes poison into the heel. Jesus comes as the "second Adam" to pronounce judgment on the devil as Adam failed to do. The focus is on how, at every level, the devil's agenda was, and still is, to crush the union of marriage between man and woman in striking against, seeking to bruise, Yahweh.

Immediately thereafter, Yahweh pronounces the curses on the woman and man, and it is in the curse on the woman where we see the burden of a broken marriage:

> I will greatly increase your pains in pregnancy;
> with pain you will give birth to sons.
> Your desire will be for your husband,
> and he will govern you (3:16).

The word for "desire" is *shuq*, and can also be translated as "longing." and the verb for "govern" is *mashal*, the first verb given for "governing" in Genesis (1:16), where stewardship of the good creation is in order, and where the Garden is to be guarded from the intrusion of the ancient serpent. *shuq* and *mashal* are likewise used in Genesis 4:7, where Yahweh says to an angry Cain, "Sin is crouching at your door; it desires to have you, but you must govern it." But context determines usage in Hebrew. The language for Cain is that of a leopard ready to pounce, "desiring" and "longing" to devour Cain, just as the devil is profiled as a lion on the prowl (see 1 Peter 5:8).

But in Genesis 3:16, the contextual usage is very different ahead of 4:7, with opposite purpose. Adam and Eve, with the broken trust now sown into their souls, are nonetheless image-bearers of Yahweh Elohim looking forward to the coming Redeemer. They have yet to hear of their exile from the Garden, their souls are trembling in the face of the judgment, sensing they have polluted the good Garden, and will thus lose its blessings in some capacity. They have broken trust with Yahweh.

Thus, they naturally cling to each other, and too, use human reasoning to plot how they might now build a life together. So given their complementary but now broken strengths, and in balance of the right and left half sides of the brain, Eve desires and longs for unity with her husband, saying, as it were, "Just hold me tight, and we will be one." Her

214

leading desire is relational. Adam responds, as it were, "Just do as I say and all will be well." His leading desire is task oriented.

They each think in terms of how they can resolve the fracture in a "power to take" mode, not in the power to give to the other first. The woman does not want to rule over the man, rather, she wants to be one with him. But she will do it her way. The man does not want to rule over her, he wants to protect her. But he will do it his way. However, neither will work, as the rest of biblical history painfully demonstrates.

With Adam's failure to cherish his wife and guard the Garden from the intrusion of the ancient serpent, the door is opened for inchoate then full-blown male chauvinism. Violence first erupts as Cain murders Abel in the first generation from Adam. Cain becomes a wanderer from his parents as a result, builds a city, and as the seventh generation reaches Lamech, marriage suffers another assault as violence is combined with bigamy:

> Lamech took two women, one named Adah and the other Zillah. Adah gave birth to Jabal; he was the father of those who dwell in tents and raise livestock. The name of his brother was Tubal; he was the father of all who play the harp and flute. Zillah also had a son, Tubal-Cain, who hammered tools out of copper, bronze and iron. Tubal-Cain's sister was Naamah.

> Lamech said to his women:
> "Adah and Zillah, listen to me;
>   wives of Lamech, weigh my speech.
> For I have killed a man for bruising me,
>   a youth for striking me.
> If Cain is avenged seven times,
>   then Lamech seventy-seven times" (4:19-24).

- Cain to Lamech on forward sets social hell into motion.

The biblical text is carefully written, all building on prior assumptions and storyline. Here we have the first example of bigamy, and the paving of the way toward full blown polygamy. It happens in the context of building civilization, but on a broken foundation. Thus, male chauvinism rears its ugly head, and women are treated as property. Along with the technicalities in grammar and syntax, all languages have their moods and tonalities, and to grasp them, it requires a depth of swimming within the given language and its cultural context.

Here, Lamech "takes" (the verb is *laqah*) two "women" (*nashim*) which can also be translated "wives," for in antiquity, when a man sleeps with a woman, they are considered married. We see Lamech leering over Adah and Zillah, as it were: "Listen up, you who belong to me." The ancient serpent shows self-righteous anger as he seeks destroys the marriage of Adam and Eve, Cain is downcast with anger and thus kills his brother, and here we can sense Lamech's tone rooted in the self-righteous anger of misogyny. Now the word choices, grammar and mood make this evident. But as well, this is seen as a continued repudiation of the order of creation. The man and woman are to be one in marriage. To "marry" two women simultaneously pollutes such unity, introduces conflict, and per force, treats women as property. It is literally the action of *laqah*, the power to take.

This violates women, and to protect his "estate," Lamech is willing to kill those who bruise him, regardless of age. Lamech will make sure anyone who kills or injures him will be avenged 77 times, making himself that much greater than Yahweh in his own pretense, as Yahweh promises to avenge Cain seven times in Genesis 4:15. Lamech also destroys the lives and properties of any and all associated with such a person, claiming divine prerogative for vengeance, and rooted in the chauvinism of bigamy and the murder of young men. He is his own god, choosing to yearn after the forbidden fruit.

The ancient serpent assaults marriage in the Garden, the second generation instigates murder, the seventh generation reifies women in further assault on marriage, and in the same breath, intensifies murder and revenge. The assumptions in the storyline are clear: immediate and huge consequence to sin. Namely, the destruction of the social order follows, that which was originally rooted in the mutual trust of one man and one woman married in mutual fidelity.

In the subsequent verses in Genesis 4, we read:

Adam knew his wife again, and she gave birth to a son and named him Seth, saying, "because Elohim has given me another seed in place of Abel, because Cain killed him." And Seth himself had a son, and he named him Enosh. At that time men began to call on the name of Yahweh (vv. 25-26).

In Eve's voice, we can sense the pain and hope. The pain of losing the second son from her womb (the greater pain of the curse on childbirth made ten thousand times worse), and now the hope placed in another son in his stead.

Thus, from Cain to Lamech we see the outworking of sin, the unfaithful lineage governed by the ancient serpent. Then, with the birth of Seth we see the contrasting lineage, the faithful line that leads to the Messiah from the offspring of Eve. This is marked by the note that, with the arrival of Seth and Enosh, men begin (again) to call on the name of Yahweh. That is, moving from just a Gentile acknowledgement of the Elohim of creation, to the covenant-keeping Name of Yahweh.

These are the "unfaithful" and "faithful" lineages. Cain's line shows what happens when unfaithfulness to Yahweh governs the social order, where men set themselves up as their own gods, defining good and evil in their own self-aggrandizing terms. Seth's line, in contrast, is rooted in an acknowledgement of *nephesh* and thus his lineage calls on Yahweh in faith, trusting in his goodness. All that follows in the Hebrew Bible is rooted in this assumption of contrasting lineages, with the emphasis on that which leads to the Messiah.

We earlier referenced Genesis 5:1-5. In vv. 3-5, we read:

When Adam had lived 130 years, he had a son in his own likeness and image; and he named him Seth. After Seth was born, Adam lived 800 years and bore other sons and daughters. In all, Adam lived 930 years, and then he died.

Now that the Messianic lineage is introduced for the redemption of mankind, the very language of the order of creation is restated. It involves the centrality of male and female, and then most powerfully, the explicit passing on of the image of Yahweh Elohim through Adam, even in spite of human sin. The broken remains of this image is the platform for Yahweh's redemptive work. And redemption is thus hugely concerned with male and female in marriage. No matter how deeply sin has broken mankind, the love and redemptive power of Yahweh Elohim is deeper yet. From this point, the rest of Genesis 5 traces the faithful lineage all the way to Noah (nine generations from Adam) – in contrast to the seven generations through Cain to Lamech.

Genesis 6:1-12 reads:

> When man began to multiply on the face of the earth, and daughters were born to them, the sons of the gods saw that the daughters of men were a good thing, and they took any woman they chose. So Yahweh said, "My Spirit will not be with mankind for a long duration, for he is flesh, and his days will be a hundred and twenty years."

> The Nephilim were on the earth in those days, and afterward, when the sons of the gods went to the daughters of men and bore children. They were the mighty men of antiquity, men of renowned name.

> Yahweh saw how great mankind's evil on the earth had become, And that all the thoughts of his mind and will were altogether evil all the day long. Yahweh was sorry that he had made the man in the earth, and his heart was pained. So Yahweh said, "I will blot out the man, whom I have created, from the face of the ground – man and animal, and ground creatures, and creatures of the heavens – for I am sorry that I have made them." But Noah found favor in the eyes of Yahweh.

> These are the generations of Noah.

> Noah was a just man, of sound judgment among the people of his time, and Noah walked with Elohim. Noah had three sons: Shem, Ham and Japheth.

> Now the earth was marred in face of Elohim, and the ground was full of violence. Elohim saw, behold, how corrupt the earth had

become, for all flesh on earth had corrupted their ways.

- The visitation of hell for those who refuse Noah.

76. So why does Yahweh not say to those in Noah's Day: "I am only judging you now, but hang in there, I will persuade you after the final Judgment that you made a bad choice?"

This also segues into an argument for an "ultimate restoration" universalism. Namely, for those who refuse the preaching of Noah, Jesus preaches to them after his crucifixion.

77. But to what end?

Scripture shows that the final Judgment is final, but here we have those who receive one more preaching before that Day. Remarkable patience on the part of God, but still with an endpoint where he discerns those who will forsake their idols, from those who choose to guard their idols forever.

The trajectory of Genesis 1-5 hits a painful apex here in the destruction of marriage and human civilization. The "sons of the gods" in v. 2 is an ancient near eastern term, here designating self-aggrandizing sons of human kings who claim to be gods (cf. Psalm 82). Adam and Seth are sons of Elohim literally (see Genesis 5:1-3; Luke 3:38), but submit to his power to give.

As human population becomes quite substantial, such "god-men" use their positions of top-down power to build harems – they "take" as many women as they choose, women who are "daughters of men," including women from the "non-royal" social order. In the Hebrew, a man having sex with a woman means literally "to marry" her. The union of man and woman, once consummated, forever changes the dynamics between them. If marriage is rooted in the mutual fidelity of one man and one woman for one lifetime, it is "very good." Breaking this life-giving boundary of freedom portends great evil.

So here, we see male chauvinism at a new threshold of polygamy – wholesale reification of women, property to be hoarded and walled off. The marriage of one man and one woman in mutual fidelity is mocked, and thus, women and their children suffer the most. Yahweh thus declares a one-hundred and twenty-year timeline until the judgment of the Flood, during which Noah preaches the coming judgment on mankind (cf. 2 Peter 2:5), but still, no one listens outside his immediate family.

The text then notes the Nephilim (proper Hebrew name for the "fallen ones"). They are the descendants of these harem building kings, with wealth, power and exploits, whose family line and reputations span the generations, and whose lineage survives the Flood through Noah's daughters-in-law. The earth is full of non-stop evil thoughts, and all forms of evil, corruption and violence – the exact lineage of Cain through Lamech. The building of harems is the epitome of it all.

With sin having become the cultural norm, Yahweh Elohim is determined to work with the most faithful, with the "remnant." This is his purpose for Seth's line, which leads to Noah, a just man with sound wisdom, so easily distinguishable in that day. Also, he is a) a true son of Yahweh Elohim who walks with his heavenly Father, b) clearly a leader, and c) maintains fidelity in his marriage.

In Genesis 9, following the Flood, conflict emerges between Noah's sons as Ham (the father of Canaan) mocks his father Noah who lay in his tent naked after having become drunk. A curse lands on Canaan, and it is the Canaanites who later excel in sorcery (treating the sun, moon and stars as sexually promiscuous gods and goddesses, in a fatalistic dependency on them); followed by sacred prostitution and child sacrifice (pre-parallel to human abortion), all in a deeper affront to marriage and life.

In Genesis 10, the table of nations is detailed, where pagan nations trace their origins from Japheth and Ham. Those who come from Shem are the Semites, out of whom Abraham and the Hebrews come, the line of the Messiah. A new round of the unfaithful and faithful lineages emerges.

In Genesis 11, the Tower of Babel, an astrological ziggurat, is built at the center of a city in a human attempt to reach "the heavens," that is, for man to build civilization on his own terms, as self-appointed "gods," in the line of Cain and Lamech (now through the Nephilim), over and against

Yahweh. The Babylonian genesis is rooted here, and its assumptions of sexually promiscuous, violent and murderous gods and goddesses. The history and subsequent metaphor of Babylon is a major theme across the Bible, and concludes as emblematic for all rebellion against God in Revelation 18, the great demonic prostitute. The assault on marriage continues relentlessly.

The proactive of Genesis 1-2 is the Creator, Yahweh Elohim.

The reactive is originally expressed in what is known as the Babylonian Genesis (aka *Enuma Elish*), written about the tenth century B.C. (the time of King David), but in oral tradition goes back centuries before that. The opening chapters of Genesis trace in written form to Moses in the middle of the fifteenth century B.C. as part of the Pentateuch, but trace back in written and oral forms to Adam in the early fourth millennium B.C.

Now for some logic.

Can something be destroyed that is not first created? This is the dilemma of pagan religion. There are two ways to define the existence of the universe and human life – through creation or destruction.

On the one hand is creation in the biblical Genesis, in which the eternal Yahweh Elohim is good, creation is good and human life is good. On the other hand, the oldest and most influential of ancient pagan origin stories, the Babylonian Genesis, starts with destruction, with no concept of original or final goodness. It assumes, but does not explain, the existence of finite, petty, jealous and sexually promiscuous gods and goddesses who beat up on each other and beat up on us. It assumes that the heavens and earth are created by one god, but out of an act of destruction, and out of prior undefined eternal matter.

This is also known as "dualism" – the most ancient non-biblical concept. Creation and destruction are seen as the opposite sides of the same coin; and likewise with good and evil (contra Genesis 2:9-17). Accordingly, there is no original and greater goodness that will triumph over evil in the end.

But how can Babylonian religion and paganism make any sense? Does not the power to destroy require a prior power to create what is then destroyed? Unless the gods, goddesses and their undefined habitat are first created, where does it all begin? All pagan origin stories cannot resolve this dilemma, and thus they ratify the uniqueness of the biblical Genesis. Secular humanism and atheism, both philosophical and ethical cognates of the older pagan religions, cannot resolve this dilemma either. And neither can Islam, which is outside of the creation → sin → redemption motif.

Which satisfies the human soul – creation or destruction?

In the Babylonian Genesis, the power to take before being taken is assumed from the outset, and it precedes and defines all. It cannot compare with three key assumptions in the biblical order of creation:

1. Yahweh Elohim is the eternal and good Creator.
2. The creation is ordered and good.
3. Man and woman are the crown of Yahweh Elohim's good creation and made free.

In contrast, three key assumptions of the Babylonian Genesis are these:

1. *Marduk* (the key chief Babylonian deity) is finite and destructive.
2. The creation is rootless, chaotic and evil.
3. Man and woman are a by-product intended for slavery.

The Babylonian Genesis starts with the assumption of a pantheon of time-bound, sexually promiscuous and pre-existent gods and goddesses, engaging in an intramural and internecine warfare. A second-level deity at the outset, *Marduk*, creates the universe by killing the chief goddess *Tiamat*, and dissecting her body – splitting it open like a mussel shell, making the heavens with one half of her carcass, and the earth with the other half. He then makes the defeated gods of *Tiamat's* army into slaves, but they complain about this status. In response, *Marduk* kills his chief remaining opponent, *Kingu*, severs his arteries, and from his blood *Marduk* creates mankind to serve as slaves to the defeated pantheonic remnant of *Tiamat* and *Kingu's* army.

Here we see the assumption of destruction. Mankind has to serve as slaves to the whims and caprice of defeated gods and goddesses, revealing a remarkably low view of man and woman. The Babylonians think they are bound by the positions of the sun, moon, planets and stars as gods (idolatry and astrology) in mundane and important decisions. They are bound to try and wrest favors from their fatalisms (sorcery). At the extreme in many related religions, they feel compelled to make human sacrifice to placate the gods – to gain fertility, good crops and peace, all in an attempt to survive in a hostile universe as they understand it.

But they also choose this worldview. Is our worth as human beings elevated or trashed by such a view? Do we take joy in a myth that the heavens and earth are made out of the dissected and bleeding carcass of a slaughtered goddess, and that we are made out of the blood of another dead god to be slaves to the defeated gods? Slaves to slaves? This is Babylon's height.

Babylonian religion starts with the assumption of destruction, then interjects a hope (of carving out survival) that is destined to disappoint, and it concludes with destruction remaining in its dualistic continuity. In other words, the reversal of Genesis 1-3:

destruction → disappointing hope → return to destruction, versus creation → sin → redemption.

Again, by definition, how can destruction precede creation? Destruction can only destroy what is already created. The Babylonian "genesis" is a reversal of reality.

Now, for a remarkable observation per our subject matter. In this myth, as *Marduk* dissects *Tiamat's* body, the text reads:

The lord rested, examining her dead body,
To divide the abortion (and) to create ingenious things (therewith).
He split her open like a mussel (?) into two parts;
Half of her he set in place and formed the sky (therewith) as a
    roof...
(Tablet IV, lines 135-138, translation of Alexander Heidel).

223

The word "abortion," an act of intrinsic destruction, is used here to describe *Tiamat*'s corpse. Her born life is aborted. Abortion is viewed as parallel to the corpse of one killed by an act of aggression, and as a means to create the universe. This is the Babylonian genesis versus Genesis in the Hebrew Bible.

All cultures eventually trace back to Genesis, to Adam's lineage at the first, then through Noah's lineage. As peoples migrate away from Eden, then away from earliest Mesopotamia – into an unpopulated, wild and wonderful world – and likewise later following Noah's flood, they gradually mix mythologies in with dimming recollections of Yahweh Elohim's revelation to Adam about creation.

Their oral traditions and written texts reflect a confusion of creation with destruction, despite their best hopes, since it is the only experience by which they can judge. And in a sinful world, with no faithful record of the order of creation at hand, destruction takes over – the power to take before being taken. Only in such a context and its influence can human abortion be rationalized. Thus, for reality and hope, we root ourselves in the opening good assumptions of Genesis 1-2.

Picking back up in Genesis 12, Abram (later called Abraham) is called by Yahweh as just about the one remaining non-idolater. He is promised a son through whom all nations will be blessed en route to the coming Messiah. But in Genesis 16, his wife Sarai (later called Sarah) gets impatient as their ages advance, and gives her maidservant Hagar to Abram to become his concubine, or second "wife" (literally again, "woman"). This is worse than straight bigamy, for Hagar has no marital or inheritance rights in view. Sarai is using her as a slave, and Abram foolishly agrees. This is a human attempt to fulfill Yahweh's promise, and though Abram's character far exceeds that of Cain and Lamech and Babel, he agrees with Sarai in an attempt to build civilization on sinful terms.

Thus, Hagar's womb is treated as Sarai's property, with Hagar as a disposable concubine who will not be allowed to rear her own son. Hagar realizes this when she becomes pregnant and thus despises Sarai. A war between the women ensues. When the angel of Yahweh comforts Hagar as she flees Sarai's mistreatment, he says of her unborn son Ishmael:

He will be a wild donkey of a man;
   his hand will be against all
   and everyone's hand against him,
   and in the face of his brothers he will dwell (16:12).

This is the quintessential profile of a fatherless boy (cf. Isaiah 1:17, representative of a consistent biblical concern). Sarai opposes Hagar when she returns after the angel speaks to her, and does not want Hagar's son in her life, or in Abram's life. So she clearly opposes the present and loving fatherhood Abram is eager to give. Isaac is born thirteen years later to Sarah, this time not by human manipulation and surrogacy, but by the intervention of the Holy Spirit. However, when Ishmael mocks the boy Isaac, he is driven away by Sarah. The war between the women becomes a war between the sons, and thus a war between the nations that come from both sons.

- Hell is visited on the world due an impatience for Yahweh's timetable, due to the resulting broken marriage covenant.

As the Arab peoples are descendants of Ishmael, and as Muhammad traces his lineage to Ishmael 2400 years later, and as we see the conflict of Islam versus the Jewish and Christian peoples to this day, we see it all rooted in the breaking of the marriage covenant.

The reputation of the evil of Sodom and Gomorrah is well known in its day (thus, a return to that which causes the Flood, a return to Cain's lineage). Abraham is apprised by Yahweh of its coming judgment, is able to intercede on their behalf, but in the end also sees their great evil. Sodom and Gomorrah is summed up across the whole biblical witness, from Genesis to Revelation, as sexual anarchy leading to social anarchy and the trampling of the poor and needy.

The sins of Sodom and Gomorrah are anteceded in Genesis 13:13, "Now the men of Sodom were evil and great sinners against Yahweh," and 18:20 speaks of the "outcry" against the city, a deeply pained anguish seeking help.

This sexual anarchy, being the most damning assault on marriage, is at play. In Genesis 19:1-5, two angels of Yahweh, appearing as men, come to Lot's house (nephew of Abraham) to evacuate him and his family from the coming destruction. Lot, sitting at the city gates, thus being an elder of sorts, invites them to lodge with him for the night:

> "No," they said, "we will lodge in the city square."

> But he pushed so forcefully that they came into his house. He made a feast for them, baking unleavened bread, and they ate. Before they laid down, men from the city of Sodom surrounded the house, young and old with all their relatives, near and distant. They called to Lot, "Where are the men who came to you tonight? Bring them out to us so that we can know them" (vv. 2b-5)

The Hebrew verb *yadha*, "to know," in some thirty out of about 830 usages in the Hebrew, refers to "sexual knowledge" (as in Genesis 4:1, 25). (vv. 2b-5). Lot knows how dangerous it is in the public square at night, but too, he is a compromised man who loves the city and its "culture" (despite knowing better, cf. 2 Peter 2:7). His thus foolishly seeks to avert the evil of a gang rape by at least hundreds, likely thousands of pansexual men. He offers, wickedly himself, to barter his two virgin (and engaged!) daughters to the Sodomites instead. His wife is so at home in the culture, that she then proves not to want to leave, and his sons-in-law think he is joking about the coming judgment, being unfazed by the attempted gang pansexual rape.

This same attempted pansexual gang rape of men is found, rooted in a lawless culture (Judges 19 at Gibeah), with evil results visited on innocent people, in an explosion of social and violent anarchy.

"Pansexuality" is a term that describes sexual relations with "any and all" possible partners, human or otherwise. Homosexuality is a subcategory, and here in Sodom it is not "homosexuals qua homosexuals" that seek the gang rape, but bisexuals or pansexuals who do so.

The reason why Sodom (and Gomorrah) becomes such a leading metaphor for wickedness, indeed, hell, from Genesis to Revelation, is seen here. From the ancient serpent to Cain to Lamech to the "sons of the gods" to Babel and now Sodom, the assault on marriage and the cognates of violence and murder are the result. Thus, the assumptions of creation → sin → redemption in Genesis 1-3, and the assumption of the goodness of the marriage of one man and one woman for one lifetime as the basis for a healthy social order, is seen to be continually under assault. After Genesis 19, across the whole biblical text, this reality is profiled a thousand different ways.

- A good question has been raised about Sodom in Matthew 11:13 – the possibility of their repentance had they seen the miraculous signs done by Jesus. Therefore, they receive a more bearable judgment in the end.

78. Is this not an argument for a form of purgatory that therefore equals an "ultimate restoration" universalism?

79. Is Jesus just using hyperbole to shame those who face-to-face rejected his loving miracles?

80. Or is there a reality for those in Sodom who were born into such a sinful culture that they did not have the ability see past their deception, and once they see Jesus, their hearts will respond differently?

81. What is the difference between the informed choice given in the Garden, the darkness of sin that follows on pagan cultures, and the informed choice Jesus is giving his hearers?

82. What is the reality of nephesh in such a scenario?

- In the end, I believe hell is a small oxymoronic community of those who stubbornly love bitterness more than mercy. The biblical storyline gives them the freedom to accordingly choose hell if they damn well love darkness more than light. They are loved by God in that they were free to reject his love despite the incarnation, cross and resurrection.

In the midst of it all, Yahweh calls Israel to be faithful to him alone, as her husband (cf. Isaiah 54:5; Jeremiah 3:20), and not prostitute themselves to pagan deities. And the church is the bride of Jesus, called to be pure in her fidelity to him (Revelation 21:2, 9). This divine metaphor of marital fidelity points to something much deeper than sex itself. Namely, unbroken trust as present in the triune God leads to the gift of unbroken trust in the marriage of Adam and Eve, and thus, as the basis for a healthy social order.

Thus, we have noted the proactive biblical assumptions in Genesis 1-2 about male and female as equals and complements in marriage, and as the source for trust and a healthy social order. Then we have noted how in Genesis 3, 4, 5, 6, 9-11, 16 and 19 it is a relentless downgrade. This sets up all that follows in the Bible, and child sacrifice and human abortion are cognates.

In my quote from Christine Overall earlier, I sought to identify core assumptions in the larger pagan and secular feminist construct that ratify it as a reaction to male chauvinism. Thus, as we grasp the good biblical assumptions, and the diagnosis of male chauvinism in its assault on marriage, is there any finer basis from which to answer such a human cry?

The eighth assumption is science and the scientific method.

Beginning with the assumption in Genesis 1:1, "In the beginning Elohim created the heavens and the earth," all else follows in human history and reality. Certainly so with scientific inquiry.

The debate over the days of creation rages within the church and in the face of the scientific community. As I write about elsewhere, the best exegetical grasp of Genesis 1 and the days of creation is that they are a literary and parallelistic framework to give eternal purpose to our literal weeks – the teleology of the Sabbath and eternal life. There is no chronological timetable per se (but certainly an order), nor are the days used in the Hebrew structure as 24-hour periods. Just as the metaphor of the human body describes the church in 1 Corinthians 12:12ff, so the literary device of the days of the week teaches us about the nature being created in the image of God, and how to order our literal weeks. *Not a biblical statement*

Genesis 1 is also structured where the universe is ordered from the most remote to the most immediate, from the lowest forms of life to the highest, *incorrect, octopus?* then with man and woman set to govern it all in stewardship of Elohim's goodness. Every form of life reproduces after its own kind, man and woman are made after Elohim's own kind, and there is no place for macroevolution. All of which merits the closet scientific inquiry and tough questions.

But where does science and the scientific method originate? "Observed reality" is what the discipline of "science" is all about. The Latin term *scientia* simply means knowledge. In every dimension, the Bible profiles knowledge and reality, things as they are, and all is rooted in the deeper reality of Yahweh Elohim's nature and human nature in his image. As well, these eleven major assumptions from Only Genesis equal the basis for "the liberal arts and sciences." All the disciplines are intertwined, where for example, music is completely mathematical in its structure and ability for giving aesthetic pleasures as manipulated sound waves massage somatic reality, able to produce great joy.

We read in Genesis 1:14-19:

And Elohim said, "Let there be light in the expanse of the heavens to separate the day from the night, to be signs for seasons and days and years. And let them be luminaries in the heavens to give light above the earth. And it was so. Elohim made two great luminaries – the greater luminary to govern the day and the smaller luminary to govern the night, and he also made the stars. Elohim set them in the expanse of the heavens to give light on the earth, to govern the day and night, and to separate the light from the darkness. And Elohim saw that it was good. And there evening and there was morning – the fourth day.

Rooted in the assumption of sound and light in Genesis 1:3, we see an example in Genesis 1:14-19. There, Elohim makes the sun, moon and stars to mark out seasons and give light to the earth. And too, sound and light are scientifically the most basic properties in the universe.

229

Moses knows the Israelites are coming out of 400 years in a pagan nation. Thus, and as led by the Spirit, he knows well their need to be completely separate from the pagan deities they and their forefathers had encountered back to Abraham's father and prior. Separate from lurking Egyptian, Canaanite and Babylonian mythologies.

These paganisms assume the sun, moon and stars are gods and goddesses, with the astrological calendars and fatalisms that follow. In Egypt, the sun and moon are capricious deities, and given how the languages of proximate nations are cognates of proto-Semitic languages, Moses knows that the Israelites need to be freed from such idolatry.

Thus, Moses does not use the words for the "sun" or "moon" or any specifically identified star that carries with it a pagan identity. Rather he is descriptive in speaking of the greater and smaller luminaries, and in making such a simple physical observation, along with the generic stars in describing them for what they are, Moses is being scientific before modern "science" has such an identity. Moses defines the sun, moon and stars as inanimate material objects, not as animated deities as in pagan religion. Reality. Science is the ability to look at things as they are. Biblical revelation shows things for what they are.

In fact, honest science traces to the biblical worldview, all because creation is a gift of Yahweh Elohim, and not animate forces to be worshiped. There is no basis for science in pagan religion. At a simple level, it is the difference between astronomy and astrology.

In view of environmental sciences, we can make another observation. In Genesis 1:26-28, when the man and woman are made, they are called to "rule" (radah in the sense of human vis-à-vis the non-human) the created order. And in Genesis 2:15, Adam is commissioned to work and guard the garden. The Garden of Eden includes a vast area, but too, this is the starting point for Adam and Eve caring for the whole earth and its ecosphere that sustains their lives. They are stewards. No possible toxic pollutions are in view that only intrude with sin.

Since the Bible defines the human body, the planet and ecosphere as good, such environment stewardship, and its work including necessary scientific study, is also good. It is a general truth that nations and states rooted in biblical ethics take care of the environment; those rooted in paganism do not.

Yet, there is a caveat. Within environmental science today, and as it grows increasingly secular and pagan, human beings become increasingly enslaved to the worship of the creation instead of worshiping the Creator. Thus, for example, much money and political energy is spent on theories concerning climate change as a (largely) future concern based mostly on computer models that cannot predict warming or cooling, and their respective seasons, across the decades and centuries. Yet at the same time, the priority for addressing dirty water and air, in second and third world countries, is thus mitigated, even though large numbers of people die daily.

In the Law of Moses, we find the ethical basis for the scientific method based on "the principle of falsification." In scientific research and discovery, if a theory is proposed to explain something, standards for testing that theory are set in place where all the variables are controlled as tightly as possible. If a theory has to do with the amount of electromagnetic energy in a certain substance, then a test is devised to measure that energy. For the theory to be "proven" true, it must produce the same results under the same conditions every time. If one measurement is evidenced 1,000 times in a row, then that measurement can be said to have a scientific basis, of a theory established.

But also, a theory "proven" is always open to being disproven. If the measurement is consistent 10,000 times, then different a subsequent time, the theory is disproved, falsified, if all the variables are certifiably the same. A new theory is proposed to take into consideration this variation, and a process pursued until no variations occur again.

At the ethical level, I have confidence equal to any measurement of scientific fact, that the storyline and doctrines of creation → sin → redemption, and their assumptions, interpret all Scripture and life accurately. I have confidence likewise in the God → life → choice → sex paradigm, the eleven positive assumptions of Only Genesis, and the six pillars of biblical power. In fact, the power to love hard questions undergirds all honest science and all academic studies.

231

Do I expect evidence ever to be presented facts that would alter these relentlessly tested convictions? Do I ever expect that $1 + 1 = 2$ will be disproved mathematically? No on both counts. But too, the more secure I am in both questions, the freer I am to entertain skeptical perspectives that might seek to dislodge these convictions.

We see the principle of falsification in Deuteronomy 18:9-22 as Moses defines opposition to the demonic non-science of sorcery and witchcraft (intertwined ethically with child sacrifice). Namely, if a "prophet" speaks a word in the name of Yahweh, and it fails to come to pass, he is falsified, and liable to the death penalty.

Thus, the standard for a true prophet in the Law of Moses is 100 percent accuracy, a 1.000 batting average. This is the most severe scrutiny possible, paving the way uniquely for the same ethical standard for honest science. Has any other religion or nation ever subjected is prophets or counselors or wise men or sorcerers to such a high standard?

Theocratic Israel is a community of choice, and those who wish to disobey Yahweh's laws, or to believe in other gods, are free to go to other nations where such is acceptable. But to remain in theocratic Israel and to prophesy falsely is an act of treason, aims to upend the goodness of Yahweh's laws, the well-being and survival of the nation, and the lineage of the Messiah.

In the Deuteronomy 18 text, Yahweh says he will raise up a prophet, like Moses, one who will speak the truth to them. This Prophet is the measure of the truth and ethics necessary for the principle of falsification. This is a Messianic prophecy that refers to Jesus as the ultimate Prophet, as Peter explicitly teaches in Acts 3:19-23. Jesus is the standard. In John's gospel, we see Jesus submitting himself to the principle of falsification as he challenges his religious elitist enemies in John 8:42-47. He uses the "if" clause ("If I am telling you the truth ..."), which Moses uses often as well, in questioning whether his enemies are truly serving God as their Father, on the one hand, and whether he is telling the truth, on the other. Later, in John 10:36-37, he reiterates the challenge of his own trustworthiness. The principle of falsification is the measure Jesus chooses to use.

- Now, our focus in these pages is not science. But in the liberal arts reality of Only Genesis, the principle of falsification begins with prophets who claim to speak for God, and thus it is natural to apply the ethics of theological inquiry to scientific inquiry. The former is also our starting point in Chapter One concerning the exhortation by James for the scrutiny of all teachers of the Word.

83. How accountable are all of us in this debate to being falsified, and if so, how willing are we to make correction?

Returning to a prior allusion concerning mathematical certainty, we can note how we all make assumptions, from the macro to the micro, and they affect our lives profoundly. The question is to what extent these assumptions are true or false. And, how well do we test our assumptions?

Kurt Gödel is the most eminent mathematician in the twentieth century, colleague of Albert Einstein. In mathematics, Gödel (in his *Incompleteness Theorems*) demonstrates that within its closed system it cannot be proven that $1 + 1 = 2$ (e.g., decimally). It must first be assumed (from outside and prior to the system), and then all mathematics works beautifully.

Namely, unless this simplicity is first assumed, then mathematical equations, by definition, are not possible. When the assumption of $1 + 1 = 2$ is in place, physics, engineering, architecture, music, art and other cognate sciences become possible. Mathematics is thus objective and utterly consistent in all means of human measurement.

In the expanding cosmos, the existence and properties of gravity have to be assumed, and accordingly all astrophysics work beautifully. In cultural anthropology, unwritten assumptions are the key to the core of the given (and usually ancient and extinct) social order.

And the greatest governing assumption is Genesis 1:1, including its unique provision for science and the scientific method.

The ninth assumption is verifiable history.

Genesis 1 is the theological grand design, and in Genesis 2:4-7 we have segue to the specificity of Genesis 2:8-14. This is just prior to the gift of human freedom:

> Now Yahweh Elohim had planted a garden in the east, in Eden; and there he put the man he had formed. And Yahweh Elohim made all kinds of trees grow out of the ground – trees that were desirable in appearance and good for food. The tree of life was in the middle of the garden, along with the tree of the knowledge of good and evil.

> A river coming out of Eden watered the garden; from there it was separated into four headwaters. The name of the one is the Pishon; it winds through the entire land of Havilah, where there is gold. The gold of that land is good; bdellium and onyx are there. And the name of the second river is the Gihon; it winds through the entire land of Cush. The name of the third river is the Tigris; it runs along the east of the Asshur. And the fourth river is the Euphrates.

The assumption in place is verifiable eye-witness history. The Bible is unique in this regard.

Regardless of pagan origin understandings we can grasp in various texts – the Babylonian *Enuma elish*, the Egyptian story of *Isis* and *Osirus*, Greek and Roman mythologies, the Vedas, the Mayan *Popul Vuh*, Celtic or Native American stories, or any number of others – we can note one similarity. They each begin with a mythological past that has no historical verifiability, nor do they have concern to rely on such an origin in historical terms. They merge the mythological past, at some point, with dim recollections of a historical one, each in their own way, until they come into more recent history and some verifiability grows in strength.

Islam, beginning in A.D. 622, is a different matter, since it says it affirms Jewish and Christian history. But this is only selective, and through its own prism. The Qur'an does not quote the Bible at all, but cites many of its stories, recasting them all according to Islamic purpose, thus vitiating biblical history. It deviates consistently from the verifiable historical witness of the Bible. The ancient and authoritative biography of Muhammad by Ibn Ishaq attempts to be very historical, but is not considered apart of sacred scripture. And too, unlike the certainty of the Bible's historical statements, Ibn Ishaq often states that the verifiability of certain stories is uncertain.

With the advent of "higher criticism" (the Graf-Wellhausen hypothesis) in the mid-nineteenth century, beginning in Germany, particular aim is taken against the historicity of Genesis 1-3. There are many means by which this is sought, and central to this thinking is the hypothesis that Hebrew monotheism evolved from a background of pagan polytheisms. Accordingly, the ethos of pagan mythology is then applied to an understanding of the origins of Genesis. There is much academic territory here, where I see no sustainable warrant for the hypothesis, but for here, let's pose a simple question: Where, in human history has unity ever emerged from the disunity of competing diversities?

Moses writes Genesis for his Hebrew audience during the exodus, ca. 1446 B.C. ff. He has, as his source, the written and oral traditions tracing back to Adam, a common possession of the covenant community. As Moses writes, he gives the exact location of the Garden of Eden, where Adam is presented the choice between the tree of life and the tree of the knowledge of good and evil. Nothing in the text allows these trees to be seen as allegorical, or the story to be seen as a myth. They are actual trees in a known location, at a certain time when Adam and Eve eat real fruit from them.

Some 2300 years later Moses verifies such a historical claim for his readers. He names the four headwaters that come out of the river that begins in Eden. The Flood has not marred their identities. This is to say that Moses is speaking about references that are common knowledge to his readers. His assumption of its historical reality is seen in the ease by which he expects his readers to immediately know what he is talking about.

The geographical scenario is that the Pishon and the Gihon are streams that feed the well-known Tigris and Euphrates. The Hebrew word for the Pishon likely means "gusher," and for the Gihon, the word likely means "spurter." This could describe streams fed by springs or an underground river, beginning in the mountains of Eden, and feeding the Tigris and the Euphrates.

The Garden of Eden, thus described biblically, traces to the current borders of Iran, Iraq and Turkey. A fertile plain surrounded by large mountains fits the description of the Garden, writ large, as its Hebrew word, *gan*, means "walled garden." From this "garden" region, the Tigris and Euphrates originate, separate and re-converge before arriving in the Persian Gulf.

So too, the Araxes and Uizhun rivers originate here, and flow from there into the Caspian Sea. The Araxes is likened to the Gihon in its winding and twisting characteristics through the land of Cush. And the Uizhun is like the Pishon, where in the land of Havilah, it weaves its way through ancient gold mines and areas of lapis lazuli. To this day it is called the "Golden River," and local people maintain that their area traces to the Garden of Eden. To the east of this region, where two salt lakes, Urmia and Van, are located, is an area called Noqdi, perhaps the original land of Nod to which Adam and Eve depart when exiled from Eden by Yahweh. As well, north of this area is a place called the "Kusheh Dagh," or the Mountain of Kush. Sounds like the Cush the eldest son of Ham (Genesis 10:6).

Regardless of our present understanding, from the vantage-point of Moses, it is an assumed and known reality to a people familiar with the geography and its names. There is far more cultural continuity between Adam and Moses, in the ancient near east, than between Moses and the modern world. Moses tells his readers that the Pishon winds through the land of Havilah, and he even takes a parenthetical aside to describe Havilah's reputation for good gold, bdellium and onyx. He also tells his readers that the Gihon winds through Kush, a local name at the time that could have preceded its later use as a description of Egypt. Thus, we have an ancient historical witness by which to compare our perspectives and research today.

In the assumptions of Moses based on the historical nature of Yahweh's revelation to Adam and Eve, he knows how important it is to give his readers geographical and historical markers known to them, so they can locate the reality of the Garden of Eden in space and time.

In fact, the entire Bible is constantly including even minor details as its stories unfold. The God of the biblical authors is the God of history. As one of a thousand examples of this detailed orientation to history, we can consider a verse proximate to what we already looked at when Hagar flees Sarai. Genesis 16:14 identifies the well named by Hagar, called Beer Lahai Roi.

Some four hundred years later, Moses inserts a marker for his readers to know exactly where the well is, where God meets Hagar's need – it still remains between Kadesh and Bered – known territory to his readers. This is why Jerusalem and Israel are so important today. So many historical markers are still known despite the ravages of war, erosion and exile which the land has seen over the millennia. Pagan cultures also have their historical markers, but they cannot trace them back to the mythological origins. Their cultures are only traceable to remaining undimmed elements of their known history as a people.

The Messianic lineage is comprehensive from Adam to Jesus, from the first Adam to the second Adam. Where else in all human history can anything compare with such a testimony to verifiable eye-witness history?

As Jesus comes to fulfill the Law of Moses, he does so being rooted in the assumption of the historical verifiability of the *Tanakh* (a translated acronym for the Law [*torah*], the Prophets [*nava'im*] and the Writings [*ketuvim*]). He repeatedly cites the Law, the Prophets and the Writings, and at a critical juncture, assumes and cites the historicity of Adam and Eve (see Matthew 19:2-6), coming also as the second Adam.

This reliance on the same, for example, is central to both Luke, in his gospel and the Book of Acts, and of John in his gospel and first letter.

Luke states:

> Inasmuch as many have endeavored to compile an account of the things that have been accomplished among us, just as they were handed over to us by those who from the first were witnesses and servants of the word, I have followed closely from above and carefully, and written a successive account for you, excellent Theophilus, in order that you may know the certainty of what you have been taught orally (1:1-4).

And then, in the Book of Acts:

> In the former book I made, O Theophilus, concerning all that Jesus
> began to do and to teach until the day he was taken up, after giving
> commands through the Holy Spirit to the apostles he had chosen, he
> presented himself to them after his suffering, giving many proofs that
> he was alive, and appeared to them for forty days and spoke about the
> kingdom of God (1:1-3).

Luke, both a physician and historian, and rooted in the biblical
assumption of verifiable history, does his careful fact-checking work within
the covenant community that requires it. He thus gives to Theophilus a
historically accurate account of the life, death, resurrection and ascension of
Jesus, and of the early church, so that Theophilus might have historical
certainty concerning what he has been taught.

The apostle John makes the same reliance on verifiable history with
reference to Jesus, as seen in his gospel (20:30-31 and 21:25). He knows
that he can only give a brief profile of his witness – the world could be
filled beyond the brim with books giving testimony to the details of what
Jesus said and did.

Then in his first letter, John is combating the rise of early Gnosticism and
its ahistorical and dualistic presuppositions that sought to deny that Jesus
came in a physical body. He counters with verifiable eye and touch-witness
history:

> That which was from the beginning, which we have heard, which
> we have seen with our eyes, which we have beheld, and our hands
> have touched – we proclaim concerning the Word of life. And the life
> was made manifest; we have seen it and bear witness to it, and we
> announce eternal life, which was with the Father and has been made
> manifest to us. What we have seen and heard we announce to you, so
> that you also may have fellowship with us, and our fellowship is with
> the Father and with his Son, Jesus Christ. We write this in order to
> make our joy full (1:1-4).

Among adherents to "higher criticism," the Book of Esther comes under particular scrutiny. The critique is that it does not mention Yahweh Elohim once, and only makes one subtle reference to his activity in 4:14-15 (though some might not even grant this). Thus, they view it as a "secular" book, being only concerned with "history."

So, the concern with verifiable history is affirmed, even by skeptics, as the book details how a Jewess is enabled to become queen in pagan Persia during the post-exilic era (ca. 460 B.C.), and from that position to intercede for and save the Jews from a plot to wipe them out. And since Esther is written in pagan Persia, the author is likely content to simply write down the historical facts that could simultaneously be entered into the royal court records, with his Jewish readers readily grasping the larger picture.

Also, there is extraordinary theology in place concerning Haman as a descendent of the Amalekites (see Chapter Nine vis-à-vis spiritual warfare), who seeks to destroy the Messianic lineage just after they flee Egypt. Which is to say: there is a unity between theological and historical purpose in the Bible, and not a divorce as "higher criticism" is wont to assume. And in modern secular thought, why is it concerned with historical verifiability to begin with, apart from prior biblical influences?

The Bible, in an assumption from the beginning, submits itself to the most stringent requirements for verifiable eye-witness history, as it does in terms of science and the scientific method. Integrity, of truth-telling, in all matters.

84. How well sustained are the church history arguments for a) the claimed preponderance for of universalism in the early church and b) the accuracy in claiming such supporters?

85. Is verifiable history on its own terms in view, or a shaped history to fit into a preconceived universalism?

The tenth assumption is covenantal law.

In the biblical series of covenantal law, Yahweh enters into mutual promises with us, in first giving freedom in the Garden, then in protecting it in the face of sin as we look forward to the coming Redeemer. There are six major covenants in the Bible – the Adamic, Noahic, Abrahamic, Mosaic, Davidic, and Messianic.

In the order of creation, Yahweh makes the original covenant of freedom with Adam. When, following the reversal, and as Noah becomes the sole remaining remnant of the faithful lineage, the next covenant is given. Sin rushes in again, later leaving Abram as the sole remaining remnant of the faithful lineage, and he is given a covenant. When his line is enslaved in Egypt, Yahweh raises Moses up and he is given a covenant for the nation of Israel. His successor Joshua ratifies it, and sees its effective implementation so long as he is alive. Later, after the days of Samuel, this covenant is rejected by Israel in favor of a pagan kingship, and Yahweh raises David up afterward, and gives him a covenant. And finally, this covenant is broken, the nation and city are destroyed, and the prophecy of the New Covenant of the Messiah is given.

The word for "covenant" is the Hebrew term *b'rith*. It involves the elements of establishing a legal relationship "between" parties, ritualized in a sacrificial meal where the food offering is "cut up" for that purpose. A crucial part involves each party, referring to the cut animal parts, giving a self-maledictory oath: "May this happen to me if I ever break this covenant." Thus, to "make a covenant" is translated by the idiom, "to cut a covenant." In ancient near eastern societies, the closest allegiance known between two parties is that which involves blood relationships, and next to that is the loyalty derived from the oaths involved in "cutting a covenant."

And uniquely, in biblical covenants, the first covenant in Genesis 2, before the advent of human sin, needs no cutting, no self-maledictory oaths. In all biblical covenants, Yahweh Elohim first holds himself accountable to the promises he makes to his image-bearers. Pagan kings (and deities) do not do so. In other words, the difference between the power to give and it will be given, versus take before you are taken.

In law, which do we have? Fidelity from the ruler for the well-being of all people equally, or totalitarian imposition and favoritism used to curry enough favor among the elites to stay in power? Jewish political theologian, Daniel J. Elazar, does yeoman work in linking Hebrew covenant with federalism (from the Latin *foedus* for covenant). And as the foundation for the United States Constitution.

The eleventh and final assumption is unalienable rights.

In our review of biblical theology, we can note again a reprise of the God → life → choice → sex paradigm. It is located in Genesis 1-2, describing the four all-defining subjects of the universe. Every issue we confront finds its basis in how these four subjects are defined and how they relate to each other, and also fully defines the abortion debate.

These subjects equal the content of Genesis 1-2:

> Yahweh Elohim is sovereign, and his purpose in creation is to give the gift of life, especially human life – to man and woman as made in his image to rule over his handiwork. Then comes the gift of moral and aesthetic choice that serves the prior gift of human life. Finally, in the order of creation, is the gift of sex within marriage: here is the power to pass on the gifts of life, choice and sex through procreation to our offspring, to celebrate the height of what it means to be made in Yahweh Elohim's image.

Or to put it another way, true sexuality is an expression of godly choice that serves the gift of human life that comes from Yahweh Elohim.

And too, we find a remarkable parallel in the 1776 Declaration of Independence, where based on the antecedents of John Locke, John Adams and Thomas Jefferson, we encounter the language of "life, liberty and property/pursuit of happiness." We read:

> WE hold these truths to be self-evident, that all Men are created equal, that they are endowed by their Creator with certain unalienable Rights, that among these are Life, Liberty, and the Pursuit of Happiness – That to secure these Rights, Governments are instituted among Men, deriving there just Powers from the Consent of the Governed …

These rights, these gifts of life, liberty and property/pursuit of happiness, are necessary assumptions for a healthy social order, rooted in the Creator under the rubric of "unalienable rights." (Note: "the pursuit of happiness" is Jefferson's philosophic clause in the declaration, made possible by property rights, as the Fifth and Fourteenth Amendments legally codify it.) The language of unalienable rights is of course a double negative – that which cannot be alienated or taken away. It is articulated in the face of broken trust, but rooted in that which precedes such brokenness, the positive reality of Genesis 1-2.

The parallels stand out:

> God = the Creator.
> Life = Life.
> Choice = Liberty.
> Sex = Property/Pursuit of Happiness.

The first three parallels are obvious. But the fourth? A closer look at the language is helpful.

In Genesis 2:24, a man leaves his parent's household to join with his wife and form a new household. The Hebrew term for household or family is *bayith*, and in the Greek of the Septuagint, it is translated *oikos*. The rule of the household *is oikonomos*, as noted earlier, from whence we derive the English word "economics."

Across the history of human civilizations, when a man is faithful to his wife and the raising of their children, the strongest possible economic unit follows. And the biblical assumption of fidelity in marriage and parenthood is the only foundation for the economic activity in creating, producing, selling, buying and trading property or goods.

Adam and Eve are created to be stewards of the good earth. This defines the nature and purpose of owning property, namely, for that which strengthens the family and social order. Thus, the idea of happiness is rooted in social health, not in a self-centered individualism.

The parallel with the subject matters of Genesis 1-2 is complete, but at a deeper level, what we witness here is the power of assumptions in the Declaration itself. Namely, these realities are viewed as "self-evident" to the signatories, the majority of whom were orthodox Protestants, along with the one Roman Catholic and the various heterodox in their midst. Self-evident as rooted in the Creator.

Despite the heterodoxies, the Declaration is written by a deeply covenantal people who are ethically orthodox, loath to break with England, but are finally pushed into it as King George III breaks covenant after covenant with the Colonies. Thus, since he is head of the church as well as head of the state, they have to go over his head – to the commonly acknowledged Creator. Back to the opening assumptions in Genesis.

There is no other source for unalienable rights, certainly not among pagan religions, not in secular constructs, and not in the Enlightenment where an ahistorical and amorphously distant deity is not, as such, concerned with human affairs.

The one true Creator gives the rights to life, liberty and property, and in the second category, religious, political and economic liberty. They are not defined by human government, cannot be given or taken away, only honored as an inviolable assumption.

Unalienable rights are protected in the Fifth and Fourteenth Amendments to the U.S. Constitution, where no person shall be deprived of "life, liberty, or property, without due process of law." Namely, people are fully free in their personal matters, so long as they do not violate the lives, liberties and properties of others.

Thus, there is a continuum between biblically legitimate and illegitimate governments – those which honor unalienable rights from the Creator on the one hand, and as ratified by the consent of the governed; and those who do not, those that are ultimately totalitarian.

- Universalists generally affirm constitutional liberties as they seek an audience for their ideas. Good.

86. But, if they mute or sublimate biblical authority, and especially argue against full freedoms in choosing an eternal destiny, do they not run into an internal conflict?

87. And do we see how the appeal to unalienable rights, and their implementation, dramatically advances the religious liberty in which the Gospel thrives?

Finally, an addendum in the six pillars of biblical power.

These six pillars equal biblical ethics (how we treat each other) that flow out of the eleven positives which equal biblical theology (what we believe). We have seen the first four in context from the order of creation. Now for the two final pillars, which redeem the prior four from the brokenness of sin.

Thus, the power to love enemies.

In Matthew 5:44, Jesus says: "Love those who hate you, and pray for those who persecute you." He then speaks of how the sun rises on the "evil and the good" alike. This is a dynamic appeal to the image of God in Genesis 1-2, prior to the history of sin as seen in 3-19. In that process, Yahweh Elohim shows great patience prior to the Flood (120 years of warning), prior to Sodom and Gomorrah (the power of Abraham's invitation to intercede, even after years of pending judgment), and later, prior to the Exodus (400 years in which the Canaanites refuse to repent). The whole book of Revelation ratchets up to pending judgment, with great patience given, but finally, we all own our own informed choices – the heavens or the abyss.

This is all Yahweh Elohim's love for his enemies – the power of informed choice. His covenant community of Israel is called on to live it even as surrounded by the opposite. In Exodus 22:21, Yahweh tells them not to oppress the sojourner, for they were once sojourners in Egypt. The Sabbath rest, invitation to join the Passover meal (beginning in Egypt) and all measures of justice equally apply to sojourners in the midst of Israel (e.g., Exodus 12:49; Leviticus 24:22), but there is no such reciprocal reality in the pagan nations (and in contrast, see how Elisha treats the enemies of

244

Israel in 2 Kings 6:21-23). In Romans 5:6-11, Paul encapsulates the love for enemies found in Jesus. And to reiterate, all of this is congruent with the power of informed choice, thus, in advancing the same, we love those who may be living as enemies of the Gospel.

In these pages, I seek to note in the course of various lived anecdotes, the power of loving those who consider themselves our enemies. Such love is a necessary engine that undergirds faithful pro-life advocacy, and as rooted in the prior pillars.

And thus, the power to forgive

And likewise, in terms of forgiving those who hate and plot against us. The bookends of the Bible, in the storyline of creation, sin and redemption, are the powers to give and forgive. Or to sum up all the Bible this way:

Yahweh Elohim gives, we blow it, and he forgives.

If we are willing to receive it. In the prophecy of the new covenant in Jeremiah 31:31-34 the capstone is Yahweh's forgiveness of our evil, where he "remembers (*zakar*) our sins no more" (note also in the prior v. 30, re: reaping what we sow pace the power of informed choice). In the Sermon on the Mount, the Lord's prayer concludes with the need to forgive as we are forgiven, otherwise there is none for us remaining (Matthew 6:12; 14-15). Again, this is the power of informed choice in action. Jesus, in dying on the cross, utters: "Father, forgive them ..." (Luke 23:24).

- Hopefully, this is how we treat one another in this debate. I affirm and do not challenge the Christian faith of any of our writers, in their trust placed in Jesus as Lord and Savior. I only ask honest questions, in reciprocity, on the biblical cogency of our arguments.

♦ ♦ ♦

Summation

Here are some observations and conclusions.

- All five writers affirm a love for hard questions, and I share with them this biblical ethic.

- The Wesleyan quadrilateral of biblical faith – Scripture, tradition, reason and experience – is upended by these writers.

- Hell is biblical language that centrally illustrates the prior and larger theme of judgment.

- The "location" and identity of hell is rooted in the language of the abyss, prior to creation, and after final Judgment.

- Genesis 2:16-17 defines freedom and judgment for all Scripture, and thus the later language of hell.

- The grammar of *moth tamuth*, "In dying you shall continually die," defines unending death, and interprets the whole Bible accordingly. Its ethics dwell as fully in the present as in the future.

- Here we find a level playing field of freedom to choose hell for those who find greater satisfaction in darkness, bitterness and idolatry, than in the Light, mercy and gratefulness to the Creator.

- Only the redemption of the Messiah liberates us from this death, we are free to receive his provision, but there is an endpoint where settled choices of resistance meet a final chosen Judgment.

- The Name and nature of *Yahweh Elohim*, he who is greater than space, time and number, defines all human language that seeks to grasp the locale and duration for both heaven and hell.

- An understanding of *nephesh*, the image of God, is the basis for grasping the offer of salvation, and it has neither negative appeal nor arbitrariness involved.

- The sovereign power of Yahweh Elohim is the location for true love and freedom, and his eternal perspective is the basis to understand predestination, and never violates the human will.

- It is not a matter of God "winning" or "losing" as though he were in a dualistic contest with the devil or sinful humanity.

- Yahweh Elohim is sovereign and free, and it is not a matter of "will not" or "cannot."

- **His desire is for us to choose his freedom, which is the power to do the good, and in his goodness, he does not manipulate freedom.**

- C.S. Lewis, in the ethics of hell as profiled in *The Great Divorce*, is consonant with this theology, and more brilliant. And in *The Last Battle*, he profiles how those who seek the true Creator will in the end find him, even if trapped within idolatry their whole lives.

- When we all appear before King Jesus on the Last Day, and look upon him, we will either love him or hate him, regardless of our theological sojourn. *Nephesh* will be embraced, or given the cold shoulder.

- **The reversal of creation → sin → redemption = the abyss → creation in God's image → rejection of such humanity → the return to the abyss.**

- **Heaven is for the many who love mercy; hell is for the few who guard bitterness.**

Epilogue: None of the five writers address the question of whether Satan and his demons gain entrance into heaven, even if after a certain season in hell. How do they address this question? And if Satan and his host do make it, is this anything less than the folly of a cosmic charade?

◆ ◆ ◆

Made in the USA
Middletown, DE
12 January 2018